PUBLIC UNIVERSITIES AND
REGIONAL GROWTH

INNOVATION AND TECHNOLOGY IN THE WORLD ECONOMY

MARTIN KENNEY, *Editor*
University of California, Davis and Berkeley Roundtable
on the International Economy

Other titles in the series:

Public Universities and Regional Growth

INSIGHTS FROM THE UNIVERSITY
OF CALIFORNIA

Edited by Martin Kenney and David C. Mowery

STANFORD BUSINESS BOOKS
An Imprint of Stanford University Press
Stanford, California

Stanford University Press
Stanford, California

Special discounts for bulk quantities of Stanford Business Books
are available to corporations, professional associations, and other
organizations. For details and discount information, contact the
special sales department of Stanford University Press. Tel: (650)
736-1782, Fax: (650) 736-1784

Printed in the United States of America on acid-free, archival-quality
paper

Library of Congress Cataloging-in-Publication Data

Public universities and regional growth: insights from the University
of California / edited by Martin Kenney and David C. Mowery.
    pages cm — (Innovation and technology in the world economy)
    Includes bibliographical references and index.
    ISBN 978-0-8047-9067-3 (cloth : alk. paper) —
ISBN 978-0-8047-9135-9 (pbk. : alk. paper)
    1. University of California (System) 2. Public universities and
colleges—Economic aspect—California. 3. Academic-industrial
collaboration—California. 4. Research—Economic aspects—
California. 5. Economic development—California. I. Kenney,
Martin, editor of compilation. II. Mowery, David C., editor of
compilation. III. Series: Innovation and technology in the world
economy.
    LD729.8.P83 2014
    378.794—dc23
                                        2013051008

ISBN 978-0-8047-9142-7 (electronic)

Typeset by Thompson Type in 10/13 Galliard

Contents

List of Illustrations

Tables

Acknowledgments

The editors gratefully acknowledge a grant from the University of California Office of the President for two authors' meetings and staff support. The Institute for Business Innovation at the Haas School of Business, UC Berkeley, provided invaluable support for the meetings. UC Davis staff helped in innumerable ways. First and foremost, the editors gratefully acknowledge the enthusiasm, encouragement, advice, and invaluable assistance of Mary Walshok in conceiving and assisting the project at every step of the way. We thank Christophe Lécuyer for his encouragement and assistance in the gestation stage of this project. Robert Cook-Deegan and John Walsh provided many helpful suggestions for strengthening the book. Martin Kenney thanks Ralph Hexter and the University of California, Davis, Provost's Forum for the Public University and the Social Good. The Forum supported Alycia Thompson, who provided superb editorial and other staff assistance that greatly simplified the burdens of coordinating meetings and producing the book. We thank Margo Beth Fleming for her sage advice and encouragement. The usual disclaimers apply, and the editors and authors are solely responsible for all of the statements and conclusions drawn in the book.

Contributor Biographies

Steven Casper is the Henry E. Riggs Professor of Management at the Keck Graduate Institute of Applied Life Sciences in Claremont, California. His research focuses on comparative studies of the development of new technology industries, with a special interest in processes by which biomedical science has been commercialized across the United States and Europe. He has published a book on the development of science-based industry in Europe (*Creating Silicon Valley in Europe: Public Policy Towards New Technology Industries*, Oxford University Press, 2007). Dr. Casper was previously a faculty member at the University of Cambridge, UK, where he was a University Lecturer in Innovation and Entrepreneurship at the Judge Institute of Management Studies. He was previously employed as a Senior Research Fellow at the Social Science Center, Berlin. He received a PhD in government from Cornell University. In 2009, Casper was awarded a Fulbright Research Scholarship to Canada.

Martin Kenney is a Professor at the University of California, Davis, and a Senior Project Director at the Berkeley Roundtable on the International Economy. He has published five books and over 120 scholarly articles on venture capital, university-industry technology transfer, new industry formation, and technology-enabled globalization. His two recent edited books *Understanding Silicon Valley* and *Locating Global Advantage* were published by Stanford University Press, where he is the editor of a book series in innovation and globalization. He has been a visiting scholar at the Economic Research Institute of Finland, Copenhagen Business School; Judge School of Management, University of Cambridge; Institute of Innovation Studies, Hitotsubashi University; Kobe University; and Tokyo University. In 2009 he was a visiting scholar at the Stanford University

Asia Pacific Research Center and in 2011 at the Economic Institute of Finnish Economy. He has consulted for or lectured at various private sector organizations, including Association of Computing Machinery, Cisco, Dell India, Intel, and GHX, and public sector organizations such as Interamerican Development Bank, National Academy of Engineering, National Academy of Science, the National Research Council, OECD, the President's Council on Science and Technology, World Bank, and the World Economic Forum. He is the West Coast editor for *Research Policy*.

James Lapsley is a Continuing Educator Emeritus UCD Extension, where he directed the Department of Agricultural and Natural Sciences from 1978 to 2009. After retirement he assumed a 30 percent position as an Adjunct Associate Professor UC Davis, Department of Viticulture and Enology, and as researcher in the Agricultural Issues Center. He is the author of *Bottled Poetry* (UC Press, 1996), a study of the emergence of the Napa Valley and a market for higher-quality wine in the United States. He coedited *Successful Wine Marketing*, which was awarded the OIV Grand Prize in 2001 for the Best Book on Wine Economics. Lapsley was President and Winemaker for Orleans Hill Winery from 1980 to 2002, a winery that specialized in wine produced from organically grown grapes. In 2003, Lapsley was a Fulbright Scholar in Uruguay, where he collaborated with faculty in the Schools of Chemistry and Agronomy to create a degree program in enology. He received his PhD in history from UC Davis in 1994 and has written numerous papers on California wine history.

Christophe Lécuyer is a Professor of the History of Science and Technology at the Université Pierre et Marie Curie and a Senior Research Fellow at the Charles Babbage Institute at the University of Minnesota. He is known for his research on the history of Silicon Valley and the history of high technologies. Among his publications are *Making Silicon Valley: Innovation and the Growth of High Tech, 1930–1970* (MIT Press, 2005) and *Makers of the Microchip: A Documentary History of Fairchild Semiconductor* (MIT Press, 2010, in collaboration with David C. Brock). Christophe Lécuyer has taught at MIT, Stanford University, and the University of Virginia and held a managerial position at the University of California Office of the President. He was a Senior Fellow at the Collegium de Lyon and the Institute for Advanced Study at Central European University and a Visiting Professor at Telecom Ecole de Management and the Ecole des Hautes

Etudes en Sciences Sociales. He is a graduate of the École Normale Supérieure (Ulm) and received his PhD from Stanford.

Cyrus C. M. Mody is an Assistant Professor of the History of Science, Technology, and Engineering in the Modern Era (c. 1600 to the present) at Rice University. His own research focuses on the physical and engineering sciences in the very modern era (c. 1970 to the present), with particular emphasis on the creation of new communities and institutions of science in the late Cold War and the post-Cold War periods. His book, *Instrumental Community: Probe Microscopy and the Path to Nanotechnology* (MIT 2011) explores the coevolution of an experimental technology (the scanning tunneling microscope and atomic force microscope and their variants) and the community of researchers who built, bought, used, sold, theorized, or borrowed these instruments. Currently, he is working on a history of the communities and institutions of nanotechnology, in collaboration with colleagues at the Center for Nanotechnology in Society at the University of California, Santa Barbara, and the Chemical Heritage Foundation in Philadelphia.

David C. Mowery is the William A. & Betty H. Hasler Professor of New Enterprise Development at the Walter A. Haas School of Business, University of California, Berkeley. He earned a BA, an MA, and a PhD in economics, each from Stanford University. He began his teaching career as an Assistant Professor in the Social and Decision Sciences Department, Carnegie-Mellon University in 1982, being promoted to Associate Professor prior to moving to UC Berkeley in 1988. He has also served as Assistant to the Counselor, Office of the U.S. Trade Representative and a Fellow at the Council on Foreign Relations.

Mowery has also been an expert witness at congressional hearings on science and technology policy issues; a member of National Research Council panels, including Competitive Status of the U.S. Civil Aviation Industry, Causes and Consequences of the Internationalization of U.S. Manufacturing, Federal Role in Civilian Technology Development, U.S. Strategies for the Children's Vaccine Initiative, and Applications of Biotechnology to Contraceptive Research and Development; a member of the Committee on Science, Engineering, and Public Policy, American Association for the Advancement of Science, 1997–2003; a member of the Presidential Commissions on Offsets in International Trade, 2000–2001;

a coeditor of special issues of the journals *Industrial and Corporate Change* and *Management Science*; and an advisor to the Organization for Economic Cooperation and Development, as well as various federal agencies and industrial firms.

Mowery's research interests include the impact of technological change on economic growth and employment, the management of technological change, and international trade policy and U.S. technology policy, especially high-technology joint ventures.

Donald Patton is a Research Associate with the Department of Human and Community Development at the University of California, Davis. He received his doctorate in economics from the University of California, Davis, in 1993.

His current research interests involve clusters, entrepreneurship, and economic development. Other research interests revolve around university intellectual property rights and policies affecting the transfer of university technology. In addition, he has been involved in constructing a database of all initial public offerings in the United States from 1988 to the present. Support for this effort has been provided by the National Science Foundation, the Small Business Administration, and the Kauffman Foundation.

Daniel Sumner is the Frank H. Buck Jr. Professor in the Department of Agricultural and Resource Economics at the University of California, Davis, and the Director of the University of California Agricultural Issues Center. He participates in research and teaching and directs an outreach program related to public issues related to agriculture.

He has published broadly in academic journals, books, and industry outlets. His research and writing have received numerous awards for research quality, quality of communication, and contribution to policy. He has served as Chair of the International Agricultural Trade Research Consortium, a consultant for farm organization, government agencies, and firms and is a frequent speaker at national and international conferences and symposia. In 1998, he was named a Fellow of the American Agricultural Economics Association for his career achievement.

From 1978 to 1992 Sumner was a Professor in the Division of Economics and Business at North Carolina State University. He spent much of the period after 1986 on leave for government service in Washington, D.C., where he served on the President's Council of Economic Advisers before moving to the USDA. Immediately prior to moving to California in January 1993, Sumner was the Assistant Secretary for Economics at the U.S. Department of Agriculture, where he contributed to policy formulation and analysis on the whole range of topics facing agriculture and rural America—from food and farm programs to trade, resources, and rural development. In his role as supervisor of the USDA's economics and statistics agencies, Sumner was also responsible for data collection, outlook, and economic research.

Sumner received a bachelor's degree in agricultural management from California Polytechnic State University in San Luis Obispo in 1971, a master's degree from Michigan State in 1973, and a PhD in economics from the University of Chicago in 1978.

Mary Walshok is the Associate Vice Chancellor for Public Programs, Dean of University Extension, and Professor of Sociology at the University of California, San Diego. She oversees a $37 million university division that educates 56,000 enrollees annually and reaches 22 million households through UCSD-TV and UCTV, as well as millions more through the web. A thought leader on aligning workforce development with regional economic growth and innovation, she is the author of *Blue Collar Women*, *Knowledge without Boundaries*, *Closing America's Job Gap*, and *Invention and Reinvention: The Evolution of San Diego's Entrepreneurial Economy* (2014, Stanford University Press). As an industrial sociologist, she has been researching various American regions for the U.S. Department of Labor, NSF, and Lilly Foundation. One of her current research projects is an NSF-funded study of the role of boundary-spanning organizations in shaping the social and cultural dynamics of the highly innovative regions. Walshok is also active on numerous community and national boards and is a cofounder of CONNECT, one of the most admired innovation cluster development organizations in the world.

Joel West is Professor of Innovation & Entrepreneurship at the Keck Graduate Institute of Applied Life Sciences. He is an internationally known researcher on innovation management, Dr. West has been invited to speak at industry and academic events on five continents. He is particularly known for his work on open innovation, as coeditor of *Open Innovation: Researching a New Paradigm* (Oxford, 2006) and cofounder (with Henry Chesbrough) of the Open Innovation Community. His other research areas include renewable energy, entrepreneurship, intellectual property, open-source software, international business, and strategies for IT vendor firms.

Before joining KGI in 2011, he spent nine years as an Associate Professor and then Professor at San José State University in its College of Business and Lucas Graduate School of Business. He has also taught at UC Irvine, Pepperdine, and Temple University Japan. He has a PhD in Management from the University of California, Irvine, and an SB in Interdisciplinary Sciences (Meteorology) from the Massachusetts Institute of Technology. Prior to becoming an academic, he had an extensive career as an engineer, manager, and entrepreneur in the software industry.

PUBLIC UNIVERSITIES AND REGIONAL GROWTH

CHAPTER ONE

Introduction

MARTIN KENNEY AND DAVID C. MOWERY

The twenty-first century is the century of knowledge-based economic growth. Recognizing this reality, national and regional governments in the industrial and industrializing economies have introduced policies and strengthened institutions to support innovation. One institution that has received significant attention in the course of these efforts is the research university. There are a number of reasons for the recent policy focus on research universities. Considerable evidence (Narin et al., 1997; Hicks et al., 2001) suggests that the dependence of technological innovation on advances in science and engineering research has increased in recent decades, a considerable change from the "trial-and-error" character of innovation in the late nineteenth and early twentieth centuries. Universities also play a unique role in both research and training, and their ability to expose graduates to the frontiers of scientific research provides a powerful mechanism for the transfer of knowledge and technology.

One of the most important recent U.S. initiatives in this area is the Bayh-Dole Act of 1980, which sought to promote the patenting and licensing by U.S. universities and federal laboratories of research advances based on federally funded research, based on the belief (which in turn had limited empirical support—see Eisenberg, 1996) that such policies would accelerate the commercialization of innovations based on publicly funded research (Berman, 2012). The post-1980 period has witnessed considerable growth in patenting by U.S. universities, and many of these patents have been licensed to private firms. Although it is far from clear that the Bayh-Dole Act in fact "caused" this growth in patenting and licensing, the Act is widely viewed as a success and has influenced the policies of other

Organisation for Economic Co-Operation and Development (OECD) and industrializing-economy governments seeking to encourage university–industry technology transfer (Mowery, 2009; Mowery et al., 2004). In addition, since 1980 state governments and universities in the United States have launched a dizzying array of initiatives for the support of new-firm formation and technology commercialization based on university research.

The intensive focus of many of these policies (including the Bayh-Dole Act) on patenting and licensing of university research advances overlooks the interactive nature of university–industry research relationships, which embody considerable feedback and iteration, rather than operating as a unidirectional flow of fundamental knowledge into industry application (Colyvas et al., 2002). In addition, these patent-focused reforms downplay the existence of multiple channels of interaction and knowledge flow between academia and industry. Our chapters indicate that a great deal of economically valuable technology transfer takes place outside the administrative channels created by most U.S. universities for technology licensing. Indeed, a number of important cases in this book highlight the movement of technology, people, resources, and knowledge from industry to university. The chapters demonstrate the importance of bidirectional and informal human and information flows, few if any of which are dependent on technology transfer offices. Technology licensing is only one of a multitude of channels through which technology and knowledge flow into and out of the university.

In spite of the endorsement by policy makers and university administrators throughout the United States of the value of "closer university–industry relationships," as well as the appearance of a large scholarly literature on this topic in the past two decades, we still know surprising little about the dynamics of these relationships, the effects of university research on regional economic development and the reverse, and the most appropriate approaches for assessing the benefits and costs of these relationships. The emphasis in recent U.S. policy on patent-based channels of interaction and knowledge transfer is reflected in the similarly "patent-centric" focus of much of the academic literature on university–industry research interactions, despite considerable evidence that patents and patent licensing play a modest role in many university–industry relationships.

The importance for industrial innovation of different channels of communication linking intrafirm R&D (research and development) to R&D in government or university laboratories was studied in a survey of R&D managers conducted by Cohen and colleagues (2002). They found that pharmaceutical executives assign greater importance to patents and license agreements involving universities and public laboratories than do other executives; even respondents from pharmaceuticals rated research publications and conferences as a more important source of information. In most other industries, patents and licenses of inventions from university or public laboratories were reported to be of little importance compared with publications, conferences, informal interaction with university researchers, and consulting (Agarwal and Henderson, 2002; Nelson 2012).

Another important feature of the relationship between academic and industrial researchers is its interactive character. Industrial research may in fact "lead" and influence the agenda of academic research in some fields, as was the case in the early stages of research on light-emitting diodes and semiconductors.[1] According to Lécuyer (2005a), Provost Frederick Terman of Stanford University encouraged William Shockley to locate his new firm near the university in 1955 to expose Stanford engineering faculty to new research in solid-state physics and electronics, and a future dean of Stanford's Engineering School served an "apprenticeship" of sorts at Shockley Semiconductor.[2] The movement of researchers between industry and academia facilitates this interactive relationship (for example, the move by Dr. Shuji Nakamura, a pioneering research in gallium-arsenide LEDs [light-emitting diodes], from Nichia Chemicals in Japan to the University of California, Santa Barbara, in 2000; see Chapter 7 in Mowery et al., 2004, for further discussion). Because many empirical studies of university–industry research linkages rely on cross-sectional analyses of patenting and licensing data, the evolution of industry- and campus-specific linkages over time often is overlooked, and these linkages inaccurately are characterized as unidirectional, with inventions and knowledge flowing exclusively from academia to industry, in another manifestation of the simplistic "linear model" of innovation.

This volume examines the evolution of university–industry relationships in research and innovation at six campuses of the University of California system, ranging from viticulture to computer science. This collection of studies enriches our understanding of the dynamics of university–industry relationships and regional economic development in several ways. First, the approach adopted in each of the chapters relies on historical analysis of the evolution of academic and industrial research, innovation, and regional development in a number of different specific fields of research. This approach enables a richer characterization of the interactive relationship between industrial and academic research and innovation than appears in many empirical analyses that focus mainly on patenting, article citations, and licensing. Second, our coverage of research fields is broader than recent historical studies, many of which have concentrated primarily on biotechnology or the life sciences generally. Although these fields have been and remain extremely important to the development of university–industry relationships in the United States during the past three decades, the unusual characteristics of research, innovation, and technology transfer in biomedical research and innovation means that the findings of these previous studies may not apply to other areas of academic research and university–industry relationships.

Our focus on a leading U.S. public research university, the University of California, also contrasts with that of previous historical studies of leading private U.S. universities such as the Massachusetts Institute of Technology (MIT) or Stanford. Inasmuch as public research universities in the United States in 2009 performed nearly 69 percent of all academic research and approximately 60 percent of federally funded R&D and accounted for 34 percent of bachelor's and more than 50 percent of doctoral degrees awarded in 2009 (National Science Board, 2012),[3] we believe that it is essential to examine their role in the evolving landscape of university–industry relationships.

It is also important to recognize some caveats associated with this volume's case studies. We cannot portray these cases as "representative" of the totality of university–industry research relationships in U.S. public universities or in the University of California (UC). Nor are the cases covered in this volume representative of the full diversity of regional economic impacts of research at leading public universities such as the UC and its various campuses. In addition, the historical approach adopted in these cases tends to highlight successes in research and innovation, rather than presenting a balanced account of successes and failures. Here, too, we cannot claim that our "sample" is in some sense representative. Moreover, the selection of case studies was influenced by author availability, meaning that equally interesting and important cases at other campuses were not chosen. Finally, as we note in the following pages, the University of California is an unusual institution, distinguished by its large size; by its network of campuses that are funded, managed, and evaluated as coequal research universities; and by the remarkable economic vitality of many regions of the enormous statewide economy. The chapters in this volume therefore are intended to present a rich portrait of the contrasting technological and economic dynamics of evolving university–industry relationships across a diverse set of research fields, regions, and university campuses, without making claims that the studies necessarily generalize to other regions or universities. We hope that these studies will stimulate similar research on other universities and research fields.

CALIFORNIA AND THE UNIVERSITY OF CALIFORNIA SYSTEM

California was admitted to the Union in 1849, and its economic growth through the remainder of the nineteenth century and much of the twentieth century was based on minerals extraction and agriculture. By 2012, it was the most populous state in the United States, and its economy (gross state product) ranks the state as one of the ten largest economies in the world. More significantly for this book, today the state has become a globally recognized center of innovation. One imperfect measure of the state's innovative performance is patenting. California's share of all U.S. utility patents granted (based on the reported residence of the first inventor on the patent) rose from 9.5 percent of the total utility patents granted in 1963 (the earliest date for which data are available) by the U.S. Patent and Trademark Office (2013) to 12.7 percent in 2012 (see Table 1.1). In 2012, California-based inventors accounted for the largest single share of U.S. utility patents among the fifty states, and the share of U.S. patents granted to California-based individuals trailed only those granted to Japanese inventors. During the 2000 to 2012 period, 45.6 percent of all U.S. venture capital invested went to California-based firms (calculated by authors from PricewaterhouseCoopers, 2013).

Coincidentally or otherwise, California also is home to ten of the world's top fifty universities (listed by their ranking in the 2012 rankings compiled by Shanghai Jiaotong University, 2012): Stanford, UC Berkeley, California Institute of Technology, UC Los Angeles, UC San Diego, UC San Francisco, UC Santa Barbara, UC Irvine, University of Southern California, and UC Davis. The geographic entity accounting for the second largest group of universities among the top fifty is a nation, the United Kingdom, with five research universities included in the ranking. The state of New York has four universities ranked among this elite group, none of which are public (Cornell is partially private and partially public). No

TABLE I.I. U.S. Patent Office utility patent grants by reported residence of primary inventor: Selected states and nations, various years.

Origin		1963	1980	1990	2000	2010	2012
Total	Number	45,679	61,819	90,365	157,494	219,614	253,155
U.S. total	Number	37,174	39,218	47,391	85,068	107,791	121,026
	Percentage of total	81.4	63.4	52.4	54	49.1	47.8
California	Number	4,357	5,053	6,946	17,491	27,337	32,107
	Percentage of total	9.5	8.2	10.7	11.1	12.4	12.7
Texas	Number	1,340	1,810	2,929	6,322	7,545	8,367
	Percentage of total	2.9	2.9	3.8	4	3.4	3.3
New York	Number	4,437	3,356	4,054	6,086	7,082	7,640
	Percentage of total	9.7	5.4	4.3	3.9	3.2	3
Massachusetts	Number	1,647	1,534	1,953	3,458	4,923	5,734
	Percentage of total	3.6	2.5	2.3	2.2	2.2	2.3
Japan	Number	407	7,124	19,525	31,295	44,813	50,677
	Percentage of total	0.9	11.5	20.9	19.9	20.4	20.0
Germany	Number	2,338	5,782	7,614	10,235	12,363	13,835
	Percentage of total	5.1	8.4	6.2	6.5	5.6	5.5

SOURCE: U.S. Patent and Trademark Office (USPTO), 2013.

other state in the United States has more than two public universities in the global top fifty.[4] Remarkably, seven of the ten leading California research universities are campuses of the University of California.

The University of California system was founded in 1869 with the establishment of the Berkeley campus, which focused on research and teaching in the humanities and natural sciences; in 1905 an agriculture-focused branch campus was founded in Davis, California (later UC Davis). A citrus experiment station established in Riverside in 1907 eventually became the nucleus of the UC campus in that city, founded in 1959. From its inception, the University of California also included a school of medicine, based in San Francisco, that became an independent UC campus in 1964. In 1919 a southern branch campus was established in Los Angeles; in 1928 this became the second University of California campus. From these beginnings, by 2012 the system had grown to include ten campuses that enrolled over 230,000 students, employed more than 13,000 academic faculty members, and spent $22 billion on operations.

Within this large university system that includes campuses distributed among diverse regional economies, the management of university–industry relationships and technology transfer within the UC system has long been a source of debate and conflict. One of the most complex and contested topics has been the relationship between systemwide and campus policies toward industry and faculty-generated intellectual property. Having been managed in a centralized fashion for much of the 1945–1980 period, a complex and incomplete process of decentralization in the formal structure of these policies and managerial responsibilities has characterized most of the decades since. But throughout the post-1945 period that witnessed the emergence of the University of California as a multicampus system of distinguished research universities, campus-level departments and faculty members have developed diverse "local" solutions to challenges of industry–university relationships in research and innovation. This diversity is hardly surprising, in view of the very different regional economic environments within which these campuses are situated and, importantly, the diversity among each campus's strengths in academic research and industrial innovation.

In the section immediately following, we summarize the case studies in the volume, by way of providing support for the discussion of overarching themes in the concluding section of this Introduction. Our conclusions also consider the implications of these studies for policy makers and university administrators.

CHAPTER SUMMARIES

Chapters Two and Three in this volume, respectively written by Christophe Lécuyer and Steven Casper, compare different UC campuses in an examination of the ways in which campus strategy and contrasting regional industrial landscapes produced different modes of university–industry interaction in the regional microelectronics and biotechnology industries in different parts of the state. The chapter by Christophe Lécuyer examines the development of the microelectronics industries of the San

Francisco, Los Angeles, and Santa Barbara regions, focusing on the interaction between industrial innovation and semiconductor-related research at UC Berkeley (UCB), UC Los Angeles (UCLA), and UC Santa Barbara (UCSB). UCB research in this area focused on silicon semiconductors for computers, benefiting from and in turn advancing the development of Silicon Valley. As Lécuyer shows, semiconductor research at UCLA pursued a different path as a result of the influence of the Los Angeles area defense industry, which had long-standing interests in communications. Microelectronics research at UC Santa Barbara focused on the exotic semiconductor materials that were of great interest to the Department of Defense and the Santa Barbara R&D laboratory operated by Hughes Electronics.

As Lécuyer points out, their contrasting paths of research reflected in part the fact that all three campuses hired faculty members with industry experience and frequently hosted visiting researchers from leading firms in their regional industries. Researchers from industry contributed technical insights to academic researchers, as well as communicating the research priorities and challenges of industry to academia. In addition, of course, the interaction between industry and academia at all three campuses aided in the placement of graduates seeking employment and was associated with growth in research support from industry. Faculty members from all three campuses also spent sabbaticals in firms that contributed to the transfer of technology to firms and (as in the case of UCB Professor Ron Rohrer's sabbatical at Fairchild), transferred semiconductor design software knowledge from regional industry to the university.

Chapter Three, by Steven Casper, on university–industry relationships in the California biotechnology industry discusses the role of UC San Francisco and UC San Diego as sources of licensed technology and start-ups. Casper shows that the San Francisco and San Diego regions developed different patterns of university-based innovation and commercialization. These contrasting patterns of regional development were based on the formation of local UC faculty spinoffs, Genentech in the San Francisco Bay area and Hybritech in San Diego, that pursued different business models. Both "anchor firms" enjoyed rapid growth and spawned other firms. In the case of Hybritech, the spawning of new firms was associated with the acquisition of the firm by the established pharmaceutical firm Eli Lilly. Lilly's acquisition of Hybritech led to the departure of many of the firm's managers (aided, in many cases, by their sale of equity stakes in Hybritech to Lilly as part of the acquisition), and these experienced executives sought other biotechnological inventions to commercialize. Genentech was an independent firm for far longer and also was the source of a number of spin-offs, although it too was eventually acquired by Roche, which purchased a 20 percent stake in the firm in 1990 and acquired the remainder of Genentech in 2012. Genentech managed corporate R&D as an "open science" model of intensive collaboration and publishing with academic scientists, while Hybritech was more commercially oriented and published comparatively little.

This chapter illustrates the complex dynamics at work between universities and regional firms and highlights the influence on these dynamics of the industrial firms (in this case new firms based on university research; in other cases described in this volume, established firms) that pursue links with university researchers. Surprisingly, the influence of these firms on the evolution of regionally contrasting patterns of university–industry relationships has received little attention in the large literature on this topic.[5]

Chapter Four by Martin Kenney and his coauthors examines the postwar history of electrical engineering at UC Berkeley by studying a number of projects that were associated with the transformation of electrical engineering at UCB from a practice-oriented "craft" into engineering science during the post-1945 period. The chapter highlights the complex and varied channels of interaction between UCB and the new and established firms that propelled the Bay Area's economic growth after 1960. Among the most important technological innovations from the UCB researchers are software-based advances, such as BSD UNIX, GENIE, and INGRES, none of which was the focus of patenting and licensing by the university. Data on patenting, licensing revenues, and even new-firm foundations fail to capture these contributions and overlook the bidirectional nature of the intellectual and personal interactions between UCB's EECS (Electrical Engineering and Computer Science) Department and local industry.

Chapter Five, by Walshok and West, examines the symbiotic relationship between UCSD and the wireless industry in San Diego, an especially interesting case of the coevolution of university and industrial research and innovation. Although his enterprise was not founded on UCSD-developed technology, the serendipitous decision of UCSD faculty member Irwin Jacobs to relocate his small start-up from Los Angeles to San Diego in 1971 initiated a powerful entrepreneurial dynamic that proved beneficial to the industry and the university. Walshok and West argue that this university–industry interaction benefited from an established cluster of government research facilities and technology-intensive aerospace firms in the San Diego region. During most of the period following the establishment of the UC campus in this region and the founding of Qualcomm, UCSD's most important role was providing trained personnel to the burgeoning regional wireless telecommunications industry. In addition to training undergraduate and graduate technical personnel, UCSD's extension programs provided advanced engineering courses, often taught by industry professionals, in wireless technology for engineers employed in local firms. The growth of the regional wireless industry initially depended less on UCSD research advances than on students trained in advanced research techniques.

Over time, UCSD became an important source of innovations, entrepreneurs, and new firms in wireless and related technologies that further accelerated the region's growth. The successful local telecommunications firms and the entrepreneurs who formed them became a source of significant gifts to the university that further strengthened the university's research strengths and stature in the rapidly advancing technologies of wireless telecommunications. As with other chapters in this collection, the UCSD narrative highlights the importance of distinguishing between the factors that may catalyze the initiation of a regional high-technology cluster's growth and the factors that sustain such growth over ensuing years.

Cyrus Mody's Chapter Six on UC Santa Barbara and the development of a regional scientific instruments "cluster" specializing in advanced electron microscopes describes a complicated interaction between university research and a start-up firm, Digital Instruments (DI), that was rooted in a unique UCSB master's degree program in scientific instrumentation. The chapter is one of very few studies of innovation in scientific instruments, a field of commercially significant innovation singled out by Nathan Rosenberg (1992) for its long-standing reliance on academic research (in many cases, based on the tinkering by academic users of instruments).[6] Digital Instruments was founded to commercialize a scanning tunneling electronic microscope (STM) that relied in part on the contributions of a visiting UCSB researcher based at IBM's Zurich R&D complex, the site of the work on STMs that led to a Nobel Prize—in this case, the movement of knowledge from industry to academia catalyzed academic innovation. Once established, Digital Instruments expanded its employment of UCSB graduate students from the instrumentation program and developed a series of important follow-on products, most of which initially relied on unpatented research advances from UCSB.

Mody's discussion of the development of probe microscopy emphasizes the informal, interactive character of the collaborations between university and industry researchers that spawned the development of advanced microscopes for applications in university and industrial research. Much of the research within UCSB that supported these innovations in industry was itself relatively applied, in contrast to the fundamental science that contributed to the founding of Genentech and other Bay Area biotechnology firms. Patent licensing was of secondary importance in facilitating these interactions at the inception of DI's development. As the links between Digital Instruments matured (and as new firms were spawned by Digital Instruments), the UCSB research advances increasingly were patented and licensed to DI and other regional firms, while DI expanded its financial and in-kind (for example, advanced instruments) contributions to research at UCSB.

The emergence of a scientific instrument industrial cluster in Santa Barbara thus did not initially depend on the licensing of UCSB technology or on sophisticated UCSB-based technology transfer activities. Instead, the cluster's growth was catalyzed by the entrepreneurial proclivities of key academic researchers at UCSB and a mutually beneficial flow of information and personnel between UCSB and DI. Moreover, as was the case with Hybritech, the acquisition of DI by another firm produced a wave of new firms founded by former DI employees in the region. The resulting scientific instruments cluster had significant economic benefits for the Santa Barbara region and enabled UCSB to become a center for nanotechnology research.

The relationship between U.S. agricultural innovation and public research universities has a long history (Ruttan, 1982; Kloppenburg, 1988; Wright, 2012), but studies of this relationship have had little influence on contemporary discussions of university technology transfer. Chapter Seven, by James Lapsley and Daniel Sumner, on the relationship between the Napa Valley wine industry and the Department of Viticulture and Enology at UC Davis highlights the ways in which university–industry relationships change over time as a result of the maturation and increasing innovative capacity of regional firms. The relationship between UC Davis research and the regional wine industry, however, also was affected by the increasing consumer demand for higher-quality wines that emerged in the 1960s.

The transformation in the technical capabilities of the Napa wine industry and the growth of the region's reputation for high-quality wine production benefited in the 1950s and 1960s from the flow of personnel, technology, and knowledge from the UC Davis viticulture program. Even in the early years of this transformation, UC Davis research publications played an important role. For example, the pioneering postwar Napa Valley vintner Robert Mondavi referred to *The Technology of Winemaking*, a book published by UC Davis professors, as his "bible." But much of the knowledge flowing from academia to the industry during this early period was "tacit" in nature, and Napa winemakers benefited from their proximity to UC Davis, as well as the UC vineyard in Oakville, the heart of the Napa Valley. Once again, much of the academic research that supported these improvements in methods and techniques in the region's wine industry was highly applied in nature and relied to a significant extent on the availability of a "test bed" in the unique climatic and growing conditions associated with the Napa wine industry. The UC Napa vineyard provided an important site for university experts and local vineyard owners to cooperate and learn from one another. The Oakville research station also was involved in extension services through its dissemination of improved rootstock to local growers.

In the 1950s, UC Davis was central to the formation of the American Society of Enologists, which linked university scientists to industry practitioners and contributed to the transformation of wine making into a science-based profession. As the Napa industry expanded and became more science based, by the late 1970s UC Davis enology and viticulture graduates were in great demand within the U.S. wine industry, leading to expanded enrollments in these academic programs. UC Davis University Extension, the self-supporting continuing education arm of the Davis campus, also began to offer short courses in wine and grape production. Finally, UC Davis researchers developed a number of research tools that were widely used in the global wine industry. None of these research tools was patented and licensed, instead being freely supplied to industry.

Since the 1980s, the Napa and other regional wine firms have expanded their support of UC Davis research and have made significant philanthropic contributions to the Davis program and campus. The long history of mutually beneficial interactions between the UC Davis campus and the regional (and increasingly, global) wine industry has operated largely through the long-established "agricultural research and extension" model that dates back to the late nineteenth century in the United States, rather than relying on the "Bayh-Dole" model of interaction that emphasizes patenting and licensing.

SUMMARY OBSERVATIONS

The diversity of knowledge-based interactions between university and "industrial" (including agricultural) innovation summarized in these chapters is remarkable, but some themes that are common to all of the studies provide useful perspectives for policy makers and university administrators who seek to encourage innovation and regional growth. These chapters also suggest some need for caution and innovation in the approaches adopted by university administrators and public officials to the evaluation of the contributions of research universities to national, state-level, or local economic development.

Even the studies examining the development of university–industry research relationships in specific technologies at different UC campuses, such as Casper's chapter on biotechnology and Lécuyer's chapter on semiconductors, highlight important contrasts in regional industrial and technological specialization that both influenced and were influenced by these relationships, reflecting different campus-level research specializations and the idiosyncratic character of regional economic development. Indeed, as in the contrast between Los Angeles or San Diego and the Bay Area, the regional industrial structure that predated the academic research discussed in these chapters influenced the direction of both academic and industrial innovation and development. There are also important contrasts among UC campuses and technology fields in policies toward intellectual property protection for academic inventions. For example, semiconductor research at UCSB was patented, but the early research on this campus dealing with scanning electron microscopes largely was not. Faculty resistance to patenting at UCB meant that a substantial portion of the research at UCB on semiconductor design software was not patented. The absence of patents on design software certainly did not discourage an intense interaction between UCB and industry researchers and arguably contributed to the broad adoption of this innovation within industry.

The portrait of university–industry interactions that emerges from these chapters thus is a complex and heterogeneous one, highlighting the diverse channels through which interactions occur, as well as the fact that interactions often flow in both directions between academia and industry. Moreover, it is inaccurate to characterize all of the research in the academic "ivory tower" that supports these interactions as basic research. The content of the academic research that has contributed to industrial innovation ranges from fundamental science to applied testing and other activities, depending on the field of research and the characteristics of the industry. The varied nature of this academic research further questions the validity of a "linear model" of innovation based on university–industry interaction.[7]

These characteristics of the interactions have several important implications. First, simple counts of academic patents or licensing revenues are poor measures of the "performance" of universities in developing or transferring technologies and knowledge to industry. Such data overlook the enormous variation among patents in their technological and economic significance or value, and patent counts alone also cannot account for the sharp contrasts in the economic value of patents among different fields of industrial innovation. Data on patenting or licensing revenues also overlook the existence of other forms and channels of transfer and interaction. The chapters by Kenney and his coauthors and by Lécuyer focus on numerous technologies (for example, INGRES, Project GENIE, BSD Unix, and semiconductor design software) that were not patented by UCB faculty, instead being provided to all interested parties in industry and academia. Lapsley's study of UC Davis and the Napa Valley wine industry similarly argues that the liberal dissemination of university research through a variety of formal and informal interactions, rather than patenting of inventions, was of great value to industry. Indeed, in several cases at UCB and UC Davis, the absence of patents on important advances contributed to an environment where industry researchers could share their expertise with university scientists, accelerating technical progress and adoption of key technological innovations. Moreover, the absence of patents did not preclude the establishment of new firms on the basis of these technological developments that enjoyed commercial success.

Patents and patent-based technology transfer are generally acknowledged to be more economically significant in biomedical technologies, as the chapter by Casper points out. Yet even in this sector, the characteristics of university–industry interactions at different UC campuses differed considerably. These contrasts suggest that no single template for designing and managing university–industry relationships is likely to be effective without flexibility to accommodate differences among industries, research fields, regional economies, and university campuses. Such flexibility should also accommodate contrasting approaches to the management of intellectual property and its licensing. Yet these contrasts and the associated importance of flexibility in strategy and policy remain insufficiently recognized in many U.S. universities' policies toward the management of university–industry relationships and patenting.

Another important theme that spans virtually all of these case studies, noted earlier, is the bidirectional nature of industry–university interactions and knowledge flows. Indeed, this characterization of these interactions applies equally to the flow of personnel, which is not uniformly a one-way flow based on the graduation of students or the departure of faculty to join firms. The academic research agendas in semiconductors and software at both UCB and UCSB, for example, benefited from the recruitment by academic departments of faculty from industry in both the United States and Japan. Equally important contributions to academic research flowed from faculty sabbaticals in industry and industry researchers' sabbaticals at universities. And in at least some of these instances, particularly in software, the two-way flow of personnel and ideas between industry and academic research benefited from the absence of patents covering key technological advances.

This bidirectional interaction between university and industry research and innovation also underscores the broader ways in which regional industry influences the evolution of university–industry relationships. The discussion in the chapters by Lécuyer and Kenney and his coauthors of the ways in which established firms in the San Francisco and Los Angeles areas influenced the research agenda and approach to commercializing their advances by UCLA and UCB researchers suggests that the influence of established firms on regional industrial and technological development may be as important as that of university "spin-offs" founded on the basis of academic research advances. Of course, in some cases, these spin-offs (for example, Cadence, Digital Instruments, Genentech, and Synopsys) mature into established regional firms. In addition, of course, the characteristics of the spin-off firms, especially their role as sources of still other new firms, is another important influence on the contrasting trajectories of university-based regional growth in Los Angeles, Santa Barbara, San Diego, and the San Francisco Bay Area, as the chapters suggest.[8] This influence of established and new firms is but one example of the ways in which the effects of university research on industrial innovation and regional growth are affected by institutions external to the university. Among the most important of these, in addition to the characteristics of existing firms, is the extent to which labor markets for scientists and engineers support movement in both directions between academic and industry and the characteristics of financial markets, notably the supply of venture capital and strength of "angel investor" networks.

Our cases also show that the contributions of university research to regional growth and those of regional industry to university research can change over time, although university-trained personnel appear to be important sources of linkage and benefit throughout the development of all of the industrial clusters examined in this volume. During the growth of the Napa Valley wine industry in the 1950s and 1960s, for example, UC Davis was the primary source of advice and technical information for the regional industry. As the technical capabilities of the Napa Valley winemakers grew, however, the importance of UCD research diminished somewhat relative to that of UC enology and viticulture graduates. By contrast, UCSD research results were of modest importance in the establishment of Linkabit and its successor, Qualcomm, in the San Diego region. Instead, the university's graduates were an important source of benefit for regional industry, a benefit that was supplemented by the contributions of UCSD University Extension courses. The expansion of the regional wireless communications cluster in San Diego, however, relied to a growing extent on the contributions of UCSD research.

Even in biotechnology, where the central role of basic science means that the knowledge underpinning industrial innovations is more likely to flow from academia to industry, numerous industry-based technical advances have been of major significance for academic as well as industrial research. For example, the polymerase chain reaction technology (itself the basis for a Nobel Prize in 1993) was invented by Cetus scientists and rapidly put to use in both academia and industry.

Casper's Chapter Three also highlights another type of knowledge-based interaction that involves contributions from practitioners to laboratory research. William Rutter, who was hired as the chairman of the Department of Biochemistry and Biophysics at UCSF in 1968, encouraged faculty members to collaborate with clinicians in their research, thereby linking the medical practitioner community with laboratory scientists. Casper also presents data on the extent of coauthorship between Genentech and scientists at both UCSF and Stanford: "Genentech scientists were authors on 6,847 publications, of which 539 included collaborations with UCSF scientists, in addition to 267 collaborations with Stanford researchers and 57 with UC Berkeley." In the San Francisco Bay Area, collaboration between local universities and small biotechnology firms continued long after the firms had grown to significant size. San Diego biotechnology firms, however, relied less on scientific publications coauthored with university researchers in their efforts to commercialize university-developed innovations. Even in this "science-based" field of research, then, Casper's chapter and other published research highlight the limits of a naïve "linear model" conceptualization of the links between university research and industrial innovation.

Another important source of benefit for universities from regional industry is the financial contributions of firms to university research, in the form of philanthropic contributions and industry-sponsored research. The chapters describe the ways in which the beneficiaries of university technology transfer may also support the university through philanthropy, which assumes a number of forms. At UCB, regional and national semiconductor firms provided significant funds for an expansion of the building that houses the Electrical Engineering and Computer Science Department. The founder of Digital Instruments has made a number of significant philanthropic contributions to UCSB; Irwin Jacobs, the founder of Qualcomm, has made major philanthropic contributions to UCSD; and Robert Mondavi (a Stanford graduate) funded the establishment of the Robert Mondavi Institute for Wine and Food Science at UC Davis. Industry-sponsored research is also very significant, especially by comparison with licensing revenues. Annual gross licensing revenues for the UC system (including awards from successful patent litigation) averaged roughly $99 million during fiscal years (FY) 1999 through 2004, less than one-half of industry-sponsored research for the UC system in FY 2003 (a total of $235 million).[9]

Our chapters illustrate the complex ways within which universities or, put more properly, university researchers contribute to the industrial technological advancement. They support a position of cautious skepticism in assessing the value of the "patent-based approach" to knowledge and technology transfer that received a significant impetus from the Bayh-Dole Act of 1980.[10] Patents and licensing assuredly are important in some fields and far less so in others. Moreover, an exclusive focus on patent-based channels of technology transfer may inadvertently lead to policies that discourage other equally beneficial or valuable (for both industry and academia) channels of interaction. The interactive relationship between regional industry and the development of university research must be kept in mind by both university and industrial managers in developing policies to maximize mutual benefit from these relationships.

We believe that these chapters provide a rich portrait of the ways in which a nationally unique public university system, the University of California, has operated as a powerful engine for knowledge-based growth throughout this large and diverse state. Although our chapters omit other important instances of knowledge-based interactions between UC and industry researchers, we believe that the emphasis in these chapters on the numerous, diverse, and heterogeneous channels of interaction between UC campuses and regional industry would only be reinforced by a lengthier study. Moreover, these chapters scarcely touch on other crucial contributions of the UC campuses to state and national economic welfare through the sheer breadth and excellence of the training provided on these campuses, as well as the equally essential contributions of this training to economic and social mobility within a diverse and expanding state population. From a social and economic policy perspective, it is essential to recognize the importance of these broader contributions from the UC system to the national and regional economies. California's future economic success depends on knowledge-based growth, something to which the University of California system must remain an indispensable contributor.

NOTES

1. For an industry insider's view on the relationship between industry and the university in semiconductors, see Moore and Davis (2002).

2. [James] Gibbons [future dean of engineering at Stanford], a junior faculty in the Electrical Engineering Department [*sic*] at Stanford, worked at Shockley Semiconductor on a part-time basis. Frederick Terman, Stanford's provost, and John Linvill, the head of the Solid-State Laboratory, had recently apprenticed Gibbons to William Shockley. They had asked Gibbons to learn the techniques required for the fabrication of silicon devices from Shockley and then transfer these techniques back to the university (Lecuyer, 2005a, p. 138).

3. According to the National Science Board (2012), public universities "represented less than 10 percent of all 4-year colleges and universities in the U.S. in 2009, but about 33 percent of first-time, full-time undergraduate enrollment that year" (p. 3). In addition, public universities enroll a disproportionate share of undergraduates from low-income backgrounds; 30 percent of Pell grant recipients attended public universities in the 2009–2010 academic year, well above the 13 percent of grant recipients enrolling at private, nonprofit four-year institutions (National Science Board, 2012).

4. Shanghai Jiaotong University, 2012.

5. For further confirmation of this point, see Owen-Smith and Powell (2006).

6. For another case study of the interaction between university researchers and a university spin-off that commercialized a scientific instrument technology, see Lenoir and Lécuyer (1995) on the commercialization of Stanford-pioneered nuclear magnetic resonance technology at Varian.

7. Rosenberg and Nelson (1994) highlighted the contributions to industrial innovation of applied research in U.S. universities in their important 1994 paper.

8. The late Steven Klepper (2011) pointed out that such entrepreneurial spawning of new from established firms frequently is responsible for the formation of an industrial cluster.

9. *Net* licensing revenues for the UC system (which nets out royalty payments to faculty inventors) were of course far smaller, averaging slightly less than $22 million annually during this period. More recent data on net revenues unfortunately are unavailable.

10. For one skeptical view, see Kenney and Patton (2009, 2011).

CHAPTER TWO

Semiconductor Innovation and Entrepreneurship at Three University of California Campuses

CHRISTOPHE LÉCUYER

California has long been a major center of innovative activity in semiconductors and in related industries such as chip design software and semiconductor manufacturing equipment (Kenney and Patton, 2005; Lécuyer, 2005a). It is home to sixteen of the fifty largest merchant semiconductor firms in the world, including Intel, the largest semiconductor corporation with roughly 12 percent of the worldwide market for microchips. California is also a major center of entrepreneurship in semiconductors and captures an overwhelming share of venture capital monies invested in this field. Since the early 2000s, 70 percent of all venture capital invested in semiconductors in the United States has gone to California start-ups each year; in terms of initial public stock offerings, the state has been even more dominant, accounting for 72 percent of the total offerings from 1996 through 2000 (PricewaterhouseCoopers, various years). Semiconductor firms are active in most metropolitan areas in California. The main center of semiconductor activity in the state is of course Silicon Valley, a high-tech district named after the main material used in semiconductor manufacturing. It is in Silicon Valley that most microelectronics firms are headquartered (the high cost of land means that little component manufacturing activity occurs in the region). Silicon Valley is also an important center for chip design software and semiconductor manufacturing equipment. But there are other dynamic semiconductor clusters in other parts of the state. Los Angeles, Orange County, and San Diego have strong firms focusing on communication integrated circuits. There is also a long-established cluster of smaller companies working on compound semiconductors, exotic semiconductor materials made of different chemical elements, around Santa Barbara.

Likewise, the University of California is a major academic institution in semiconductor research and innovation in the United States. Over the last forty years, UC has emerged as an important center of innovation in solid-state electronics and optoelectronics. It was the first university to establish an integrated circuits laboratory. Groups of UC faculty members and students have since made significant contributions to semiconductor technology and industry, especially in the areas of communications circuits and chip design software. They also established major firms specializing in integrated circuit design and the software used to design these circuits.

The strength of UC's programs in semiconductors can be gauged through several measures such as the number of faculty members elected to the National Academy of Engineering, presentations at prestigious conferences, and the rankings of individual departments. For example, over the last ten years, UC engineers have presented more papers at the International Solid-State Circuits Conference (ISSCC), the most prestigious conference in silicon-based microchips, than other top-ranked schools in electrical engineering. In particular, they presented more papers at the ISSCC than Stanford, Caltech, the University of Illinois, and the University of Michigan combined (International Solid-State Circuits Conference, various years). Similarly, the Materials Department at UC Santa Barbara is consistently ranked first in national surveys of materials science and engineering programs, largely on the basis of the strength of its compound semiconductor group. How did UC and its campuses emerge as important players in semiconductor research and innovation? What did the university's research and teaching programs owe to the semiconductor industry in California? In turn, what did UC researchers contribute to the California-based semiconductor industry?

To address these questions, this chapter examines and compares three UC campuses active in semiconductor research: UC Berkeley, UCLA, and UC Santa Barbara. These campuses were not the only UC campuses with research and teaching programs in semiconductors. All UC campuses (with the exception of UCSF) conduct research in solid-state electronics and optoelectronics. UC San Diego, for example, has a distinguished program in communication integrated circuits (which is discussed in greater detail in the chapter on UC San Diego). UC Davis has been active in this field since the 1970s. But this chapter focuses on UC Berkeley, UCLA, and

UC Santa Barbara. Over the last forty years, these three campuses developed close relations with California-based semiconductor corporations. For example, the solid-state electronics program at UC Berkeley grew in close contact with semiconductor firms in Silicon Valley and contributed new and often successful start-ups, as well as a considerable amount of technology, know-how, and engineering talent to this high-tech cluster. Engineers working on semiconductors at UCLA drew on the resources offered by large defense corporations located in Southern California and established a major fabless semiconductor firm, Broadcom (fabless companies do not operate manufacturing plants, "fabs" in semiconductor parlance; they contract out production to other firms). Finally, the compound semiconductor specialists at UC Santa Barbara benefited from the presence of Hughes in the area. They later established innovative start-ups in their region and in Silicon Valley.

Thus, this chapter contributes to recent work on the relation between universities and their regions. Economists and other social scientists have demonstrated the importance of regional environments in the development of academic research programs. Jason Owen-Smith and Walter Powell have shown that the biotechnology clusters located in Boston and the San Francisco Bay Area exhibited different patterns of university-based innovation and entrepreneurship (Owen-Smith and Powell, 2006). Other scholars have argued that industrial environments surrounding universities help shape their intellectual orientations and the content of their research programs (Braunerhjelm, 2006; Furman and MacGarvie, 2007; Tuzi, 2005). The present author has shown, for example, that the solid-state electronics program at Stanford owed greatly to continued interaction with Silicon Valley–based firms. Corporations such as Shockley Semiconductor Laboratory, Hewlett-Packard, Fairchild Semiconductor, and Intel contributed people, ideas, technologies, and monies to the university. Stanford faculty members used these resources to make significant innovations in manufacturing processes and microchip design that were then widely used in industry (Lécuyer, 2005b). Oddly enough, far less is known about the interaction between UC Berkeley's semiconductor researchers and the Silicon Valley.

The University of California offers a particularly interesting case to investigate the interactions of academic programs with their environments because it is a single institution located in many different regions of a state with a very large and diverse economy. All campuses belong to the same organization and follow the same basic internal rules on how to relate to

industry and to manage intellectual property. Until recently, they benefited from University of California systemwide programs such as MICRO
and UC Discovery that fostered relations with the state's microelectronics
and computer industries and provided significant funding to semiconductor research at the campuses. But over the years these campuses developed
very different characteristics and followed different intellectual and technological orientations in semiconductors. They also developed different
approaches to entrepreneurship and technology transfer in this field. Many
of these differences can be accounted for by intercampus competition, by
the different technical interests of faculty members in solid-state electronics and optoelectronics, and also and most importantly by the different environments in which the campuses were situated. For example, UC Berkeley is located close to Silicon Valley, whereas UC Santa Barbara is based in
a metropolitan area that has had only a small high-tech industry, especially
instrumentation firms (Cyrus Mody's Chapter Six in this volume highlights the campus's strength in scientific instruments). In contrast, UCLA
is situated in a region whose high-tech industrial structure has long been
dominated by large, integrated defense firms. In other words, the different
campuses developed contrasting innovative foci and entrepreneurial approaches that were conditioned by the contrasting technological resources,
interests, and entrepreneurial styles of their respective regions.

This chapter argues that UC campuses, especially UC Berkeley and
UCLA, benefited from their proximity to major centers of semiconductor innovation. Not unlike Stanford, they took advantage of this proximity to build close relations with semiconductor firms, which enabled UC
researchers to identify problems of importance to industry; to gain access
to people, funding, and ideas; and to bring technologies developed in the
corporate world to the university. It was on the basis of these technology
transfers that academic administrators and faculty members at UC Berkeley, UCLA, and UC Santa Barbara built major research programs in semiconductors. They used these industrial inputs to make important innovations that were later commercialized through technology licensing, faculty
consulting, the hiring of students by industrial concerns, and the formation of new firms. As a result, these UC universities had a significant impact on a critical sector of California's high-tech manufacturing economy.

Within this general pattern, the specific forms of innovation and
entrepreneurship and their impact on the semiconductor industry differed widely across the UC system. Over the last forty years, UC Berkeley, UCLA, and UC Santa Barbara developed specific subspecialties in

semiconductors, partially on the basis of their regions' particular industrial strengths, the technological interests of leading faculty members, and competitive forces within UC and the academic disciplines of semiconductor electronics and optoelectronics. Making the most of the resources offered by Silicon Valley, UC Berkeley focused on silicon integrated circuits, especially communications circuits, and on the software tools required to design complex microchips. UCLA brought in technologies from large defense firms in Southern California and developed strengths in broadband communications chips. Entering semiconductor research significantly later than UC Berkeley, UC Santa Barbara concentrated on compound semiconductors, a field in which the campus faculty saw much potential and where they would not compete with more established campuses. The three campuses also developed different ways of transferring and commercializing these technologies. Some faculty groups, especially at UC Berkeley and UCLA, preferred the free distribution of their findings and software programs, whereas others (at UC Santa Barbara and, to a limited extent, Berkeley) favored more formal forms of technology transfer. Different types of university-based entrepreneurship can also be identified. Some faculty, especially at Berkeley, created many competing spin-offs, while others (at UCLA) sought to build large firms by consolidating existing start-ups. In the case of UC Santa Barbara, researchers established their firms in Silicon Valley and sometimes in the Santa Barbara area—with the goal of having them acquired by larger firms located outside the region.

UC BERKELEY: THE INTEGRATED CIRCUITS
LABORATORY AND MIXED-SIGNAL CIRCUITS

UC Berkeley was the first UC campus to enter semiconductor research. It did so under the leadership of Donald Pederson. Pederson, a circuit specialist, had received his PhD in electrical engineering from Stanford. He had done research on transistor circuits at the Bell Telephone Laboratories in the first half of the 1950s. In 1955, Pederson was recruited as a junior faculty member to UC Berkeley's division of electrical engineering by two powerful faculty members, John Whinnery and Paul Morton (the current and former chairs of electrical engineering at Berkeley). Both Whinnery, a leading microwave tube technologist, and Morton, a computer engineer, advocated the building of a science-based curriculum in electrical engineering and thought that Pederson would help them realize this vision (for the history of the Electrical Engineering Department at Berkeley, see Chapter Four by Martin Kenney, David Mowery, and Donald Patton in this volume). Another semiconductor expert who soon joined the department was Thomas Everhart. Everhart had pioneered the use of electron beams to make semiconductor devices at Westinghouse. Along with Pederson and Morton, Everhart played a significant role in the development of solid-state electronics at Berkeley. One of their first moves was the creation of the integrated circuits laboratory in 1962 (Perry, 1998; Whinnery, 1996). Integrated circuits were then a new technology, recently developed in industry. Texas Instruments had announced the creation of the first integrated circuit in 1959 (integrated circuits were composed of various transistors, diodes, resistors, and capacitors placed on the same sliver of silicon crystal). Two years later, Fairchild Semiconductor, a firm located in Silicon Valley, commercialized the first family of integrated circuits. It was quickly followed in the market by Texas Instruments and two Silicon Valley startups, Amelco and Signetics (for the early history of the industry, see Berlin, 2005; Holbrook et al., 2000; Lécuyer, 2005a; Lécuyer and Brock, 2010).[1]

Even before microchips were commercialized by TI, Fairchild, and other Silicon Valley firms, Pederson determined that Berkeley should become active in the new field. As early as 1960, Pederson sensed that integrated circuits would revolutionize electronics and that there would be a large demand for engineers knowledgeable about this important technology (this was remarkably prescient, as many leading semiconductor engineers would come to the same conclusion several years later) (Lécuyer, 2005a). Along with Morton and Everhart, Pederson also reasoned that to train integrated circuit engineers, they would need to create a new facility where students could learn how to fabricate microchips. Establishing an integrated circuits facility, however, was particularly difficult in a university environment. Semiconductor fabrication facilities were expensive. They also quickly became obsolete, as semiconductor manufacturing technology evolved very rapidly. Not surprisingly, Pederson's project encountered significant opposition within the department and the university. It also generated a great deal of skepticism in the semiconductor industry (Hodges 2008–2010; Hodges and Newton, 2007; Perry, 1998; Turin, 1980a).[2]

Using their formidable political skills, Pederson, Morton, and Everhart overcame these resistances and created the first integrated circuits laboratory in a university environment in the early 1960s. They secured $300,000 in grant funding from the Air Force to build the laboratory. They also benefited from the support of Whinnery, who mustered the necessary lab space for the project.[3] To outfit the integrated circuits laboratory, Pederson, Everhart, and Morton pooled the laboratory equipment and instruments they owned. This in itself was an important social innovation. The integrated circuits laboratory was a collective endeavor, and its three founders were equal partners in it. This arrangement was extremely rare in American universities at that time. It set an important precedent for the building of large, collective research programs in solid-state electronics at Berkeley (Hodges, 2008–2010; Hodges and Newton, 2007; Perry, 1998; Whinnery, 1996). With the leadership of Robert Pepper, a former student of Pederson and a newly hired assistant professor, and of George Becker, a skilled and resourceful engineer, the group acquired and installed secondhand integrated circuit fabrication equipment. Becker designed and built the photolithographic tools, which were too costly to purchase. Students from Pederson, Everhart, and Morton's groups developed fabrication processes and then designed and fabricated simple experimental integrated circuits (Hodges, 2008–2010; 2012a,b).

In this, they were greatly aided by inputs from industry. They were helped especially by engineering managers working at semiconductor firms in Silicon Valley. For example, Gordon Moore, who had been a chemistry undergraduate at UC Berkeley and was the head of Fairchild's research and development laboratory, introduced the Berkeley engineers to the appropriate experts within his organization. In turn, these engineers advised them on how to design the necessary equipment and processes (Hodges, 2008–2010). The connection to Fairchild Semiconductor was essential. Fairchild was the fountainhead of semiconductor manufacturing knowledge, having developed the main processes used in the production of silicon devices a few years earlier (Lécuyer, 2005a; Lécuyer and Brock, 2010). Also important for the establishment of the integrated circuits laboratory at Berkeley was the assistance of military contractors such as Westinghouse and Texas Instruments (they had been instructed by the Air Force to share their semiconductor manufacturing expertise with the Berkeley group). To facilitate learning from industry, Pederson, Everhart, and Morton agreed that they would not consult for semiconductor firms. They wanted to be seen as a neutral party and benefit from interactions with as many semiconductor corporations as possible. With significant help with industry and after two years of planning and construction, Pederson, Everhart, and Morton opened the integrated circuits laboratory in 1962. Doctoral students made the first functional integrated circuits that very same year (Hodges, 2008–2010; Perry, 1998; Turin, 1980a; UCB, 1985).[4]

Pederson, Everhart, and Morton produced a growing stream of master's and PhD students knowledgeable about microchips and solid-state electronics in the 1960s. Because Berkeley was one of the very few sources of such students, they were in great demand in the semiconductor industry.[5] Pederson's students and assistant professors quickly rose to positions of influence in industry. After running the integrated circuits laboratory on a daily basis, Robert Pepper left to become the lead engineer of Sprague Electric's microelectronics division. William Howard, another former PhD student and junior faculty member, joined Motorola, where he rose to positions of influence. Another notable doctoral student was David Hodges. Hodges completed his PhD under Pederson's direction in 1965. After a postdoctoral fellowship in Denmark (where he aided in the planning of an integrated circuits laboratory), he moved to the Bell Telephone Laboratories. At Bell Labs, he became the head of a research group investigating integrated circuits for digital switching and transmission. Other Berkeley students accepted positions at IBM, Fairchild Semiconductor, National Semiconductor, Tektronix, Hewlett-Packard, the Bell Telephone Laboratories, Rockwell, and other electronics corporations located in Southern California. This network of former Berkeley students proved invaluable for the strengthening of Berkeley's integrated circuits processing capabilities in the second half of the 1960s. Hewlett-Packard and Tektronix, for example, transferred some of their microchip manufacturing processes to Berkeley (Hodges, 2008–2010).

The presence of graduates in key positions in industry was also essential for the growth of the microelectronics program at UCB in the 1970s and 1980s. At that time, the integrated circuits group expanded its activities into two main directions: the design and fabrication of mixed signal integrated circuits and the engineering of software tools that enabled the design of more and more complex microchips.[6] Critical for the initiation of the research program on mixed signal circuits was Hodges's return to UC Berkeley as faculty member in 1970. His return was strongly supported by Pederson and others who viewed microelectronics as a field of great strategic importance for the university and wanted to strengthen Berkeley's presence in it. With him, Hodges brought to Berkeley expertise in logic and memory circuits and a strong interest in and familiarity with the telephone system. At first, Hodges and his students worked on memory and logic integrated circuits. But he soon found out that grant money was scarce in this field of research and that it was very hard to compete with corporations that had very large and well-funded engineering programs in logic microchips and memory chips (Hodges, 2008–2010).

This realization led Hodges to reorient his research to an area of micro-electronics technology not yet exploited by industrial firms: MOS mixed signal integrated circuits. MOS (metal-oxide semiconductor) was a new device and manufacturing technology that was increasingly used in the semiconductor industry to make digital microchips (Bassett, 2002; Brock and Lécuyer, 2012). Hodges was interested in applying MOS to the fabrication of mixed-signal circuits. Mixed-signal circuits were integrated circuits processing both digital and analog signals. They enabled the interface between digital systems and the analog world. Hodges did much of his work on mixed-signal circuits in collaboration with Paul Gray. Gray, an analog circuit expert who had worked at Fairchild Semiconductor, joined the EECS faculty in 1971. Working together, Hodges and Gray reasoned that MOS was quickly becoming the dominant technology for the production of digital microchips, especially microprocessors, but that other types of integrated circuits such as analog and mixed-signal circuits were still made with an older manufacturing technology, bipolar. Bipolar analog and mixed signal circuits were difficult to use in conjunction with MOS logic and memory chips. As a result, there was clearly a need for MOS analog and mixed-signal circuits that would interface well with MOS microprocessors and memories. Hodges and Gray reckoned that this need was not filled by semiconductor firms. No such products existed on the market (Gray, 1998; Hodges, 2008–2010).[7]

Making the most of this opportunity, in the early 1970s Hodges and his colleagues launched a research program on MOS analog and mixed-signal circuits with funding from the Air Force. Designing and making these circuits was especially difficult because MOS technology, unlike bipolar technology, was not well suited for analog applications. At first, Hodges, Gray, and their students designed and fabricated various MOS analog and mixed-signal chips in the integrated circuits laboratory. But, as Hodges later recalled, "Our work never really jelled until we focused on one important application. That was the voice interface to the telephone network" (Hodges, 2008–2010). Since his days at the Bell Labs, Hodges had been interested in the conversion between analog and digital voice signals (which required pulse code modulation—PCM—coding and de-coding). But he had not been schooled by his Bell Labs colleagues in the details of PCM technology. The situation changed when Vidar, a medium-sized communications company based in Silicon Valley, hired Hodges as a consultant in 1973. Vidar asked Hodges, the memory expert, to assess the reliability of Intel's memory chips for the private telephone networks they were designing. This assignment enabled Hodges and Gray to gain a thorough understanding of pulse code modulation technology. The firm's lead engineers, who used PCM in their systems, tutored them in it (Gray, 1998; Hodges, 2008–2010).

Exploiting their new understanding of PCM technology, and benefiting from discussions on the telephone requirements of digital telephony with engineers at Bell Labs and Bell Northern Research, Hodges, Gray, and their students concentrated on the design and fabrication of an analog-to-digital converter for the telephone network. They surmised that by integrating this function in MOS technology, they would lower the cost of converting analog representations of voice signals into digital ones by a factor of ten (until then analog-to-digital conversion had been very expensive; it had been performed by bipolar integrated circuits or by hybrid circuits, that is, miniaturized circuits made of discrete components). To design MOS analog-to-digital converters, they pioneered the use of matching capacitors (Everhart, 1975; Gray, McCreary, and Hodges, 1978). Hodges and Gray reported their work on converters at international meetings in 1974 and 1975. They also convened engineers from the Bell Telephone system and other firms for a special meeting in Berkeley where they showed them their chip and convinced them of its potential for digital telephone networks. In conjunction with this promotional campaign, Hodges and Gray filed a patent application for their invention in 1977. It was granted the following year (Hodges, 2008–2010; 2012a,b).

Building on this work on PCM converters, Gray, Robert Brodersen (who joined the faculty from Texas Instruments in 1976), and another group of doctoral students later designed MOS analog filters. Filters were used in conjunction with the PCM codec chips. They removed unwanted frequency components from the voice signals and reinforced wanted ones. In 1978, Gray, Brodersen, and their doctoral students invented a new technique to perform this function: the switched-capacitor filter. This filter used capacitors and MOS transistors to filter analog signals (Gray, 1998; Hodges, 2008–2010; Hodges, Gray, and Broderson, 1978).[8]

These innovations—switched capacitor filters and analog-to-digital converters—were soon commercialized by semiconductor and telephone equipment firms in the United States, Canada, Japan, and Germany.

AT&T and Northern Telecom, the Canadian equipment corporation, licensed Hodges and Gray's patent on analog-to-digital conversion technology. In 1981, after much haggling, AT&T purchased a one-time license from the University of California for $250,000. Northern Telecom signed a licensing agreement with the university that brought about $1,000,000 in royalties to UC over the life of the patent. Semiconductor companies also commercialized the technologies coming from UC Berkeley. To do so, they often brought in members of the Berkeley group to design new products on the basis of the mixed-signal circuit techniques they had invented at the university. For example, Silicon Systems, a small semiconductor firm located in Southern California, hired Hodges as a consultant and recruited one of his doctoral students to design a chip using analog-to-digital conversion technology for dual-tone multifrequency (that is, touch-tone) receivers. Silicon Systems made hundreds of thousands of these chips in the following years. Siliconix, a Silicon Valley corporation, also employed another Hodges student to engineer PCM telephone coder and decoder chips (Hodges, 2008–2010; 2012a,b).

Other early adopters of Berkeley's technologies were Intel and National Semiconductor. Working under the direction of James Solomon, a former student of Donald Pederson, several students of Gray and Hodges designed telephone PCM and filter microchips at National Semiconductor. Intel also went into the PCM codec business. In this case, it was Gray who transferred the technology to Intel (Intel was then interested in diversifying from memories and microprocessors into communication chips). After consulting for the firm for several years, Gray took a sabbatical leave at Intel in 1976 and 1977. There, he helped the firm's engineers translate the ideas developed at Berkeley into commercial products. He also headed the group that designed Intel's filter chip. Intel introduced these codec and filter products to the market in 1978 (Gray, 1998; Hodges, 2008–2010; Hoff, no date).[9]

By the early 1980s, the codec and filter chips pioneered at Berkeley had become a worldwide business, attracting large players such as AMI, Mostek, Siemens, Hitachi, Fujitsu, and Nippon Telephone. In 1981, the Berkeley group estimated that integrated circuits using the PCM analog-to-digital conversion techniques developed on campus were manufactured at the rate of 4,000,000 per year. In a report four years later, they reckoned that the merchant market for PCM chips was in the order of 10,000,000 circuits.[10] They also identified ten microchips on the market that incorporated Berkeley's switched capacitor technology. By the mid-1980s, the work of Hodges, Gray, Brodersen, and their students had helped create a new branch of the semiconductor industry: MOS mixed-signal circuits. They had also enabled the growth of digital telephony by dramatically lowering the cost of electronic circuits critical for digital telephone networks (Hodges, 1981; Turin, 1981a, b; UCB, 1985).

MICRO

Critical for the further growth of semiconductor research at Berkeley and other UC campuses was MICRO.[11] MICRO was one of the first organizations created in the United States to fend off Japanese competition in semiconductors. It was Jerry Brown, California's governor, who initiated MICRO. Brown was concerned that Japanese and European competition threatened California's semiconductor industry, one of the largest and most dynamic industries in the state (Hodges, 1980a,b; Oldham, 1980; Turin, 1980b, 1982f). Following a recommendation from David Hodges, who was a member of the governor's task force on research and development, in 1980 Brown asked the University of California to define the broad outlines of a program that would combine state and industry funding to support university research in microelectronics and computer engineering.[12] His goal was to train more microelectronics engineers and to "increase the amount of semiconductor research" done in California. It was expected that research done at UC would generate new products and processes that would be commercialized by local firms (Brown, 1981; Carrick, 1980a, 1980b; Department of Economic and Business Development, 1981; Kennedy, 1980).

In December 1980, David Saxon, the president of the University of California, appointed a faculty committee to devise such a scheme. Among the committee's members were Hodges; Chand Viswanathan, the chairman of UCLA's Electrical Engineering Department; Herbert Kroemer, the leader of the compound semiconductor group at UC Santa Barbara; and Roger Ditzel, UC's patent administrator.[13] The committee proposed to create a program that would match industrial funding with state financing. This program would work in the following way: UC faculty members, who had secured financial commitments for their research from industrial sponsors, would apply for additional funding from MICRO. MICRO would then peer review their proposals and match industrial contributions with state funding for selected projects. The peer-review process and the disbursement of state funds would be administered by the University of California and supervised by a committee of representatives from UC, industry, and the state. Importantly, neither the industrial sponsors nor the state would pay overhead to UC for their research grants. UC would thus subsidize microelectronics research with its own funds. Standard rules governing intellectual property protection at UC would apply to MICRO projects: Industrial sponsors would get nonexclusive royalty-bearing licenses to inventions that arose out of the research they supported through MICRO (Brown, 1981; Department of Economic and Business Development, 1981; Hodges, 2008–2010; Viswanathan, 2007).[14]

UC's proposal was endorsed by Jerry Brown and, after some lobbying, passed into law by the California legislature in 1981. The legislature allocated $1 million to the MICRO program that very same year. Annual funding for MICRO grew to the $4 to $5 million range within the next five years. It remained at that level until the mid-1990s. MICRO proved very attractive to semiconductor firms. Industrial sponsors liked state matching and the fact that none of their financial contributions went into overhead. More important, the program gave them access to UC students and researchers. In the first year of the program, twenty-five companies participated in MICRO. Although many firms were less than satisfied with MICRO's IP provisions, the number of participating companies grew very quickly (Cole, 1985; Hodges, 2008–2010, 2012a,b; Viswanathan, 2007). By 1992, more than a hundred firms supported semiconductor research at UC through MICRO. They contributed $5.9 million in cash and $3.9 million in equipment and services to MICRO projects during that year. Among the largest participants were Intel, Hughes, Rockwell, IBM, and Hewlett-Packard (Arditti, 1993).[15]

MICRO's impact on microelectronics research at UC went far beyond the disbursement of funds. MICRO enabled UC faculty members to work on projects they could not finance with federal grants and contracts. They used MICRO to finance speculative and high-risk projects that were not yet ready for federal agencies. They employed it to launch new research programs in integrated electronics. Junior faculty also used MICRO to start their own research groups. Maybe more important, MICRO helped shape the types of projects that faculty members pursued at UC. It stimulated them to find out what problems interested potential industry sponsors and to conduct research that was of relevance to semiconductor firms. In contrast, before the establishment of MICRO, the great majority of faculty members had focused exclusively on what would make winning proposals for the National Science Foundation (NSF), Department of Defense (DoD), and Defense Advanced Research Projects Agency (DARPA). This focus had oriented their research toward the priorities of military agencies and the scientific and technical interests of NSF program managers. In addition, MICRO helped reproduce the industrial collaborations pioneered by Hodges, Gray, and Pederson at Berkeley across the whole UC system (Hodges, 2008–2010; Samueli, 2007).

Of the UC campuses participating in MICRO, the greatest beneficiaries in dollar terms were UC Berkeley, UCLA, UC Santa Barbara, and UC San Diego (in that order). For example, in 1982–1983 UCB received $2 million in combined state and industry funding from MICRO, UCLA $1.1 million, and UCSB $700,000. By 1990–1991, combined MICRO funding grew to $4.4 million at UCB, $2.5 million at UCLA, and $1.2 million at UCSB. MICRO financed influential research programs at UC Berkeley, including one on microchip design software (a program that had preceded the establishment of MICRO).[16] It helped support the Integrated Circuits and Systems Laboratory at UCLA. In addition, MICRO financed UC Santa Barbara's entry into compound semiconductor research and continued work in this field in the 1980s and 1990s (Ackwood, 1992; Hodges, 2008–2010; Samueli, 2000; Turin, 1983).

UC BERKELEY: MICROCHIP DESIGN SOFTWARE

In the late 1960s and early 1970s, Berkeley's integrated circuits group expanded into the software used for microchip design. In 1965, Pederson, the prime mover of the solid-state electronics program at Berkeley, perceived that integrated circuits would soon become so complex that it would be impossible to design them manually. This realization led Pederson to orient the activities of the integrated circuits group toward the development of several integrated circuit simulation and computer-aided design (CAD) programs (Perry, 1998). For example, Ronald Rohrer, a junior faculty, and a group of graduate students designed CANCER (Computer Analysis of Nonlinear Circuits Excluding Radiation), a circuit simulation program, in 1969 and 1970. Rohrer was then doing a sabbatical at Fairchild Semiconductor. While at Fairchild, Rohrer taught a yearlong advanced circuit class on campus. This course was project based and consisted in the writing of code for CANCER (much of this work was guided by the parallel project on circuit simulation that Rohrer conducted at Fairchild Semiconductor at the same time) (Nagel, 2011a; Rohrer, 2011; Rohrer et al., 1971).

By the spring of 1970, CANCER had gained a strong following at UC Berkeley. Pederson found it superior to similar programs developed on campus. CANCER had several advantages: It could simulate both digital and analog circuits, and it could handle large circuits (with a few hundred transistors). Starting in the fall of 1970, Pederson used CANCER in his electronic circuits design courses. Interest in the program encouraged Rohrer to commercialize his circuit simulator the following year. Softech, a software firm based in Massachusetts, developed a commercial version of CANCER (with the help of Rohrer and one of his students). It brought it to the market in 1971.[17] Although the version of CANCER developed at Softech was easier to use than its academic cousin, it was a commercial failure. It had very few takers among integrated circuit designers. Shortly thereafter, Rohrer abandoned the circuit simulator project and its commercialization, as he left Berkeley for a position in industry (Nagel, 2011a; Pederson, 1984; Perry, 1998; Rohrer, 2011).

Pederson picked up the project after Rohrer's departure and turned CANCER into a public domain circuit simulator (Pederson called it SPICE for Simulation Program, Integrated Circuit Emphasis). SPICE was both a software development project and a social experiment where users contributed code to the program. To develop SPICE, Pederson followed a two-pronged strategy. He recruited talented doctoral students and assistant professors to improve the SPICE algorithms and add new device models to it. This long-term software development program was funded by the Army Research Office and the National Science Foundation. Starting in the early 1980s, MICRO also financed the SPICE project (with contributions from General Electric, Phillips, and Harris Semiconductor). At the same time, Pederson, who had long felt that it was a mistake for public universities to patent their electronics inventions, made SPICE freely and universally available. Berkeley released the first public version of SPICE in 1972. This release was soon followed by SPICE 2 in 1975. Other versions came on line in rapid succession in the second half of the 1970s and early 1980s (Nagel, 2011a,b; Perry, 1998; Turin, 1983).

User feedback was essential for perfecting SPICE and making it applicable to a wide range of circuits. Thousands of students taking electronics courses at Berkeley used it to complete their class assignments. Research groups, including those of Hodges, Gray, and Brodersen, relied on

SPICE to design new microchips. On-campus users helped identify the code's limitations. Feedback also came from industry. Chip designers, who used SPICE to analyze and simulate circuits, identified problems with the software. They sometimes shared their own code with the Berkeley team. Engineers working at Hewlett-Packard and Tektronix, for example, contributed algorithms to SPICE. The end result of this collective design effort was that by the mid- to late 1970s, SPICE was the program that offered the best combination of algorithms and device models to simulate the behavior of integrated circuits. Other programs developed in industry or academia may have had better individual algorithms, but none matched its overall performance (Hodges, 2008–2010; Perry, 1998).

Pederson's open source approach to technology development and transfer created a large user base for SPICE. Students who had learned to use SPICE at Berkeley brought it with them to the firms they joined after graduation. They used it there to analyze and simulate circuits. They also introduced their colleagues and supervisors to SPICE. As a result, many engineers got to learn and appreciate the program. By the early 1980s, SPICE was so widely used that it had entered the industry's vocabulary and had become a verb (one "spiced" a circuit). In 1985, Berkeley administrators estimated that 3,000 copies of SPICE were in active use in the United States. In other words, the great majority of chip engineers employed SPICE to analyze and simulate the circuits they were designing (Hodges, 2008–2010; Perry, 1998; Turin, 1982e; UCB, 1985).[18]

SPICE was so widely employed in industry that it enabled the Department of Electrical Engineering and Computer Sciences to raise substantial funds from corporations that had benefited from it. In the first half of the 1980s, the school of engineering faced a decline in state support.[19] To maintain its national preeminence and finance its research and teaching programs, it turned to industry. The Department of Electrical Engineering and Computer Sciences established a consortium of industrial firms to fund a major addition to the electrical engineering building and to finance more research on microchip design tools. Many semiconductor, electronics, and computer firms joined the consortium. Most donors had directly benefited from SPICE. For example, Digital Equipment Corporation, which had sold hundreds of its VAX machines to engineering groups using SPICE, gave $1 million to the department. The Semiconductor Research Corporation, many semiconductor firms, and the foundations that were associated with them contributed significant sums as well (Turin,

1982a,b,c,g). By 1983, the department had raised more than $8.5 million in cash for the CAD program and the addition of a fifth floor to the electrical engineering building (Hodges, 2008–2010; Wong, 1985).[20]

SPICE was also the source of a new industry, electronic design automation or EDA software, in Silicon Valley.[21] In the early 1980s, the use of SPICE was so widespread in the semiconductor industry that it became expensive for firms to support the program internally. They needed to employ teams of engineers who would debug SPICE and help circuit designers solve the problems they encountered when running it. The situation inspired James Solomon, a former student of Pederson who had supervised the design of PCM codecs and filters at National Semiconductor, to propose the formation of a new company that would support and improve on SPICE and other integrated circuit design programs developed at Berkeley. He asked Pederson and two young faculty members, Richard Newton and Alberto Sangiovanni-Vincentelli, to participate as consultants. Pederson declined, while the latter two agreed (Knivett, 2008). Sangiovanni-Vincentelli, an Italian engineer with significant mathematical expertise, had joined the faculty in 1977, with the express mandate of developing the department's research activities in the computer-aided design of microchips (Everhart, 1977). Newton, an Australian engineer and computer scientist, was also a new addition to the faculty. He had received his PhD at Berkeley, where he had worked in Pederson's group and managed new releases of SPICE. By the early 1980s, Newton and Sangiovanni-Vincentelli had established themselves as important players in the integrated circuits group at Berkeley (funding from MICRO was important for the launching of their faculty careers at UCB). They had substantial research groups, and they worked on a platform-approach to the design of Very Large Scale Integration (VLSI) chips—microchips with more than 100,000 transistors. This platform included a single database and a graphical user interface. It coordinated and incorporated unrelated software tools used in the design of microchips (Turin, 1981e, 1982e, 1983; MICRO, 1985, 1986; Wong, 1989).

In 1983, Newton and Sangiovanni-Vincentelli associated themselves with Solomon to start a new company, Solomon Design Automation (SDA) Systems. Solomon headed the start-up. Newton and Sangiovanni-Vincentelli acted as chief recruiters (the early staff of SDA Systems was made up mostly of former Berkeley students). They also provided technical leadership to the firm. Funding for the start-up came from companies interested in using SDA's software: Ericsson, National Semiconductor, General Electric, and Harris Semiconductor. Silicon Valley venture capitalists, led by Donald Lucas, also funded the new venture. During the first four years of its existence, SDA Systems experienced product delays and great difficulties in creating markets for its products (SDA was one of the very first firms to commercialize chip design software). It owed its survival to a major cash infusion from Harris Semiconductor, which acquired a 40 percent stake in the company in 1985. By 1986, the market for electronic design automation (EDA) software was growing rapidly, as semiconductor firms reduced the size of their in-house CAD development groups and began to purchase circuit design software from outside vendors. The following year, SDA Systems merged with ECAD, another EDA company based in Silicon Valley, to form Cadence Design Systems, which quickly became one of the dominant firms in the electronic design automation industry (Borrus, 2010; Kuehlmann, 2010).[22]

In the 1980s and early 1990s, Newton and Sangiovanni-Vincentelli pioneered the area of logic synthesis, defining new approaches to the automated design of digital integrated circuits. Logic synthesis enabled the creation of very complex microchips, with millions of transistors. Their work in logic synthesis originated in a collaboration between Sangiovanni-Vincentelli and a group of engineers from IBM. Sangiovanni-Vincentelli spent the summer of 1981 at IBM, where he collaborated with Robert Brayton, a mathematician and EDA specialist, and Gary Hachtel, an IBM veteran and one of the first PhDs coming from Berkeley's integrated circuits laboratory. At first, Sangiovanni-Vincentelli, Hachtel, and Brayton reverse-engineered a logic synthesis program engineered at Tektronix. They also improved on it, creating the seeds of two important logic synthesis software programs that they developed at Berkeley over the next five years: ESPRESSO and MIS. To collaborate more closely with Newton and Sangiovanni-Vincentelli, Brayton moved to Berkeley, first as a visiting lecturer and then as a faculty member. Much of their work was funded by DARPA and MICRO (with financing from firms such as IBM, GTE, AMI, Fairchild, Intel, Intersil, Hughes, Rockwell, Olivetti, Phillips, Xerox, Silicon Compilers, General Electric, Hewlett-Packard, Texas Instruments, and Harris Microwave Semiconductor) (Brayton, 2010; de Micheli, 2010; MICRO, 1985, 1986, 1989; Sangiovanni-Vincentelli, 2010; Wong, 1987a,b, 1988).

With MIS and ESPRESSO, Sangiovanni-Vincentelli, Newton, and Brayton followed the same open-source approach as the one Pederson had pioneered with SPICE.[23] By the early and mid-1980s, all faculty members in the integrated circuits group at Berkeley were convinced of the importance and value of free and universal distribution of research results. With their recent experience with SPICE, they also understood that the open-source approach brought greater financial returns to the department and faculty than the protection of intellectual property (Hodges, 2008–2010). Newton, Brayton, and Sangiovanni-Vincentelli freely distributed ESPRESSO and MIS in academia and industry. Among the early adopters were IBM and Intel. In the first half of the 1980s, Intel faced the daunting challenge of designing increasingly complex microprocessors—microprocessors with hundreds of thousands, even millions of transistors. This challenge led the firm's managers to adopt Berkeley's logic synthesis software to accelerate microprocessor design. In 1983, Intel used ESPRESSO to design the 386 microprocessor. Several years later, Intel was the first firm to use MIS for the development of the successor chip to the 386, the 486. Improvements made by Intel's engineers to the code were added to the software—leading to the development of more reliable and more capable programs (Gelsinger et al., 2011).

Logic synthesis software, like SPICE a few years earlier, was commercialized by a new firm established by Newton and Sangiovanni-Vincentelli. This time, the pair partnered with Aart de Geus, a Dutch engineer and entrepreneur, and a group of technologists who had developed a pioneering logic synthesis program at General Electric's semiconductor facility in North Carolina. In 1986, Newton learned that the group was interested in forming a new company to commercialize its program, as General Electric had decided to exit the semiconductor business. According to several accounts, Newton tried at first to convince his first start-up, SDA Systems, to hire the GE engineers and enter the logic synthesis market. But because SDA's management demurred, in 1987 Newton, who had by then built a solid network in Silicon Valley, found venture capital for the group, with the express condition that they relocate their firm, Synopsys, to Silicon Valley. Two other investors, General Electric and Harris Semiconductor, took stakes in the start-up as well (Sangiovanni-Vincentelli, 2010).

After moving to California, Synopsys recruited students from Newton and Sangiovanni-Vincentelli's research groups who had worked on ESPRESSO and MIS. Not surprisingly, the first product that Synopsys brought to the market in 1987 used features from MIS and ESPRESSO as well as code from Socrates, the original program written at General Electric. Synopsys's product was rapidly adopted in the semiconductor industry, especially by firms specializing in the design and fabrication of custom integrated circuits (application-specific integrated circuits). By 1989, Synopsys's software was used by fifty semiconductor and electronics corporations and had become the dominant logic synthesis package in the EDA industry. In the following years, Synopsys maintained its dominance in this field and evolved into one of the two largest EDA firms (Cadence retained its primary position by expanding into logic synthesis software as well). In the 1980s and 1990s, both Cadence and Synopsys acquired a stream of smaller EDA firms, many of them started by Newton, Sangiovanni-Vincentelli, and their students. With them, they expanded their technological capabilities and their product offerings (Synopsis launches, 1989; McLeod, 1989).

The logic synthesis software developed at Berkeley helped create major firms in Silicon Valley. But its impact went far beyond successful entrepreneurship. Since the mid-1980s, virtually all complex microchips have been designed with the tools innovated by Brayton, Newton, Sangiovanni-Vincentelli, and their students. Their software had a transformative effect on the semiconductor industry. It revolutionized the ways by which semiconductor firms developed their chips by accelerating circuit design and by making the engineering of increasingly complex microchips possible (de Micheli, 2010).

UCLA: BROADBAND COMMUNICATION MICROCHIPS

UCLA moved into microchip design more than twenty years after UC Berkeley. It was in 1986 that the Department of Electrical Engineering at UCLA established its Integrated Circuits and Systems Laboratory (ICSL). The ICSL was part of a second wave of microelectronics laboratories at U.S. universities. In the early 1960s, Berkeley had pioneered the first integrated circuits laboratory. Stanford and the University of Arizona had soon followed suit. But most universities went into this field in the late 1970s and the first half of the 1980s (Hodges, 1980a; Wildes and Lindgren, 1985).[24] They were attracted by the growing technological and economic importance of silicon microchips, which were increasingly used across a wide range of products and industrial sectors (Lécuyer and Brock, 2010). Funding also became more easily available for microelectronics research. In the late 1970s, DARPA established the Very Large Scale Integration (VLSI) program, with the goal of expanding high-quality research on very complex chips at universities. In 1982, the Semiconductor Industry Association, the trade association representing the semiconductor industry in the United States, formed the Semiconductor Research Corporation to finance academic research in silicon electronics. Another factor facilitating the creation of numerous microelectronics research programs at U.S. universities was the creation of MOSIS (Metal Oxide Semiconductor Implementation Service) in 1981. MOSIS was funded by DARPA. It acted as a broker between university research groups and industrial fabrication facilities, enabling academic researchers to fabricate their chips at relatively low cost. MOSIS lowered the barriers of entry into chip design. Universities no longer had to establish their own fabrication facilities and continually update them, as Berkeley had done at great expense since the early 1960s (Burger, 1998; Lécuyer, 2005b; Lécuyer and Choi, 2012).

Several UC campuses went into silicon-integrated electronics in the first half of the 1980s. UC Davis and UC Santa Cruz created microelectronics research groups. At UCLA, the Department of Electrical Engineering, under the direction of its chair, Chand Viswanathan, made a concerted effort to build up its microchip design activities (Viswanathan was backed in this endeavor by George Turin, UCLA's dean of engineering, who had previously served as chair of the EECS Department at Berkeley and had strongly supported the growth of the microelectronics program there) (Viswanathan, 2007).[25] In 1985, the Department of Electrical Engineering at UCLA recruited two young designers, Asad Abidi and Henry Samueli. Abidi was a Berkeley PhD and an analog circuit specialist who had engineered microchips for fiber optics networks at the Bell Telephone Laboratories. Samueli was a UCLA product. He had received his bachelor's, master's, and PhD degrees in electrical engineering from UCLA. He also had significant industrial experience. He had led a research group working on military communications circuits and systems at TRW, the large defense firm located in Redondo Beach (Abidi, 2007; O'Neill, 2008; Samueli, 2007).

In 1986, Samueli, Abidi, and another faculty member, Kenneth Martin, established the Integrated Circuits and Systems Laboratory (ICSL). From the start, the ICSL focused on the design of broadband (high-speed) communications circuits and systems. Samueli and Abidi reasoned that UCLA was a latecomer in microelectronics, by comparison with Berkeley and Stanford. Their laboratory had to differentiate itself from these universities' well-established programs. To do so, they focused on broadband communications circuits and systems, an area that was not explored by these universities. Samueli and Abidi presciently surmised that communications would become a major driver of innovation in microelectronics and that broadband chips, which were then a military technology, would find large markets in the commercial sector (Abidi, n.d., 2007; O'Neill, 2008; Samueli, 2007).

Early on, Samueli and Abidi made several important decisions that shaped their research and entrepreneurial activities. Unlike many microelectronics programs at other schools, they did not focus exclusively on circuits but also designed whole systems on single chips. Inspired by Berkeley's open-source approach, Abidi and Samueli did not patent their work, instead publishing it in the engineering literature.[26] They felt that filing patents was a loss of time and resources and reasoned that patenting their inventions would make it more difficult for them to start new businesses (Abidi, n.d., 2007; Samueli, 2007). Samueli and Abidi also employed the services of MOSIS to fabricate their chips (in contrast, UC Davis, which entered microelectronics research around the same time, built a large clean room to process integrated circuits). The decision to use MOSIS led Samueli and Abidi to design chips for standard manufacturing processes, which was relatively rare in communications microchips at the time. Engineers working on communications chips tailored fabrication processes to circuit designs. The design of microchips for MOSIS prepared Samueli and his students well for the fabless business model that came to dominate much of the U.S. semiconductor industry, where engineers conceived microchips for the standard processes offered by semiconductor foundries (foundries specialized in chip manufacture) (Abidi, n.d., 2007; Samueli, 2007).

Crucial for the launching of the ICSL was MICRO, the UC program that cofunded advanced research in microelectronics in collaboration with industry. MICRO provided the only source of external funds for the laboratory in its first three years of existence and was the source of a significant share of its funding thereafter. When Samueli joined UCLA's faculty in 1985, he approached TRW, his former employer, for funding, noting that the matching funds available through MICRO would reduce their costs substantially. The grant he received from TRW enabled him to hire his first doctoral students and finance the fabrication of the chips they designed. More importantly, MICRO shaped Samueli's research program, orienting it to practical problems of great significance for industry (Samueli, 2007). "The MICRO program was very important for my early research program at UCLA," Samueli later recalled:

> It enabled me to fabricate the chips I designed. As a result, I was able to test out the chips, i.e. prove out ideas in real chips. This was critical because it gave me credibility, which in turn enabled me to get much larger grants from

DARPA and other funding sources. The MICRO program also enabled me to work with ten firms and learn about relevant problems in industry. As a result, I could tie in my research with real world problems. If I had not received MICRO funding, my research would have been theoretical and I would not have created Broadcom. (Samueli, 2000)

Abidi also relied heavily on MICRO funding and received grants from Silicon Systems, Western Digital, and Rockwell International in the second half of the 1980s.[27] Later, Samueli and Abidi assembled consortia of corporations financing their research on broadband systems-on-a-chip through MICRO. These grants supported graduate students. Contracts from DARPA financed the salaries of technicians, postdocs, and faculty members, as well as other expenses (Abidi, 2007; Samueli, 2007; Viswanathan, 2007; Yablonovitch, 2007).

To design broadband chips, Samueli and Abidi relied on Samueli's pioneering work and the development of broadband communications microchips and systems at TRW. TRW was one of the prime contractors for the Very High Speed Integrated Circuits (VHSIC) program of the Department of Defense. This program, started in 1981, sought to accelerate the development of Very Large Scale Integration (VLSI) microchips, chips with more than a 100,000 transistors, for military applications. The VHSIC program financed research on manufacturing processes and the development of computer-aided tools for the fast prototyping of microchips. Within this large-scale program, TRW focused on the design and fabrication of "superchips" that could process signals and data twenty times faster than the most advanced integrated circuits then on the market. It produced digital chips that processed radio signals (Broad, 1985; Klass, 1986; Mitchell, 1985; Samueli, 2007).[28]

After joining TRW, Samueli became involved in the VHSIC program. One of his first assignments was the engineering of circuit boards for high-speed digital military satellite and radio communications systems, followed by the design of a broadband digital radio modem for the U.S. Army. This modem transported multiple signals simultaneously and handled a wide band of frequencies. Samueli was the manager responsible for the modem's development. He also conceived high-speed digital microchips that corrected for distortions in the radio signal. At TRW, Samueli was involved in the design of a very complex processor chip, with more than 4,000,000 transistors, and the creation of silicon compilers for the VHSIC program. Silicon compilers were software programs that accelerated the design of integrated circuits by automatically generating them on the basis of detailed specifications (Broadcom turns, 1995; Burke, 1997; Perry, 1999; Samueli, 2007; Schonfield, 1999).

At UCLA, Samueli and his ICSL colleagues further refined the broadband communication technologies and software programs developed at TRW and used them to design broadband systems-on-a-chip for civilian applications. The ICSL was the first group not employed by a military contractor to design single-chip broadband modems and produce algorithms for these modems (Samueli focused on the digital side of these systems, while Abidi and other faculty members concentrated on analog design).[29] In the first half of the 1990s, the ICSL group designed faster and faster modem chips, reaching unheard-of speeds. To design these broadband systems on single chips, Samueli and Abidi seized on the CAD tools developed at Berkeley and the growing EDA industry in Silicon Valley. They relied on H-SPICE, the professional version of SPICE that had been released by a small Silicon Valley firm. They also employed the tools of Mentor Graphics, a competitor to Cadence and Synopsys. More importantly, they wrote their own enhancements for these tools. For instance, relying on prior experience with the VHSIC program at TRW, Samueli and his students developed powerful silicon compilers in the late 1980s and the first half of the 1990s (Abidi, 2007; MICRO, 1989; Perry, 1999; Samueli, 2000, 2007).

Soon the concepts and technologies developed by Samueli and his associates found their way into Southern California's semiconductor industry. In 1988, two former colleagues of Samueli at TRW started PairGain Technologies, a firm that focused on the design of microchips for the telephone network. They asked Samueli to join them as the firm's chief architect (Samueli worked at PairGain one day a week). Henry Nicholas, Samueli's first doctoral student and a former TRW engineer, joined the start-up as a consultant, designing its chips. At PairGain, Samueli and Nicholas worked on integrated circuits that improved the performance of copper phones lines. They addressed one of the main economic problems of telephone companies. These corporations had traditionally lost money in rural areas. In the 1980s, they experienced a significant increase in the number of rural customers, as many people left cities to live in the countryside. To address the phone companies' financial predicament, Samueli, Nicholas, and their colleagues at PairGain designed a complicated chip that enabled up to twelve people to share the same line. Thereby, they increased the use of existing phone lines and reduced the investments required for the laying of new lines in rural areas. The chip was very successful. PairGain built a solid business in the telephone industry, enabling it to go public in 1993 (Perry, 1999; Yablonovitch, 2007).[30]

Inspired by their experience at PairGain, Samueli and Nicholas went into business on their own in 1991. They established Broadband Telecom (later renamed Broadcom). By that time, Samueli's research on broadband communication circuits at the ICSL had attracted significant attention in industry. Corporations started to contact him, asking him to commercialize his designs so that they would be able to integrate them into their own products. "Many of the research results [at UCLA] were very relevant and practical and were in fact the reasons why we founded Broadcom," Samueli later recalled:

> The chips we had done as these early projects found their way into being relevant for commercial products and the companies would come back to us and say: "Here are wonderful results you have achieved. Why don't you take the next step and turn them into commercial products?" They urged us to move from proof of concept to commercial products. We founded Broadcom to do just that. (Samueli, 2000)

Samueli and Nicholas started Broadcom as a custom chip operation, designing broadband integrated circuits for other firms. They invested $10,000 in the start-up and, more important, brought the knowledge they had accumulated at UCLA on broadband communications microchips and systems (they had not patented their inventions at UCLA).[31] Broadcom was based on the proof-of-concept chips and software tools they had developed on campus. Another important asset was the students they recruited from the ICSL (Abidi, 2007; Perry, 1999; Samueli, 2007; Yablonovitch, 2007).

Samueli, Nicholas, and their team had unique expertise in broadband communication microchips and therefore were in a very strong bargaining position when they negotiated design contracts with customers. Unlike many other custom circuit operations, they were able to retain the intellectual property rights to the chips they engineered (Samueli and Nicholas, who had eschewed patenting at UCLA, now patented their technology as much as they could). Among the first important contracts they received was a contract from Scientific-Atlanta. Scientific-Atlanta needed a broadband chip for a digital cable set-top box, connecting televisions to the digital network. The set-top box was to be used in the interactive TV network that Time-Warner was then building in Orlando, Florida. Another contract came from Intel, which wanted a chip for high-speed Ethernet that it could sell with its microprocessors to PC makers. These contracts, especially the one from Scientific-Atlanta, enabled Broadcom to augment its expertise in signal processing and digital systems-on-a-chip technologies. They laid the groundwork for the development of product lines in high-speed chips for Ethernet and digital set top boxes (Broadcom turns, 1995; Perry, 1999; Yablonovitch, 2007).[32]

The large market for broadband chips that Samueli had envisioned in set-top boxes for interactive TV did not materialize, as Time-Warner terminated the project in 1994. By then, however, the Internet was growing very quickly, and Samueli realized that the system-on-a-chip technologies his firm had designed for Scientific-Atlanta could be used to bring high-speed Internet to the world. They could be used in digital set-top boxes and cable modems connecting personal computers to the Internet. To address this major market opportunity and design low-cost chips that could be mass produced by semiconductor foundries such as TSMC, Samueli and Nicholas raised $5 million from Intel, Scientific-Atlanta, General Instrument, and Cisco Systems in July 1994. These investments enabled Broadcom to develop microchips for the cable industry and strengthen its offerings for Ethernet cards. They also financed the development of a standard for cable modems. By 1995, Broadcom had a significant technical lead over its competitors, and Samueli took a leave of absence from UCLA to devote himself fully to the business (Broadcom, 1998; Burke, 1997; Nee, 2000; Perry, 1999; Yablonovitch, 2007).

In the second half of the 1990s, Broadcom's sales grew explosively, as more and more consumers wanted high-speed access to the Internet. Revenues expanded from $6 million in 1995 to $21 million in 1996 and $203 million in 1998. They reached the $500 million mark in 1999. By 2000, Broadcom's microchips were in 90 percent of all television set-top boxes and cable modems and in 65 percent of all local area computer networks. Because of the firm's dominant position in fast growing markets, Broadcom's stock rose quickly in value, growing by a factor of ten between its IPO in April 1998 and July 2000. The soaring value of Broadcom stock made its founders fabulously rich. By mid-2000, Samueli and Nicholas, who each owned 18 percent of the company, had a combined net worth of $10 billion. Samueli used some of his capital gains to make very large gifts to UCLA's and UC Irvine's engineering schools ($30 million to UCLA and $20 million to UC Irvine) in 1999 (Broadcom, 1998, 1999, 2000).

More important, the rapid increase in the valuation of Broadcom's stock enabled the entrepreneurs to purchase other fabless firms designing communication microchips. Their goal was to build the dominant semiconductor firm in broadband chips, the "Intel of communications," as Samueli put it. Broadcom acquired twenty-four companies with its stock from 1998 to 2004. About half of these were located in Silicon Valley. A quarter of the acquisitions were spin-offs of UCLA or large defense firms in Southern California.[33] These acquisitions complemented Broadcom's strengths. They added expertise in software, chips for fiber optics networks, and, more important, chips for wireless communication (Holson, 2000).[34]

One of Broadcom's main acquisitions was Innovent Systems, a fabless start-up designing microchips for short-range wireless data communications. Like Broadcom, Innovent Systems was a spin-off of the Integrated Circuits and Systems Laboratory. It was established by Ahmadreza and Maryam Rofougaran, two Iranian doctoral students who had worked in Abidi's group, in January 1999 (the Rofougarans were brother and sister). Starting in the mid-1990s, with funding from MICRO and DARPA, Abidi oriented his research group toward the design of radio frequency complementary metal-oxide semiconductor (RF CMOS) circuits, wireless systems in single chips made with CMOS, the main process used in the fabrication of semiconductor memories and microprocessors. It was particularly difficult to meet the performance requirements of radio circuits with this manufacturing technology (all radio frequency chips had been made until then with bipolar silicon technology or with exotic materials such as gallium arsenide). Abidi, the Rofougarans, and other students showed that it was possible to design a variety of radio circuits in CMOS and that these circuits could be augmented by digital functions on the same chips. The group designed more and more integrated and complex CMOS RF microchips in the second half of the 1990s (Abidi, 2007; Kundert, 2011; O'Neill, 2008; Samueli, 2007).[35]

Innovent Systems commercialized the work on RF CMOS coming out of Abidi's laboratory (like Samueli's research on broadband circuits, this work had not been patented by UCLA).[36] Samueli, who had been the Rofougarans' second advisor at UCLA, arranged for Broadcom to provide seed funding to the start-up. Other investors were Silicon Valley venture capitalists such as Crosspoint Venture Partners and several angel funds located in Southern California. Innovent focused on the design of chipsets (groups of microchips engineered to work together) for short-range wireless transmission using the Bluetooth standard (this standard had been devised by Ericsson's engineers a year earlier to exchange information between mobile phones, mobile personal computers, and other peripherals over short-range radio links). To design these chips, the Rofougarans recruited former colleagues from the ICSL. They also hired experienced engineers from communications systems firms in San Diego. In less than six months, Innovent's team designed its first CMOS RF chip and proceeded to develop a full family of Bluetooth transmitter and receiver chips. Because of the novelty of its offerings, the start-up quickly attracted the attention of large firms that were interested in acquiring its technology. One of them was Broadcom. In June 2000, Ahmadreza and Maryam Rofougaran sold Innovent to Broadcom for more than $450 million in Broadcom stock. At Broadcom, they joined the firm's upper management and became the technical directors of its wireless division. This division grew very quickly in the next few years. By 2006, wireless microchips represented one-third of Broadcom's total revenues (Abidi, 2007; Fried, 2000; Rad, 2000; Samueli, 2007).

In summary, the Integrated Circuits and Systems Laboratory made major contributions to the emergence and rise of the fabless semiconductor industry in Southern California. It "liberated" military broadband communications and microchip technologies developed by the region's large defense contractors. With financing from MICRO and DARPA, the ICSL further developed these technologies for use in commercial broadband communications systems. It also pioneered the design of wireless chips that could be made with standard silicon manufacturing processes. The laboratory was the source of two important start-ups, Broadcom and Innovent Systems. These start-ups commercialized the ICSL's research and employed a very large fraction of its students (by 2004, 10 percent of Broadcom's employees had worked or been trained at the ICSL). They created a major semiconductor firm with $7.4 billion in revenues in 2011.[37]

UC SANTA BARBARA: COMPOUND SEMICONDUCTORS

Unlike Berkeley and UCLA, which focused on silicon microchips, UC Santa Barbara oriented itself toward compound semiconductors. Compound semiconductors were exotic semiconductor materials, made of two or more chemical elements. The strategy of developing the compound semiconductor area was developed by Herbert Kroemer, a German applied physicist, who joined UCSB's Electrical and Computer Engineering Department in 1976. Kroemer recalled that he convinced Ed Spear, the chairman of the department, to develop such a program while interviewing for a job at UCSB. "I know what everybody else is advising you," Kroemer told Spear during the interview:

> Everybody is advising you to get into the mainstream silicon technology. Don't. It's too late. It's too expensive. And most importantly, the graduate program depends on being able to attract top graduate students. You will not be able to do this one and they will all go to other places. My own interest is in compound semiconductors. I think this is going to be an important field. Different from silicon. It's not something in which everyone has to be involved. There [are] three universities that [have] critical mass [in compound semiconductors]—critical mass meaning more than two professors: Stanford, Illinois, and Cornell. There is a place for a fourth. If you are willing to put all your eggs in one basket and you are going to gamble, you have a 50/50 chance of making number four. If you go into silicon technology you have a 100 percent chance of being an also-ran. (Kroemer, 2003)

Kroemer further argued that the school of engineering at UCSB would be at a significant disadvantage if it competed with UC Berkeley in silicon electronics. The College of Engineering at UC Santa Barbara was still relatively new. It had been created in the early 1960s and did not have the resources and drawing power of the Berkeley campus (Kroemer, 2007).[38]

By the mid-1970s, compound semiconductors were a well-established field of research in the electronics industry. They had been developed at RCA, the Bell Telephone Laboratories, and other corporate research laboratories, as alternatives to silicon. Starting in the second half of the 1950s, research managers at RCA and other corporations saw compound semiconductors as representing the future of semiconductor technology. Because of their unusual properties, compound semiconductors would permit the fabrication of new types of transistors. They would also allow the making of laser diodes and light-emitting diodes and open up new applications for semiconductors in communications and consumer electronics (Choi, 2007). The Department of Defense, NASA, and other federal agencies also viewed compound semiconductors as offering unique opportunities for the making of high-speed integrated circuits and optoelectronic devices for military and aerospace applications, and they heavily funded compound semiconductor research at military contractors in the 1960s and 1970s. These investments led to the building of significant research programs in compound semiconductors at large defense firms in Southern California, especially Rockwell and Hughes (Hughes had a research center working on compound semiconductors in Santa Barbara). Most of these programs were interested in using compound semiconductors for electronic applications. For example, engineers at Rockwell pioneered integrated circuits made of gallium arsenide in the mid-1970s. Another important player was Hewlett-Packard, which heavily invested in compound semiconductors for light emission starting in the 1970s (Dupuis and Krames, 2008; Lécuyer and Ueyama, 2013).

Kroemer was an experienced compound semiconductor researcher. He had done most of his career in industry, starting with RCA in the mid-1950s. It was at RCA that he had first been exposed to compound semiconductors. Kroemer later established a gallium arsenide laboratory for Philips in Germany. Gallium arsenide was a compound of gallium and arsenic. It had high electron velocity and enabled the fabrication of very fast transistors. It could also be used in the fabrication of light-emitting diodes. In 1959, Kroemer joined the compound semiconductor operations of Varian Associates, a Silicon Valley corporation. At RCA and Varian, Kroemer originated the concept of the heterostructure: a device structure made of different semiconductor materials. He also invented the heterostructure transistor and the heterostructure laser (Kroemer received the Nobel Prize in physics for these conceptual advances in 2000). At Varian and later at Fairchild and the University of Colorado (where he joined the faculty in 1968), Kroemer worked on gallium arsenide. He studied the physics of the Gunn effect, microwave oscillations induced by the application of a voltage to semiconductor crystals (Kroemer, 1963, 2000a,b, 2003; Perry, 2002).

Shortly after coming to UCSB, Kroemer recruited compound semiconductor experts from Rockwell and the Bell Telephone Laboratories. In 1978, he hired Jim Merz, who had worked on the optical properties of compound semiconductors at the Bell Labs. Three years later, he recruited Steve Long, an engineer who had made the first semiconductor memories made of gallium arsenide at Rockwell. With these appointments, the compound semiconductor group gained expertise in materials growth, theory, materials characterization, and circuit design. To fund their research, Kroemer, Merz, and Long relied on small military contracts and more importantly on MICRO. In the first half of the 1980s, they received grants from Rockwell, Xerox, Lockheed, EG&G, Fairchild, and Hughes's Santa Barbara Research Center, which were matched by MICRO. These grants represented the majority of their funding during this period. They were also important because they gave the group access to the laboratories and research equipment of their sponsors, notably those at Hughes's Santa Barbara Research Center (the compound semiconductor group at UCSB worked closely with the SBRC in the 1980s and the first half of the 1990s) (Hu, 2007a,b; Kroemer, 2003, 2007).[39]

The group, especially Kroemer, focused on molecular beam epitaxy (MBE).[40] MBE was an emerging technique for growing compound semiconductor materials. It had first been developed by scientists at the Bell Labs in the late 1960s and early 1970s (McCray, 2007). MBE relied on the use of molecular beams to deposit crystalline layers on crystal substrates. The process involved evaporating source materials such as gallium and arsenic and depositing these vapors with an atomic beam onto a thin crystal substrate within an ultrahigh vacuum chamber. MBE enabled the close control of crystal growth and the creation of structures made of different compound semiconductor materials. It offered a way for Kroemer to realize his concept of the heterostructure. After acquiring an MBE reactor with military funding, Kroemer and his students worked on largely unexplored classes of materials such as indium arsenide and gallium antimonide to make advanced heterostructures. They also experimented with the growth of gallium phosphide and gallium arsenide over silicon. They made high-speed transistors with these material structures. Merz and his group used MBE to investigate new compound semiconductor for infrared and nuclear detectors. They also made gallium arsenide–based heterostructures and circuits and developed fabrication techniques such as diffusion and etching for making them. Long focused on very-high-speed gallium arsenide-integrated circuits and on gallium arsenide microchips for analog applications. Kroemer, Merz, and Long, who had been schooled in the importance of intellectual property protection in industry, carefully patented their inventions (Kroemer, 1981, 2000b; MICRO, 1985, 1986).

In 1983, the trio received a large grant to do research on gallium arsenide from the Semiconductor Research Corporation, the industry-funded organization supporting semiconductor research at universities. This grant put the compound semiconductor group at UCSB on a path of rapid expansion. It helped convince campus administrators to make major investments in compound semiconductors. At that time, Robert Huttenback, the campus chancellor, was shaping UCSB, which had a strong teaching orientation until then, into a major research university. Among the changes that he pushed through was the upbuilding of the engineering school.[41] He gave Robert Merhabian, the school's dean, the authority to create a new Department of Materials Science with fifteen faculty positions. Mehrabian, a materials scientist who had taught at MIT and the University of Illinois and had directed the Center for Material Science at the National Bureau of Standards, chose to allocate a significant number of these positions to compound semiconductors and electronic materials experts. This decision enabled the compound semiconductor group to hire additional faculties and to grow in two different departments: Materials and Electrical and Computer Engineering (Hu, 2007a,b; Gossard, 2007; Kroemer, 2007).

With the new positions, Kroemer and his colleagues recruited leading compound semiconductor engineers and scientists from the Bell Telephone Laboratories. The timing of the creation of the Materials Department at UCSB was perfect. In 1984, the Bell Telephone System broke up into seven regional carriers and a long distance service provider. This fundamental shift led to the slow decline of the Bell Telephone Laboratories. Taking advantage of the situation, Kroemer "raided" the Labs. He hired Larry Coldren, a laser scientist who had developed fabrication processes for compound semiconductor devices. He brought in John Bowers, who had worked on lasers and fiber optics networks at Bell Labs. Another recruit was Evelyn Hu, who had developed manufacturing processes for silicon microchips at Bell Labs. At UCSB, she applied her microfabrication expertise to the making of compound semiconductors (Hu, 2007b; Kroemer, 2003, 2007; Perry, 2002). Kroemer also recruited Arthur Gossard, an MBE expert. Gossard had codiscovered the fractional quantum Hall effect at Bell (his team partners, Horst Störmer and Daniel Tsui, received the Nobel Prize in physics for this work in 1998) (Gossard, 2007; McCray, 2007; Störmer, 1998). The new recruits transferred expertise, knowledge, and techniques developed at Bell Labs to UCSB.

At the same time, Kroemer and his group created a shared fabrication facility to support their research, along the model of the integrated circuits laboratory at UC Berkeley. To finance the cleanroom, Kroemer, Merz, Long, and Hu mustered a large gift from the Whitaker Foundation and attracted funds from industry.[42] Faculty members donated their laboratory equipment and instruments to the fab. They received also equipment donations from several firms. In addition, Kroemer and Merz bought an MBE machine from Varian Associates at a deep discount. The new facility, designed by Hu, greatly improved the group's capability in crystal growth and device processing. Along with the new faculty positions, it enabled them to secure large multiyear grants from the DoD and the National Science Foundation in the late 1980s and 1990s. In 1989, the compound semiconductor group received more than $20 million from the NSF to create the Center for Quantized Electronic Structures. They also obtained large grants from DARPA to establish the Multidisciplinary Optical Switching Center and the Optoelectronics Technology Center. This center conducted research on lasers (Hu, 2007a,b; Kroemer, 2007).

The shared fabrication facility enabled Gossard to greatly expand the MBE research program at UCSB (Kroemer and Merz had asked him to takeover this line of research and greatly expand it). It also led to renewed collaborations with industry through the MICRO program. For example, in collaboration with engineers working at Hughes's Santa Barbara Research Center and with funding from MICRO, Merz and Gossard used MBE techniques to create a new material for infrared detectors (this material was a superlattice, made of many different crystalline layers). The SBRC characterized the material developed at UCSB. This collaborative program provided an alternative to infrared detectors made of mercury cadmium telluride then manufactured by Hughes (Gossard, 2007). Coldren also used molecular beam epitaxy to make laser diodes. These faculties transformed UCSB into the academic leader in MBE. The know-how acquired in MBE was then transferred to industry, as many doctoral students trained in the program went to work for the SBRC, Rockwell, and Hewlett-Packard (Bowers, 2007; Kroemer, 2007).

Starting in the early 1990s, the compound semiconductor group built a capability in another epitaxial technique, metal organic chemical vapor deposition (MOCVD).[43] MOCVD was a chemical process using metal organic gases to grow semiconductor crystals. It was faster than MBE. It also enabled the growth of new classes of compound semiconductor materials such as phosphides (compound semiconductors with phosphorus) and nitrides (incorporating nitrogen). Like MBE, MOCVD had been pioneered in industry. Harold Manasevit had developed MOCVD reactors at Rockwell in the late 1960s. Researchers at Philips and Rockwell later perfected these techniques. In the 1980s, Japanese corporations widely adopted MOCVD to create new materials and optoelectronic devices (Dupuis, 2009; Lécuyer and Ueyama, 2013; Manasevit, 1981; Shimizu and Kudo, 2011). To gain expertise in MOCVD, the UCSB group turned once more to industry. In 1991, they hired Steve DenBaars, a MOCVD expert, from Hewlett-Packard. They gave him the mandate of creating a MOCVD capability on campus.[44] Supporting DenBaars's efforts was Hughes, which provided seed funding to his laboratory. DenBaars also secured grants from the NSF, the ONR, and UC Discovery. UC Discovery, like MICRO, was a systemwide program that matched industrial funding with state monies to support industry–university research collaborations at the University of California. But its scope was larger, as it also funded research on software, computer architecture, digital media, and the life sciences. In the early 1990s, DenBaars received a UC Discovery grant matching funding from Cree, a North Carolina–based firm producing light emitting diodes. According to DenBaars, this grant was important. It enabled him to upgrade his laboratory equipment. The capability in MOCVD, built by DenBaars and his students, was critical for the subsequent growth of the compound research program at UCSB and for the creation of new firms that commercialized technologies developed on campus (DenBaars, 2007; Hu, 2007b; Kroemer, 2007; Lowe et al., n.d.; Lowe, 2002).

Coldren, Bowers, and others used MOCVD techniques to make indium phosphide–based heterostructures. Indium phosphide is composed of indium and phosphorus. It is used in laser diodes and high-frequency electronics. Bowers and his group worked on indium phosphide, doing material characterization and making new components such as detectors and telecommunication devices. Coldren used the material to make tunable lasers that could be used across a wide range of fiber optic channels. Much of this work was patented by UCSB (Bowers, 2007; Kroemer, 2007). Research on indium phosphide–based devices soon gave birth to start-ups targeting the telecommunications market. The Santa Barbara region, however, was not an optimal place to start a semiconductor company. There was little venture capital in the area. It was also difficult to attract engineers to Santa Barbara, as the local job market was limited. These limitations led some start-ups to relocate to Silicon Valley or to Los Angeles (Bowers, 2007).

A start-up coming out of indium phosphide research was Agility Communications. Agility Communications was established by Coldren and two of his graduate students, Greg Fish and Beck Mason, in 1998. The start-up took an exclusive license on UCSB's patents and commercialized the tunable lasers developed on campus. It also employed students, many of whom had worked with DenBaars. The firm was based in the Santa Barbara area, but its capital came mostly from VCs in Silicon Valley. At a time when venture capital was plentiful for fiber optic communications (this was the height of the Internet bubble), the firm raised more than $200 million between 1998 and 2000. These investments financed product development and the construction of an indium phosphide fabrication facility, meant to produce 10,000 laser diodes per week by 2002. The 2001 crash halted these plans and severely limited the firm's subsequent growth. By 2004, Agility Communications had $20 million in sales. The investors sold it to JDS Uniphase, a Silicon Valley firm, the following year (Den-Baars, 2007; Tenorio, 2000; Trujillo 2012; Zate, 2002a).

Another telecommunication start-up was Calient Networks. Calient Networks was established by Bowers; Daniel Blumenthal, a junior faculty member in ECE; and Charles Corbalis, a former Cisco Systems executive, in 1999.[45] The firm was based on work by Bowers and his group on optical switches. These switches were made of micromirrors and selectively switched light between optical fibers. Calient Networks addressed the problem of switching massive amounts of data in fiber optics networks (optical switches, which could handle more data than electronics switches, greatly increased the capacity of fiber optics networks). Calient was first established in the Santa Barbara area, but its headquarters rapidly moved to Silicon Valley, where potential customers for its products were located. Like Agility Communications, Calient Networks licensed UCSB's patents and recruited compound semiconductor experts trained on campus. It also raised $285 million from VCs (venture capitalists) and networking firms in Silicon Valley. Like Agility, Calient Networks encountered significant difficulties in marketing its products after the dot.com crash and the over-building of fiber optics capacity in the United States. As a result, most of its sales were with Japanese telecommunication carriers. But Calient remained a niche player, and after the dot.com crash the company never had more than a hundred employees (Bowers, 2007; Gubbins, 2006; Marshall, 2003; McGarvey, 2000; Zate 2001, 2002b).

The MOCVD capability built by DenBaars was also the basis for a large research program on gallium nitride at UCSB. In the early 1990s, gallium nitride emerged as a major compound semiconductor material critical for the fabrication of LEDs and laser diodes. Gallium nitride, made of gallium and nitrogen, was first developed at RCA in the late 1960s. But it became an important material twenty years later with the development of MOCVD-based techniques and the creation of the first bright blue LEDs by Isamu Akasaki at Nagoya University. Shuji Nakamura, an engineer working at Nichia Chemical Industries, then commercialized Akasaki's techniques and introduced bright blue LEDs based on gallium nitride to the market in 1993. This breakthrough persuaded hundreds of firms and academic laboratories to enter gallium nitride research (Akasaki, 2000, 2007; Akasaki and Amano, 2006; Johnstone, 2007; Lécuyer and Ueyama, 2013).

UCSB was one of the first universities to build a competency in gallium nitride. After Nichia's commercialization of the first blue LED, Den-

Baars and Umesh Mishra, an Indian engineer who had worked at Hughes before joining UCSB, turned their MOCVD expertise to the making of gallium nitride–based devices. They could do so immediately, without having to apply for research grants. This gave them a considerable advantage in a highly competitive field. DenBaars and his students conducted research on LEDs made of gallium nitride, while Mishra worked on blue lasers and pursued the potential of the new material for the fabrication of electronic devices (among other characteristics, gallium nitride had very high electron velocity and could withstand high voltages). In the second half of the 1990s, Mishra and his group fabricated gallium nitride–based microwave transistors for wireless applications. These research programs were particularly productive. Between 1995 and 2001, DenBaars, Mishra, and their students filed twelve patents and published more than 220 papers on gallium nitride (DenBaars, 2007; Hu, 2007b; Kroemer, 2007; Lowe et al., n.d.; Lowe, 2002).

To commercialize their research, DenBaars and Mishra associated themselves with Fred Blum, a semiconductor executive and entrepreneur who had worked at Rockwell. They established Nitres in 1996 (the headquarters were in Los Angeles and the R&D operations in the Santa Barbara area). The start-up was focused on the fabrication of bright blue LEDs made of gallium nitride, and it performed research on high-speed transistors. Unlike Coldren and Bowers, the founders did not raise venture capital for their firm. Instead, they financed research and development and the design of LED products with contracts from the DoD and the Department of Commerce and with a Small Business Innovation Research (SBIR) grant from the National Institute of Standards and Technology matched by Hughes and General Electric. To cut costs, Nitres's engineers used UCSB's fabrication facility to develop their devices. By 2000, they had made sufficient progress with bright blue LEDs that Cree, the North Carolina–based manufacturer of LEDs, purchased the start-up. Cree, which fabricated and marketed blue LEDs made of silicon carbide, was anxious to get access to Nitres's MOCVD expertise and to fabricate brighter LEDs made of gallium nitride. It paid more than $200 million in stock for Nitres.[46] Cree then proceeded to transform the start-up into its technology development center on the West Coast. It also commercialized the bright light-emitting diodes developed at Nitres (Bursky, 2000; Lowe, n.d., 2002; Ranji, 2000a,b, 2001).

By the late 1990s, UCSB had established itself as a significant center for gallium nitride research and entrepreneurship. This enabled the compound semiconductor group to attract Shuji Nakamura, the engineer who had developed the first commercial blue LEDs and blue and violet lasers at Nichia Chemical, to the faculty. Nakamura joined the Materials Department in 2000. He also consulted for Cree (Hu, 2007b; Johnstone, 2007; Kroemer, 2007).[47] In collaboration with DenBaars, Nakamura established a new research center investigating solid-state lighting with funding from manufacturers such as Cree, Rohm, and Mitsubishi Chemical. The main thrust of their research was to improve the efficiency and luminosity of gallium nitride LEDs and to develop new lasers based on the same material. In collaboration with engineers from Mitsubishi, the group pioneered a new approach to the fabrication of gallium nitride crystals and diodes. Instead of growing gallium nitride on sapphire, which had been the main process used since the late 1960s, they employed gallium nitride substrates provided by Mitsubishi. They also used crystals with a different crystalline orientation. These innovations enabled Nakamura, DenBaars, and Speck to fabricate much brighter blue LEDs and to make a blue-violet laser diode as well (Riordan, 2007). In parallel, Mishra pursued his research on heterostructure transistors based on gallium nitride and established a center on gallium nitride electronics supported by the ONR.

These research programs led to the formation of a second wave of gallium nitride start-ups. The new firms, Soraa and Transphorm, benefited from the surge in venture capital funding for energy-related technologies in the mid- and late 2000s. They also relied on the cadre of engineers and managers who had been trained at UCSB and had worked for Nitres, Calient Networks, and Agility Communications. Mishra established Transphorm in the Santa Barbara area in 2007. The firm focused on the making of high-speed switches that converted AC to DC current more efficiently than silicon-based converters. To develop its products and build a gallium nitride fab, Transphorm raised more than $100 million from Silicon Valley venture capitalists and Japanese investors (Clarke, 2011; Swift, 2012). Another start-up coming out of the research program at UCSB was Soraa. It was formed by Nakamura and DenBaars at the instigation of Vinod Khosla, the Silicon Valley venture capitalist (like Transphorm, Soraa received very significant venture capital investments). Started in the Santa Barbara area in 2008, the firm soon moved to Silicon Valley to get access to experienced engineers and managers. Soraa exploited the new approach to gallium nitride growth developed at UCSB. In 2011, it commercialized very bright white LEDs that competed with Cree's and Nichia's products (Baker, 2012; Markoff, 2012).

Thus, over a thirty-year period, the compound semiconductor group at UCSB brought in expertise and competencies from industry. It also benefited from significant funding from industrial corporations such as Hughes and Cree, often through MICRO and UC Discovery. Technology transfer and funding from industry enabled the group to make significant innovations of their own that were later commercialized by UCSB-based start-ups. Among them were communications, electric transmission, and solid-state lighting firms that sometimes competed with the program's industrial patrons.

CONCLUSION

UC Berkeley, UCLA, and UC Santa Barbara experienced very different trajectories in semiconductors. They also developed different relations with their industrial surroundings. UC Berkeley was the first campus to enter semiconductor research. Donald Pederson, a Bell Labs engineer, established the first integrated circuits laboratory at any U.S. university in the early 1960s. Following this pioneering move and with significant input from Silicon Valley corporations, faculty interested in semiconductors at UCB built two distinct research programs: one focused on mixed signal MOS circuits for communication applications and another concentrating on the software tools used to design these circuits. The group working on mixed-signal circuits transferred their innovative designs to industry through sabbaticals in Silicon Valley firms, the hiring of students by local start-ups, and the licensing of intellectual property to corporations located outside the region. In contrast, the faculty group working on microchip design software established leading electronic design automation firms such as Synopsys and Cadence Design Systems in Silicon Valley.

As with their counterparts at UC Berkeley, much of the innovative and entrepreneurial activities of microelectronics engineers at UCLA concentrated on communications integrated circuits. But the industrial origins of these activities did not reside at the Bell Telephone Laboratories or in Silicon Valley firms. Rather, the communication circuits program at UCLA grew out of research on very high speed integrated circuits (VHSIC) funded by the DoD at TRW. In 1986, Henry Samueli, a former TRW engineer, established the Integrated Circuits and Systems Laboratory at UCLA in collaboration with Asad Abidi. Using software tools initially developed at UC Berkeley and with financing from MICRO, they designed new broadband circuits and CMOS radio frequency circuits. Samueli and ICSL students later established fabless firms such as Broadcom to commercialize these innovations.

In contrast, Herbert Kroemer and other faculty members at UC Santa Barbara focused on compound semiconductors. They brought in experts from the Bell Labs, Rockwell, Hewlett-Packard, and Nichia Chemical. With support from MICRO, the NSF, and the DoD, they developed productive research programs in compound semiconductors that often led to the formation of start-ups. Facing a regional environment that was less favorable to high-tech businesses than Silicon Valley and Southern California, they often moved their start-ups to Silicon Valley or to the Los Angeles area.

Rare were the universities that made contributions to semiconductor technology and industry that were as significant as those of UC Berkeley, UCLA, and UC Santa Barbara.[48] Their impact on the evolution of semiconductor design and manufacturing can be explained by their "bottom-up" approach to program building, the nearby presence of major centers of entrepreneurship and industrial innovation, and the internal dynamics specific to the UC system. UCB, UCLA, and UCSB's semiconductor research programs emerged out of campus-based initiatives (rather than from decisions made at the system level) (Turin, 1983). A group of well-connected faculty at UC Berkeley established the integrated circuits laboratory and later mustered significant campus resources to expand their research activities. Administrators at UCLA and UCSB also made significant investments in semiconductors in the 1980s and 1990s. All these initiatives relied on the close coupling with local electronics firms and high-tech clusters. Close relations with these corporations enabled faculty groups to acquire state-of-the-art expertise from Silicon Valley and the defense industry in Southern California.

Supporting the "bottom-up" approach to program building was MICRO. MICRO gave financial incentives for UC researchers to work with semiconductor firms. It helped recreate the industrial collaborations pioneered by Berkeley faculty around mixed-signal circuits across the whole UC system. MICRO also oriented semiconductor research at the campuses toward practical problems of relevance to industry. It was this practical orientation and the focus on industrial problems that led faculty groups at UCB, UCLA, and UCSB to make significant innovations in materials, devices, circuits, and design tools and to transfer these technologies to start-ups and well-established firms.

Also important for the emergence of centers of semiconductor innovation and entrepreneurship at UC were the system's internal dynamics. Competition among campuses led faculty groups to explore different opportunities such as broadband communication microchips at UCLA and compound semiconductors at UC Santa Barbara. At the same time, research groups across the UC system relied heavily on the technologies, especially design tools, engineered at other campuses. The flow of administrators between campuses also played an important role in the creation of centers of excellence in microelectronics. For example, George Turin, who had chaired the Electrical Engineering and Computer Sciences Department at Berkeley, later became dean of the Engineering School at UCLA. At UCLA, he supported the growth of the microelectronics program, including the recruitment of microchip designers who established the Integrated Circuits and Systems Laboratory.

The semiconductor programs at UC Berkeley, UCLA, and UC Santa Barbara exemplify the many economic functions of research universities since the late 1970s. The primary function of research universities in high tech economies is the training of highly skilled engineers and scientists. Over the last forty years, UCB, UCLA, and UCSB graduated thousands of microelectronics and semiconductor engineers with master's and doctoral degrees. The great majority of these engineers went to work for semiconductor and electronics corporations in California. At some firms, such as Broadcom, engineers trained at UC represented a very sizable part of the overall technical and managerial workforce. Many other UC-trained engineers went to work for Hughes, TRW, Rockwell, Intel, Hewlett-Packard, and other Silicon Valley corporations. With them, these engineers brought the skills, knowledge, and tools they had acquired at the campuses. For example, they diffused SPICE and microchip design software developed at UC Berkeley. Similarly, MBE and MOCVD techniques devised at UC Santa Barbara flowed with them to compound semiconductor firms located in Southern California.

The second economic function of research universities is the development and promotion of experimental technologies not yet explored in industry. Across the whole period, UC researchers identified technological opportunities that were not fully (or not at all) exploited in industry and where academic groups could make significant contributions. Making the most of these opportunities, they developed experimental devices, proof-of-concept microchips, and microchip design tools. For example, Samueli, Abidi, and their groups developed experimental chips showing the potential of RF CMOS and broadband communication circuits. Hodges and Gray engineered proof-of-concept microchips for filtering and analog-to-digital conversion. Similarly, Newton, Sangiovanni-Vincentelli, Brayton, and their students devised "academic" tools for the logic synthesis of very complex circuits. Faculty members heavily promoted these innovations in the corporate world. Hodges and Gray, for instance, organized meetings with engineers working in industry to publicize their research on analog-to-digital converters. Newton and Sangiovanni-Vincentelli spent significant time on the road touting their advances in logic synthesis. These promotional efforts enabled UC faculty to bring their technologies to the market.

The third economic function of universities and academic engineers in high-tech economies is the translation of experimental technologies into commercial products. Some researchers, including Hodges and Gray, transferred their technologies to existing firms. Gray, for instance, took a sabbatical leave from UC Berkeley to lead an Intel team designing integrated circuits filters on the basis of his research on campus. Another vector for the transformation of university ideas, software code, and proof-of-concept chips into stable products has been the formation of start-ups. For example, Solomon, Newton, and Sangiovanni-Vincentelli created SDA Systems, which transformed the software programs developed at Berkeley into a suite of commercial tools. Similarly, at Broadcom Samueli and his group translated the proof-of-concept chips devised at UCLA into very reliable and high-performance products that could be manufactured at low cost by semiconductor foundries. The translation of university concepts and techniques into commercial products enabled the growth of new branches of the semiconductor industry such as mixed-signal circuits and broadband communications chips. Entirely new industries also arose out of research activities at UCB and UCSB: solid-state lighting and electronic design automation.

Universities can also play a significant role in the growth and renewal of industrial regions. The ICSL at UCLA transformed the Southern California economy by "liberating" broadband microchips and systems developed for military purposes at TRW and other defense firms and commercializing them through the formation of start-ups. When military contractors experienced a deep crisis with the end of the Cold War, UCLA spin-offs such as Broadcom absorbed many experienced microelectronics and systems engineers laid off by defense contractors and turned their creative potential to the design of high-performance broadband chips for Internet access and wireless communications. In other words, UCLA helped a defense-dependent economy to reinvent itself with the emergence and growth of the fabless semiconductor industry. On a smaller scale, the region around Santa Barbara greatly benefited from research in compound semiconductors at UCSB. Although many UCSB start-ups moved their headquarters, and sometimes their entire operations, to Los Angeles and Silicon Valley, the entrepreneurial activities of faculty members and students enriched the small high-tech region in Santa Barbara with compound semiconductor and instrumentation firms. A small cluster of firms and R&D operations designing and producing LEDs, lasers, converters, and optical switches emerged in the area and survived the dot.com crash of the early 2000s. These businesses provided a skilled and experienced workforce for a new wave of start-ups exploiting UCSB's gallium nitride technology in the following decade.

NOTES

The author would like to thank David Hodges, Martin Kenney, and David Mowery for their insightful comments on earlier versions of this chapter. His thanks also go to the Institute for Advanced Study at Central European University for supporting the writing of this chapter.

1. William Hewlett, the cofounder of Hewlett-Packard, supported the department's expansion into semiconductor engineering. In collaboration with Gordon Brown, the chairman of the electrical engineering department at MIT, Hewlett submitted a report to Berkeley's dean of engineering in April 1956. In this report, Hewlett and Brown recommended a thorough reorganization of the electrical engineering curriculum at Berkeley. They also advised the department (then called a division) to invest in new fields such as semiconductor technology and information science. Hewlett and his business partner, David Packard, had made a similar pitch at Stanford a few years earlier (Brown and Hewlett, 1956; Lécuyer, 2005b).

2. Critics also noted that semiconductor fabrication facilities required extensive chemical knowledge, which was not the main strength of the department of electrical engineering.

3. Paul Morton had chaired the division of electrical engineering, which helped in getting space assigned to the integrated circuits laboratory (Hodges, 2012b).

4. Another industrial supporter was Ampex (Hodges, 2008–2010).

5. Stanford and the University of Arizona established their own integrated circuits laboratory along the Berkeley model in the mid-1960s. But most American universities entered the field of silicon electronics much later, in the late 1970s and 1980s (Gray, 1998; Lécuyer, 2005b; Linvill, 2002).

6. A third research program focused on computer architecture. This program was led by David Patterson, Carlo Sequin, Randy Katz, and others. It sought to

optimize computer architecture with the restriction to single-chip integrated circuit implementation. This led to a succession of Reduced Instruction Set Computer (RISC) designs, subsequently commercialized by Sun Microsystems, Digital Equipment, and other firms. For the development of RISC, see the chapter on the department of electrical engineering and computer sciences at Berkeley in this volume and Khazam and Mowery (1994). For a discussion of entrepreneurship in the EECS department at Berkeley, see Kenney and Goe (2004).

7. Engineers at TRW were working on MOS mixed signal integrated circuits at that time (Hodges, 2008–2010).

8. The group was interested in patenting this invention, like the one on PCM encoders. But they soon discovered that there was enough prior art to make patenting difficult. James Clark Maxwell had anticipated some of their ideas in the 1890s (Hodges, 2008–2010).

9. National Semiconductor and Hitachi refused to negotiate licenses and pay royalties on the Hodges and Gray patent. They worked around the patent claims (which is easy to do for circuit patents) and mounted defenses that UC could not challenge. Much later, National and Hitachi made large gifts to support the EECS department's building projects. No such gifts were made by Bell Labs and Bell Northern Research (Hodges, 2012a).

10. This estimate did not include the many millions of chips used within the Bell Telephone system.

11. MICRO stood for "Microelectronics Innovation and Computer Research Operation." "Operation" was later replaced by "Opportunities."

12. Hodges's experience with industrial collaboration at Berkeley, around mixed signal circuits, led him to make this recommendation to Jerry Brown (Hodges, 2012a).

13. Hodges recalls that Roger Ditzel was important in the discussions leading to MICRO. The passing of the Bayh-Dole act in Congress motivated him in his support of the MICRO proposal (Hodges, 2012a).

14. The committee also recommended that all research universities in California, including Stanford and Caltech, be eligible for this program and that the annual funding level on the state side should be in the order of $10 million. None of these propositions was retained in the bill (Hodges, 2008–2010).

15. Industrial firms resented having to pay royalties on inventions they had financed. Complaints from industry, notably from IBM (which wanted free, nonexclusive licenses), led the University of California to make an exception to its intellectual property policy for MICRO projects in 1992. With the policy change, industrial sponsors could negotiate exclusive royalty-bearing licenses on patents coming out of the research projects they had funded at UC (Kroemer, 1992; Turin, 1983).

16. For example, MICRO financed the RISC and RAID projects in their beginnings. It also provided significant funding for UCB's research program on semiconductor manufacturing processes (Hodges, 2008–2010). For RISC and RAID, see Chapter Four in this volume.

17. According to Rohrer, the agreement with Softech stipulated that part of the profits would flow back to Berkeley to support research there (Rohrer, 2011).

18. This open-source approach was criticized by the central technology licensing office of the University of California, which viewed the free releases of SPICE as a loss of revenues.

19. It took three years of an intense lobbying effort for the electrical engineering and computer sciences department to receive $3 million from the State of California to modernize its semiconductor fabrication facility in 1983 (Turin, 1981c,d).

20. Industrial funding for research increased in the late 1970s and early 1980s. Industry, which financed 2 percent of electronics research at Berkeley in 1978–1979 funded approximately 12 percent of this research in 1983–1984. The share of research funded by the DoD went from 33 to 49 percent during the same period. Overall, research funding in electronics increased substantially going from $4 million in 1978–1979 to $15 million in 1984–1985 (Wong, 1985).

21. A measure of the significance of SPICE to the semiconductor design software industry can be seen in the backgrounds of the winners of the Phil Kaufman award, which is presented by the Electronic Design Automation Consortium to individuals who have had a significant impact on the semiconductor design automation industry. Of the eighteen award winners through 2011, nine either received their highest degree and/or were professors at UC Berkeley—by far the largest share accounted for by any leading U.S. EE department. The author would like to thank Martin Kenney for sharing this observation with him.

22. It is not clear how Solomon, Newton, and Sangiovanni-Vincentelli dealt with Berkeley's IP rights on the code commercialized by SDA Systems. According to Michael Borrus, they "legally worked around a recalcitrant licensing office" (Borrus, 2010).

23. By then, the open-source approach advocated by Pederson had become widely accepted in the department. In a letter to Andrew Grove, Intel's president, in October 1982, George Turin, the chairman of the electrical engineering and computer sciences department, summarized this consensus. Discussing the "elements of the philosophy that [were] unique to [Berkeley]," Turin cited the following characteristics:

> . . . practically-oriented research with an emphasis on university–industry cooperation; a non-proprietary stance that concentrates on dissemination of our research results rather than on establishing University or Faculty proprietary rights in them; an integrated Faculty effort spanning the entire range of electrical engineering and computer science disciplines, which avoids internal "fiefdoms." (Turin, 1982d)

In 1983, Turin tried to convince UCOP to create an exception to its intellectual property policies for MICRO projects, by letting the inventions coming out of MICRO fall into the public domain—to no avail (Turin, 1983).

24. Among the universities entering microelectronics research in the early and mid-1980s were Cornell, Carnegie Mellon, MIT, North Carolina State, Auburn University, Case Western Reserve, Washington University in Saint Louis, and the Universities of Illinois, Colorado, Utah, Arizona, Florida, and Michigan (Hodges, 1980a).

25. Abidi and Samueli were not the first faculty members active in silicon microelectronics at UCLA. Gabor Temes, for example, had worked on high-speed converters at UCLA in the late 1970s. Alan Willson, Samueli's doctoral advisor,

was a digital signal processing specialist. But before the creation of the ICSL, UCLA was mostly known for research in device physics. Chand Viswanathan, for example, had done noted theoretical work on MOS field effect transistors.

26. Like Pederson, Morton, and Everhart at Berkeley in the early 1960s, the founding faculty members of the ICSL created a common instrumentation pool (Abidi, 2007). But the team does not seem to have been as closely integrated as those that emerged at Berkeley around MOS mixed-signal circuits and the development of SPICE and logic synthesis software.

27. Abidi and his students also designed read-write circuits for hard disk drives, with funding from Silicon Systems and Western Digital (Abidi, 2007).

28. For contemporary reports on the VHSIC program, see Brueckner and Borrus (1984) and U.S. General Accounting Office (1985).

29. Samueli and his group developed a unique expertise in Quadrature Amplitude Modulation (QAM) technology at UCLA. QAM is a modulation scheme for digital communications systems. This expertise in QAM later enabled Broadcom to out-compete much larger firms such as Texas Instruments and to secure an important design contract from Scientific-Atlanta.

30. Samueli later commented that Frank Wazzan, the dean of the engineering school, was very supportive of his entrepreneurial ventures (Samueli, 2007).

31. Unlike most Silicon Valley entrepreneurs, Samueli and Nicholas were not interested in raising monies from venture capital partnerships, which would have diluted their stakes in Broadcom.

32. Broadcom also received design contracts from TRW for a digital synthesizer integrated circuit for military satellites and from the Air Force for the design of a filter microchip for a satellite global positioning system (GPS) receiver. These and other contracts supported a small operation with $3.6 million in sales in 1994.

33. Among Broadcom's acquisitions in Southern California was NewPort Communications, a firm started by Armond Harapetian, a UCLA PhD, in 1996.

34. This wave of acquisitions later led to significant legal problems for Samueli, Nicholas, and Broadcom. They were accused of back-dating stock options granted to engineers coming from firms they had acquired and to new hires as well. Nicholas was forced to resign from his position as CEO and to leave the firm in 2003.

35. Abidi and his students used Spectre RF, a software tool developed by Cadence, to design RF CMOS circuits.

36. Infineon and Atheros Communications, a Silicon Valley firm, also exploited the work on RF CMOS work coming out of the ICSL (Abidi, 2007).

37. Broadcom was the tenth-largest semiconductor firm in the world in 2012.

38. UCSD followed a similar strategy in compound semiconductors, for the same reasons, in the mid- and late 1970s. See Chang (2007) and Larson (2007).

39. Kroemer consulted for Hughes from 1978 to the late 1990s.

40. Before Merz and Long joined UCSB, Kroemer did mostly theoretical work, focusing on band offsets (Kroemer, 2000b).

41. Huttenback's abrasive style owed him the enmity of part of the faculty. He was accused, and later charged, with embezzlement. Huttenback resigned from the University of California in 1986.

42. The gift from the Whitaker Foundation also financed an endowed chair for Kroemer (Hu, 2007b).

43. MOCVD is also called MOVPE (metal organic vapor phase epitaxy) or OMVPE (organometallic vapor phase epitaxy).

44. Before the hiring of Steve DenBaars, the UCSB group relied on their industrial collaborators through MICRO to grow crystals with MOCVD. For example, Rockwell grew a heterostructure of gallium arsenide and indium phosphide for optoelectronic devices with MOCVD for Larry Coldren in 1987–1988. See Coldren, 1989.

45. Calient Networks was not Bowers's first start-up. He had started Terabit Technology in 1995 and sold it to Ciena three years later. Terabit made detectors for data transmission (Bowers, 2007).

46. Following Nitres's acquisition, Cree licensed UCSB's patents on LEDs.

47. Nakamura's recruitment from Nichia was highly contentious. Nichia sued him for leaking trade secrets to Cree. Nakamura countersued, asking Nichia to compensate him for the inventions he had made at the firm. After several years of litigation, Nakamura prevailed. In 2001, Cree gave an endowed chair to the materials department at UCSB. Nakamura was the first recipient of that chair (Johnstone, 2007).

48. Only Stanford, Caltech, and to a lesser degree the University of Illinois matched their impact. The University of Illinois at Urbana-Champaign originated LED technology. Stanford played a critical role in the development of RISC chips and semiconductor manufacturing processes. Caltech, through the activities of Carver Mead, had a significant impact on synaptic devices and microchip and electronic system design. In contrast, the many universities that entered semiconductor research in the late 1970s and first half of the 1980s had little influence on the subsequent evolution of semiconductor design and manufacturing. For Stanford, see Lécuyer (2005b).

CHAPTER THREE

The University of California and the Evolution of the Biotechnology Industry in San Diego and the San Francisco Bay Area

STEVEN CASPER

Biotechnology has emerged as a leading high-technology industry within the state of California. The origins and growth of biotechnology in California are strongly tied to the University of California (UC). From 1980 to 2005 UC scientists were listed as inventors on over 2000 biotechnology-related patents and have been founders of over 300 biotechnology companies (Casper, 2009). Although important contributions have been made to the commercialization of biotechnology across the UC system, UC San Diego (UCSD) and UC San Francisco (UCSF) have had a disproportionate impact. This influence is partly seen through commercialization indicators: UCSF and UCSD lead all California universities (including Stanford) in patenting biotechnology discoveries and are among the leaders in the number of spinout firms created (California Healthcare Institute, 2004). The two campuses are also anchors of regional biotechnology clusters. The San Francisco and San Diego regions contain two of the three largest biotechnology clusters in the world (with Boston being the third). This chapter examines the early history of biotechnology in the San Francisco and San Diego regions, exploring commercialization processes linking UCSF and UCSD to an early company in each cluster, Genentech and Hybritech, respectively. The chapter argues that different patterns of university–industry relationships that emerged within these early firms affected the development of their respective biotechnology clusters, creating important differences in each region in both the dominant corporate strategies of biotechnology firms and the orientation of ties linking universities and firms.

Much research on the role of universities on the economic development of biotechnology clusters has focused on two regions, San Francisco and Boston (see for example Powell, 2002; McKelvey, 1996; Owen-Smith and Powell, 2004). Previous studies demonstrate the importance of "star scientists" within both regions in creating biotechnology firms and forging highly collaborative ties linking university laboratories and the spin-off companies that are financed by venture capitalists (Zucker, Darby, and Armstrong, 2002; Powell, Koput, and Smith-Doerr, 1996). The research reported in this chapter on UCSF in San Francisco is consistent with this view. Biotechnology firms in the San Francisco Bay area are frequently spun out from laboratories of leading academic scientists and are strongly science driven, investing heavily in research and allowing scientists to participate in "open science" collaborations with universities that emphasize both publication and patenting. This pattern was diffused across Bay Area biotechnology firms through the emergence of Genentech in 1976, a firm launched on the basis of pioneering advances in genetic engineering at UCSF that adopted a highly collaborative, science-driven mode of operations modeled in part on a vision of interdisciplinary science gleaned from the UCSF Department of Biochemistry and Biophysics. This model spread through the Bay Area as dozens of Genentech scientists went on to found or take senior positions in subsequent biotechnology firms. UCSF has remained a central actor within Bay Area biotechnology networks, not just through technology licensing but through the active participation of its scientists in thousands of collaborations with regional biotechnology firms.

While the model of organizing biotechnology firms primarily around scientific research networks can succeed, in San Diego a different model has developed and also is viable. Many successful biotechnology companies in San Diego have adopted a market-centered orientation centered more on proprietary science, focusing on the continued exploitation of founding technologies rather than longer-term investments in the generation of fundamentally new technologies (Powell, Packalen, and Whittington, 2009; March, 1991). Scientists from UCSD have routinely transferred technology to regional companies and are involved in advisory boards, but scientists from the university have played a less central role in collaborative R&D networks linking firms to universities. Networks driving the development of biotechnology in San Diego have been more entrepreneurial, linking a pool of managers and venture capitalists eager to start companies that are often based on technology from UCSD or elsewhere that is "pulled into" a new venture. The chapter will examine the development of a key UCSD spin-off, Hybritech, which was managed with a strong commercial orientation and whose acquisition by an established pharmaceuticals firm led to the formation of the key entrepreneurial network that fueled the growth of the San Diego cluster from the late 1980s onwards.

The remainder of this chapter is organized into four sections. The first two sections contain a narrative history of the roles of UCSF and UCSD in becoming anchors of their respective technology clusters. The study emphasizes how different patterns of science commercialization leading to the development of Genentech and Hybritech affected the organization and strategy of these firms and eventually affected the contrasting patterns of evolution of the biotechnology industry in the San Francisco and San Diego regions. This is followed by a section drawing on patent and bibliometric analysis to demonstrate at a more aggregate level of analysis of how the contrasting patterns of science commercialization have affected the organization of scientific networks within the two regions, followed by a concluding section that discusses implications of the chapter's findings.

UCSF AND THE EMERGENCE OF BIOTECHNOLOGY IN THE SAN FRANCISCO BAY AREA

The University of California, San Francisco, can trace its history back to the 1860s, emerging as part of the initial founding of the University of California. By the mid-twentieth century, UCSF had established itself as a leading medical school. UCSF was slow, however, to integrate basic research, and especially advances in molecular biology, within its well-regarded clinical programs. The ranking of the UCSF Medical School steadily declined to twentieth in the country by 1966, leading UC President Clark Kerr to replace UCSF Chancellor John Saunders (Jong, 2006: 267). A new campus administration led by Willard Fleming is credited with reviving basic research at UCSF (Vettel, 2006), leading to the hiring in 1969 of William Rutter, a prominent biochemist from the University of Washington, to organize a newly named Department of Biochemistry and Biophysics. Rutter was given wide latitude in organizing the department and hiring. UCSF quickly became a leading center of molecular biology research, particularly the recombinant DNA techniques that were developed during the 1970s. UCSF's reputation as a leading center for molecular biology research increased throughout the 1980s, and by 1993 the UCSF Department of Biochemistry was the top-ranked program in the country (Goldberger, Maher, and Flatteau, 1995, cited in Jong, 2006: 269).

Sociologists of science have traced UCSF's rise in biomedical sciences to the establishment of an interdisciplinary and clinically focused research program under Rutter (Hollingsworth and Hollingsworth, 2012; Jong, 2006). As pointed out by Jong (2006) in a study comparing biochemistry departments at UCSF, Stanford, and UC Berkeley, most molecular biology research conducted during the 1960s and early 1970s involved simple organisms, which simplified molecular research by focusing on basic biological processes. Moreover, most biochemistry departments within which research occurred adopted a strong disciplinary focus. Arthur Kornberg, for example, through the 1970s had established a leading biochemistry department at Stanford by hiring a team of faculty who worked to establish a shared approach to isolating and employing enzymes to understand biochemical processes involving DNA (Jong, 2006: 264). Two scientists within this department won Nobel Prizes for their work during this period, Paul Berg and Kornberg.

Basic sciences at UCSF under Rutter departed from this tradition. Rutter, in establishing the new department, stated that its goal should be to understand molecular processes within higher organisms, particularly in humans (Jong, 2006: 267). To accomplish this goal, Rutter established an interdisciplinary focus for his department, encouraging the biochemists he hired to form collaborations with biologists and chemists in other departments. Moreover, the goal of applying molecular biology techniques to human health required clinical collaborations with the hospital. Within three years of the department's founding, at least seven faculty members had developed collaborations with clinicians at UCSF (Ibid.: 268; see also Hall, 2002: 290–293). Rutter also encouraged the medical school to hire several basic research scientists, a practice of integrating basic and clinical researchers within medical schools that is now widespread.

The targeting by UCSF scientists of molecular biology techniques to help understand biological mechanisms within complex organisms was a crucial step in the eventual establishment of the biotechnology industry. Cetus, founded in 1971 around technology created by UC Berkeley Nobel Laureate Donald Glaser, is usually credited as the first biotechnology firm. Though it became famous for inventing the polymerase chain reaction (PCR) in the early 1980s, Cetus was originally established to use molecular biology techniques to simplify and improve the productivity of industrial processes, such as using microorganisms to help produce chemical feedstocks (Rabinow, 1996). The UCSF faculty was the first to explicitly target human medicine as a goal for intervention through molecular methods.

This idea would become the founding premise on which much of the biotechnology industry is based.

The Origins of Genentech

The history of Genentech's founding within the context of a scientific race to use genetic engineering techniques to produce a synthetic form of human insulin is well documented (see, for example, Kenney, 1986; McKelvey, 1996; Hall, 2002, Hughes, 2011). Briefly reviewing Genentech's origins is important, however, as patterns of company organization and technology strategy established at Genentech during the late 1970s were closely linked to the research strategy developed at UCSF during the 1970s and had a strong impact on the broader San Francisco biotechnology cluster.

Genentech was founded in 1976 on the basis of a partnership between Robert Swanson, an entrepreneur with ties to the local venture capital company Kleiner Perkins,[1] and Herbert Boyer, a professor of microbiology at UCSF. In the early 1970s Boyer had collaborated with Stanford scientist Stanley Cohen to develop a successful genetic engineering technique. The success of Boyer and Cohen's experiments led to worldwide interest in genetic engineering, particularly the idea that *E. coli* or other organisms could be programmed to express human molecules that could be used as medicines. In 1976 the pharmaceutical firm Eli Lilly organized a conference on the topic of whether the new techniques could be used to produce human insulin. Synthetically produced human insulin would be superior to the animal insulin that most diabetics were forced to use at the time, which was often poorly tolerated by humans and had to be extracted from pig or cow pancreases procured from slaughterhouses. Lilly launched a race to clone the gene for human insulin and express it in bacteria using recombinant DNA techniques. Aside from the scientific fame for being the first scientist to use genetic engineering techniques to clone a human gene, Lilly created a strong commercial incentive by promising to license the technology from the winning team (see Hall, 2002).

Genentech competed in the race to clone human insulin with other two teams of academics. The first was Walter Gilbert's laboratory at Harvard. Initially trained as a physicist, Gilbert had achieved fame, and would subsequently be awarded the Nobel Prize, for research developing a reliable method to sequence DNA. The second competitor was a collaboration of two laboratories at UCSF, Rutter and Howard Goodman. Goodman had previously collaborated with Boyer on gene-sequencing experiments but broke off the collaboration when he learned of the commercial orientation of Boyer's project and soon after formed a partnership with Rutter (Hall, 2002: 86–90). Thus, Boyer's new company was competing with a leading scientist at Harvard and two senior professors working in the same building as Boyer.

While Genentech had commercial motives for entering the insulin race, through 1977 the company had yet to establish an office or hire scientists. Boyer formed a collaboration with City of Hope professor Arthur Riggs, who had proposed a synthetic method of constructing DNA fragments in which the amino acid pairs forming DNA sequences would be fused together artificially. Rather than funding corporate laboratory space or scientists, initial investments in the company by Tom Perkins, and then more formally Perkins's venture capital firm Kleiner Perkins, were used to employ postdoctoral scientists and graduate students in Boyers's and Riggs's laboratories at UCSF and the City of Hope, respectively. As a result, the initial research conducted under the guise of Genentech had a strong academic flavor. Following a norm established by Boyer and Cohen a few years earlier, the Genentech team would obtain patents on their scientific discoveries in the area of synthetic insulin as well as publishing their research. In this respect, the Genentech team was little different from either the Gilbert or the Rutter and Goodman teams. In fact, while the Rutter and Goodman team ultimately lost the race to clone human insulin, Axel Ullrich, a postdoctoral scientist working in their lab, led the UCSF team to be the first lab to successfully clone a mammalian protein using recombinant methods, rat insulin (Hall, 2002). In addition to an important publication in *Science*, UCSF filed for a patent on the discovery.

Genentech ultimately won the race to clone insulin, accomplishing the feat in August 1978, a few days before the Gilbert team. Boyer's decision to collaborate with Riggs in developing a synthetic method of DNA sequences that were fused artificially gave Genentech important advantages over the "cut-and-paste" methods employed by others in obtaining sequences from actual human DNA. While risky—Riggs had turned to Genentech in part because the NIH had rejected grant proposals for the process (Hall, 2002: 83)—the synthetic method emerged as superior to the technique first used by Cohen and Boyer. Moreover, the synthetic approach did not fall under the guidelines of the 1975 Asilomar Conference, which mandated that scientists conducting recombinant DNA research on mammals and humans do so within specially designed laboratories (Berg and Singer, 1995). The Gilbert team, for example, was forced to conduct their final experiments using human DNA in a germ warfare laboratory in the United Kingdom. By contrast, many of the final Genentech experiments were conducted in a corridor near the main wing of City of Hope hospital complex in Southern California (Hall, 2002: 150). After successfully cloning and expressing the human insulin gene, the Genentech team simultaneously published the results in the *Proceedings of the National Academy of Sciences* and filed for a patent. The patent became the basis for a subsequent licensing agreement with Eli Lilly.

Following its success in cloning human insulin Genentech was able to obtain additional financing from a syndicate of venture capitalists led by Kleiner Perkins. Beginning in late 1978, Genentech used the new funds to build an actual company. Many of the early scientists recruited to Genentech were UCSF graduate students and postdocs who had previously worked in the Boyer, Goodman, and Rutter laboratories. Science at Genentech mirrored science within the academic laboratories at UCSF. Genentech would take on "first in kind" science problems that had a clear clinical focus, the hallmark of research in Rutter's UCSF labs. The human insulin race was the first example, but Genentech's second and third major projects, human growth hormone and interferon, were also of this type. Peter Seeburg had been conducting research on human growth hormones while a postdoc at the Goodman lab at UCSF. He moved to Genentech and immediately starting working with Axel Ullrich, who had also migrated to the firm, and other Genentech scientists on cloning human growth hormone. Success would again lead to a series of high-profile science articles, and ultimately to Genentech's first product.[2]

Genentech established what Ullrich describes as a "university like atmosphere" (Hughes, 2005: 32; see also Hughes, 2011). Senior scientists were given broad leeway to choose projects and organized laboratories along the principal investigator model commonly seen within universities. This is not to suggest that the firm did not develop downstream commercial capabilities. Genentech became a vertically integrated company, investing in clinical and manufacturing operations to support the downstream development of products. But commitment to an "open science" model of publishing has long been a hallmark of the firm. This sometimes led Genentech scientists to compete directly with university scientists. During the years 1979–1980, for example, Ullrich's lab at Genentech competed with Rutter's at UCSF on a series of experiments designed to further clarify the biological mechanisms surrounding insulin (Hughes, 2005). Genentech's open-science model also encouraged the firm's scientists to collaborate with university scientists when necessary. The firm continued, for example, to collaborate with Riggs at the City of Hope and with Boyer, who remained at UCSF. One measure of Genentech's research prowess is the publication between 1979 and 1984 of 295 scientific articles by company scientists that were subsequently cited 43,335 times. Forty-five of these articles were in the leading journals *Nature* or *Science*.[3]

The strong commitment by Genentech toward publishing promoted the creation of collaborations with university research labs. During the early 1980s Genentech primarily collaborated with UCSF scientists, leading to seventeen publications between 1979 and 1984. However, as the company grew, the web of collaborations developed by its scientists soon included Stanford and UC Berkeley. From 1977 to 2010, Genentech scientists were authors on 6,847 publications, of which 539 included collaborations with UCSF scientists, in addition to 267 collaborations with Stanford researchers and fifty-seven with scientists from UC Berkeley. An important by-product of this collaborative activity, discussed in the following pages, was the creation of strong scientific inventor networks linking scientists at Genentech and Bay Area universities. However, as additional biotechnology companies were founded in the region, often mimicking Genentech's open-science model, a dense web of network ties linking university and corporate life science researchers developed throughout the Bay Area biotechnology industry (Powell, 2002).

The UCSF–Genentech Model and the Growth of Biotech in the Bay Area

In funding Cetus and Genentech, the venture capital company Kleiner Perkins applied the model of milestone-based financing techniques that were commonly used in the electronics industry to their life science portfolio firms (see Kenney, 1986). Following Genentech's highly publicized achievement in cloning human insulin in 1978 and successful initial public offerings (IPOs) on the stock market for both Cetus and Genentech in 1981, venture capitalists rushed to establish competing biotechnology firms. During the early to mid-1980s, Kleiner Perkins focused much of its biotech investment activity on the San Diego region (see the following discussion). However, during the early 1980s, at least a dozen venture capital firms were investing actively in the San Francisco Bay Area, and many added biotech firms to their portfolio. Early Bay Area venture capitalist investors making biotech investments between 1979 and 1981 include

Vanguard, Crocker Capital, Arthur Rock Associates, Bryan & Edwards, Bay Partners, Alta Partners, and Greylock Capital, a Boston firm with a Bay Area office (data from Thompson One VentureXpert). Between 1979 and 1985, twenty-four Bay Area biotechnology companies were launched with financing from venture capitalists (Ibid.).

Most of the new Bay Area biotech firms founded during this period followed the template for organizing a biotechnology company that had been established by Genentech. The new firms were usually founded by one or more prominent university professors, who advised the companies, worked with the university to license technology to the new firm, and sent talented graduate students and postdoctoral scientists to work on commercially oriented research at the new firm (see Murray, 2004; Kenney, 1986). The open publication model established at Genentech became entrenched within many Bay Area biotech firms. Genentech's success in cloning human insulin convinced venture capitalists and executives that prominent publications, paired with patents, could create powerful reputational capital for companies, useful in attracting deals with pharmaceutical companies, raising capital, and attracting talented scientists to the company (Gans, Murray, and Stern, 2008). Genentech, after all, had launched its successful 1981 IPO with no products on the market (Lilly would launch synthetic insulin in 1982, and Genentech's first product, synthetic human growth factor, would not be launched until 1985). Scientists generally have a strong preference for being able to publish, not least because publishing helps preserve a scientist's standing within academic science, which is useful in searching for other jobs if a commercial venture fails (see Stern, 2004).

While prominent scientists at Stanford and Berkeley launched biotechnology companies during the 1979–1980 period (DNAX and Hana Biologics, respectively), UCSF was a dominant source of new Bay Area biotechnology companies during the early 1980s (Jong, 2006). The emphasis within UCSF on using the new molecular methods to investigate the biology of complex organisms, especially humans, created a group of faculty and researchers at UCSF who were well positioned to launch biotechnology companies. At least five faculty members active within Rutter's Department of Biochemistry and Biophysics during the 1970s launched biotechnology companies (William Rutter, John Baxter, David Martin, and David Zakim) (Ibid.: 267).

The most important UCSF spin-off after Genentech was Chiron, launched in 1981 by William Rutter in collaboration with UCSF Professor Pablo Valenzuela and UC Berkeley Professor Edward Penhoet. Chiron closely followed the Genentech model, relying on postdocs within Rutter's lab to fill scientist positions within the company and focusing its research on high-profile scientific projects with commercial value. Chiron's first project, completed in 1982, employed recombinant DNA techniques to create a vaccine for hepatitis B. The project was successful, leading to high-profile publications and a licensing collaboration with the pharmaceutical company Merck. Chiron's next project, completed in 1983, led the company to be the first to use genetic engineering to clone epidermal growth factor, which is involved in healing. Chiron returned to vaccine research in the mid-1980s, working in the fields of HIV/AIDS and malaria. Chiron's adherence to the open-science model of organizing research can be seen in its publication history. Over the firm's first ten years, it published 464 articles, including forty in *Science* and *Nature*, resulting in 61,707 subsequent citations. Chiron successfully developed several medicines and was acquired in 2006 by the pharmaceutical firm Novartis for $5.9 billion.

At least seventy-nine companies licensing UCSF technology were founded between 1976 and 2003, and UCSF faculty were directly involved in the founding of forty-one biotech firms between 1976 and 2005 (Economic & Planning Systems, 2010). Many of these firms employed the research-intensive model pioneered by Genentech and Chiron. A hallmark of many of these companies was their reliance on a highly innovative scientific methodology developed within the founding professor's lab at UCSF that was subsequently licensed to the start-up company and applied to commercially valuable areas of scientific discovery involving human medicine. While most of the early spin-offs were from UCSF's basic research departments, by the mid-1980s the university's medical school became involved in commercialization activities. One well-known start-up that can be traced to the medical school is COR Therapeutics, a firm focused on cardiovascular drug discovery that was founded in 1988 by UCSF faculty member Lewis Williams. COR Therapeutics was eventually acquired by Millennium Pharmaceuticals in 2002 for $2 billion. A second prominent example is Onyx Pharmaceuticals, which was founded in 1992 by UCSF Medical School Professor Frank McCormick. The firm has developed two targeted therapies against cancer. While both COR Therapeutics and Onyx employed the open science policy, Onyx was particularly prominent within academic science due to the novelty of its targeted cancer therapeutics technology. In the first ten years following its founding, Onyx published 329 articles, including nineteen in *Nature* or *Science*, that in aggregate have subsequently been referenced 38,976 times.

The open-science model of organizing biotechnology firms has influenced numerous biotechnology firms in the San Francisco Bay Area that do not have direct ties to UCSF. A key mechanism helping to spread the open-publication norm has been interfirm mobility of scientists and managers.[4] Venture capitalists are a primary cause of extensive mobility, as they frequently recruit managers and scientists from portfolio firms to fill positions in new start-ups. In the first twenty-five years since its initial founding, at least twenty-one biotech firms in San Francisco were founded or held senior managers that were former managers or scientists at Genentech (Abate, 2001).

One of the most prominent examples of a Bay Area biotechnology firms affected by the involvement of individuals with experience at Genentech is Gilead Sciences, a 1987 start-up that has grown into a multibillion dollar company on the basis of its successful HIV/AIDs therapies. Gilead was initially founded by H. DuBose Montgomery, a founder of Menlo Ventures, and Michael Riordan, a medical doctor who had taken a junior associate position at Menlo Ventures. Gilead's organization and scientific trajectory were strongly influenced by the recruitment of Mark Matteucci, a scientist with several years of experience at Genentech, who was Gilead's first employee. Gilead quickly adopted the open-science model of organizing research. The firm initially focused on gene therapy applications but gained traction in 1991 after in-licensing technologies from two European laboratories that became the basis of the firm's successful antiretroviral therapies against HIV/AIDs (Gilead Sciences, 2006).

Other examples of prominent Bay Area biotechnology firms founded by prominent early Genentech scientists include Tularik, cofounded in 1991 by David Goeddel, the first full-time scientist hired to work at Genentech in 1977; UC Berkeley scientist Robert Tjian; and University of Virginia scientist Steve McKnight. That same year, Axel Ullrich left Genentech to found the Bay Area biotechnology firm SUGEN, which was subsequently acquired by the pharmaceutical company Pharmacia & Upjohn in 1999. In addition to companies directly linked to UCSF or Genentech, the open-science model was used by other regional biotech start-ups without links to either the university or Genentech. One of the most successful Bay Area start-ups that used this strategy was the Affymax Research Institute, a pioneering firm in the area of combinatorial chemistry founded by UC Berkeley Professor Peter Schultz.

The history of Cetus provides another indicator of the pervasiveness of the UCSF/Genentech model. Cetus published very few articles in the

TABLE 3.1. Publication activity of prominent San Francisco biotechnology firms, 1976–1994.

Firm	Year of founding	Source of founding science	Total publications (first 10 years)	Total citations (first 10 years)	Papers in Science or Nature
Cetus (1971–1980)	1971	UC Berkeley	13	233	0
Cetus (1981–1990)	1971	UC Berkeley	888	94,590	43
Genentech	1976	UCSF	435	68,933	65
DNAX	1980	Stanford	338	70,745	9
Chiron	1981	UCSF	464	61,707	40
GeneLabs	1983	Stanford and Yale	169	11,113	7
Gilead Sciences	1987	Individuals	214	11,594	8
COR Therapeutics	1988	UCSF	157	7,584	2
Affymax Research Institute	1988	UC Berkeley	198	19,650	11
Tularik	1991	UC Berkeley	242	45,290	22
SUGEN	1991	Individuals	216	22,907	7
Onyx	1992	UCSF	329	38,976	19
Exelixis	1994	UCSF	98	9,401	5

first decade after its founding in 1971, focusing on industrial applications of biotechnology, but starting in 1981 the company refocused itself on genetics-oriented projects aimed at biomedical markets. While Cetus scientists published only thirteen articles during its first decade, in the firm's second decade it adopted an open-science strategy modeled on Genentech. Cetus scientists were authors on 888 publications during 1981–1990, including forty-three in *Nature* and *Science*. It was during the early 1980s that Cetus scientist Kary Mullis invented the polymerase chain reaction, a crucial enabling technology within genetics that won Mullis the Nobel Prize in 1993 and became an extremely valuable licensing franchise for Roche, to which Cetus sold the technology.

Table 3.1 summarizes the publication activity of the Bay Area biotechnology companies discussed in this chapter. The publication success of these firms, measured not just in terms of the quantity or frequency of publication but also in the placement of highly cited papers in the leading journals such as *Science* and *Nature,* underscores the pervasiveness of the open science model within the region. The data in Table 3.1 provide a useful point of comparison with biotechnology companies founded in San Diego, which developed a very different research and development orientation.

UCSD AND THE EMERGENCE OF BIOTECHNOLOGY IN SAN DIEGO

From the early 1970s onwards, UCSD's biomedical science departments had achieved an international reputation that was comparable to that of UCSF. As early as 1971, just over a decade after the university's founding in 1960, both its Molecular Biology and Biochemistry Departments were ranked by the American Council of Education (ACE) among the top ten nationally (Anderson, 1993).[5] A 1994 National Research Council Report ranked UCSD's programs in neuroscience, biomedical engineering, physiology, pharmacology, genetics, cell biology, biochemistry, and molecular biology among the top-ten U.S. programs in these fields (Jones, 2005: 226–227). In 1994 UCSD was ranked fifth nationwide in attracting federal research funding and first within the University of California system (Jones, 2005: 227). UCSD's life science programs have remained nationally prominent to the present day. In 2010 the National Research Council ranked UCSD's biological science program as number one in the country (Piercy, 2010).

UCSD's strategy for staffing and organizing its biomedical research departments was broadly similar to that of UCSF. In the decade after its founding, the university aimed to recruit distinguished professors from leading universities across the country. David Bonner, the founding chair of UCSD's Biology Department, was a renowned geneticist recruited from Yale.[6] UCSD also followed UCSF's model of integrating its medical school, which opened in 1968, with its basic science departments. Through the mid-1980s, ten faculty positions within the school of medicine were directly controlled by the Biology Department. A similar pattern of integration between basic science and clinical research existed in the Chemistry Department, which assumed responsibility for all biochemistry instruction within the medical school. Clinical training and research were conducted at a 1,000-bed Veterans Administration hospital opened along with the school of medicine on the UCSD campus in 1972. UCSD thus integrated clinical and basic research within its medical school in a very similar fashion to that of UCSF.

Another similarity between UCSF and UCSD was their catalytic effects on their regions' life sciences industries. By the mid-1990s, the San Diego region had developed the third-largest bioscience industry cluster in the world, trailing only San Francisco and Boston in size (Casper, 2007). Given the strength of biomedical science at UCSD, along with the Scripps Research Institute and the Salk Institute, one might expect that biotechnology emerged in San Diego in a process similar to those observed in the San Francisco region or in Boston, another region with a strong biotechnology industry built on collaborative scientific linkages between firms and universities (Owen-Smith and Powell, 2004). Although UCSD played a similarly central role within its region's biotechnology cluster, the San Diego biotechnology industry emerged from a different pattern of university–industry interaction. UCSD scientific research assuredly did flow into the region's biotechnology industry from the time of the establishment of the campus, but the process by which it did so differed from that of UCSF in the San Francisco region. Strong networks linking prominent professors and venture capitalists did not develop in San Diego until the 1990s, in part due to the paucity of local venture capitalists during the 1980s (Powell, 2002). Rather than networks linking scientists with financiers, in San Diego the key networks were entrepreneurial, surrounding a core of commercially oriented managers and scientists who worked at Hybritech, a prominent early San Diego biotechnology company with links to UCSD.

Origins and Strategy of Hybritech

Hybritech was founded in 1978 by Ivor Royston, an assistant professor in the UCSD School of Medicine specializing in cancer research who was appointed to the faculty in that year. Royston was one of the few scientists in the United States conducting research on monoclonal antibodies, an important new technique created at Cambridge University in 1975 by Cesar Milstein and Georges Köhler. Monoclonal antibodies were used as probes to help understand the biology of cancer and other complex diseases and had promise in both the diagnostics and therapeutics fields. The new technology was quickly seen as important, leading Milstein and Köhler to be awarded the Nobel Prize for Medicine in 1984 (Cambrosio and Keating, 1995). In contrast to Stanford and UCSF, which patented the genetic engineering methods created by Cohen and Boyer, Cambridge University decided to put the monoclonal antibody discoveries into the public domain. While the technique for creating monoclonal antibodies was published in *Nature*, they proved very difficult to reliably create in the laboratory and required access to cell lines at Cambridge developed by Milstein and Köhler (Cambrosio and Keating, 1995). Leonard Herzenberg, a professor of immunology at Stanford, had taken a sabbatical at Cambridge in 1977 and received access to the cell lines as part of a collaboration with Milstein. On Herzenberg's return to Stanford, several scientists, including Royston, a Stanford postdoctoral fellow at the time, received access to the cell lines through collaborating with him. Royston soon began working with Howard Birndorf, a master's-level research associate at Stanford who quickly learned how to reliably produce monoclonal antibodies (Jones, 2005). When Royston took a faculty position at UCSD, he recruited Birndorf to be his senior technician within his new lab.

Royston became interested in founding a biotechnology company soon after arriving at UCSD. Having observed a booming demand for monoclonal antibodies for use in experimental research within academic laboratories, he proposed starting a company to supply monoclonal antibodies as a research tool for his own cancer research as well as other researchers (Jones, 2005). After unsuccessfully pitching his idea to contacts at several large medical supply companies, Royston was introduced to Brook Byers, who had recently been hired as a junior partner at Kleiner Perkins focusing on biotechnology. Byers took an immediate interest in the project and began commuting to La Jolla to oversee the founding of what became Hybritech beginning in mid-1978. Byers soon realized that the market for antibodies as research tools would likely become a commodity market as competing companies entered, due to the lack of patent protection over the basic process for the antibodies' creation. A more lucrative market existed in the field of molecular diagnostics. Byers proposed using antibodies as the basis for diagnostic test kits antibodies for hepatitis and a variety of other diseases, based on the patentability of such kits (see Kiley, 2006).

Hybritech was the first firm to enter the molecular diagnostics field, though within two years competitors would be founded in San Diego (Quidel) and San Francisco (Monoclonal Antibodies, Inc.) In June 1978 Kleiner Perkins invested $300,000 in exchange for a 60 percent ownership stake in Hybritech, setting as an initial milestone the development of a monoclonal antibody based diagnostic for hepatitis (Jones, 2005: 413–416). Howard Birndorf left UCSD to become the firm's first employee (Royston remained at UCSD, just as Boyer had done at UCSF). Within a few weeks Birndorf successfully created a monoclonal antibody diagnostic for hepatitis. At this point, Kleiner Perkins made a larger investment in Hybritech, which then launched a search for a permanent CEO. Howard (Ted) Greene, a former McKinsey consultant and product manager from Baxter, was hired as Hybritech's first CEO.

Under Greene's direction Hybritech became a profitable company, developing innovative diagnostics for a wide variety of diseases, such as prostate cancer, and developing a widely used pregnancy test. The firm was fortunate in that the regulatory approval process for monoclonal antibody–based diagnostics was fast, usually taking less than ninety days. In contrast to the multiyear clinical trials facing pharmaceutical companies, Hybritech could quickly market products and as a result developed manufacturing and marketing operations soon after being founded.

Greene hired several former colleagues from Baxter into senior management positions at Hybritech. Monica Higgins (2005) has examined the impact of former managers from Baxter, a large medical products company, on the development of many early biotechnology companies. She notes that during the 1970s most managers at Baxter, including Greene and several other Baxter alumni hired into Hybritech, had participated in a rotation program at Baxter that had given them experience in a variety of functions spanning R&D, marketing, and plant management. The core of former Baxter managers at Hybritech drew on their broad experience in quickly launching several products within three years of the firm's launch and launching a successful initial public offering in 1983.

An important implication of Hybritech's early and successful focus on commercial products was that it did not need to pursue scientific achievement as a signal of its future success. As a result, the company published far less intensively than Genentech and many of the San Francisco area biotech firms. During its first five years (1978–1983), for example, Hybritech scientists were authors on thirty-nine publications (eleven of which had academic collaborators). During the same 1978–1983 period Genentech had 186 publications (108 of which had academic collaborators). Moreover, Genentech scientists collaborated with researchers from ninety-seven academic organizations during this period, while Hybritech scientists collaborated only with scientists from UCSD and the University of Southern California. The purpose of most Hybritech publications was to establish scientific legitimacy for new monoclonal antibody assays developed by the firm, which is important within the medical diagnostics field because the standards for clinical validation for these products are less stringent than is true of new pharmaceutical products. Many Hybritech publications described results of clinical trials using the firm's antibodies, which were often conducted within the Veterans Administration Hospital at UCSD. A good indicator of the low priority of academic publication within Hybritech is the frequency with which the firm's publications were subsequently cited. During 1978–1986 Hybritech published 144 articles, which were cited 2,284 times, a stark contrast with the Genentech papers discussed earlier. Hybritech's commercial orientation had a pronounced impact on the character of the San Diego biotechnology cluster, as a series of prominent firms founded in the region during the 1980s would be launched by managers and scientists who had worked at Hybritech.

Growth of Biotech in San Diego

Following the success of Hybritech several professors from UCSD and nearby Scripps became active in founding companies. An early rival of Hybritech in the area of monoclonal antibody diagnostics was Quidel, founded by Scripps Professor David Katz and funded by a Los Angeles–based venture capital firm, Brentwood Associates. Robert Hamburger, one of the founding faculty members of the UCSD School of Medicine and a prominent immunologist, cofounded two companies, Immunetech (1981) and Cytotech (1982), with postdoctoral research associates. Immunetech eventually grew into a successful company, Dura Pharmaceuticals, which was acquired by Elan in 2000 for $1.7 billion. Another prominent early UCSD biotechnology spinout was Agouron Pharmaceuticals, launched by several UCSD chemistry professors interested in computer-aided drug design. Agouron received seed funding from Ventana Investments, a Southern California–based real estate investment firm that became active in venture capital. Agouron became a pioneer in the field of rational or structure-based drug design and helped create an important class of HIV/AIDS drugs known as protease inhibitors. Agouron was acquired by the pharmaceutical firm Warner Lambert in 1999 for $2.1 billion.

Two other early San Diego biotechnology companies were founded as spin-offs from Hybritech. The first company, Gen-Probe, was the first firm to use nucleic acid–based assays as diagnostic probes, a strategy that is now commonplace within the field of molecular diagnostics. The company was founded in 1983 with technology developed by David Kohne, a research scientist who was working at the Center for Neurological Study, a nonprofit research foundation in La Jolla. Gen-Probe was cofounded by Birndorf and Thomas Adams, who had become the chief technology officer at Hybritech in 1980 after previously working at Baxter. In addition to Kleiner Perkins, which served as the lead venture capitalist, Hybritech was an early investor in the new firm. The second spin-off was Idec, a firm founded in 1985 to use Hybritech's monoclonal antibody technology to develop cancer therapies, a strategy closely aligned with Royston's long-term research interests. Royston and Birndorf were cofounders of the company and served as advisors, along with Robert Sobel, a faculty member at the UCSD School of Medicine who left his faculty position to manage the new firm. Kleiner Perkins was again the lead venture capitalist. Idec became one of San Diego's most successful biotechnology firms. Its technology was used to develop Rituxan, a targeted cancer therapy for non-Hodgkin's lymphoma. In 2003 Idec merged with Boston-based Biogen in a deal worth $6.6 billion.

Despite the success of Hybritech and these early spinouts, the growth of biotechnology in San Diego was limited during the early 1980s. During 1975–1986, twenty-five biotech firms were established in the San Francisco Bay Area, a considerably larger number than the eleven established in San Diego (Casper, 2009). Though San Diego rivaled San Francisco in the quality of its basic science, the region had few local venture capitalists. This was partly due to the lack of another large technology-oriented industry in the region to attract venture capital investments, similarly to San Francisco's large electronics industry.[7] Venture capitalists from the San Francisco region or the East Coast had been syndicate investors in several San Diego biotechnology companies, but other than Kleiner Perkins, none was actively supporting the foundation of new firms in the region.

Perhaps the most significant influence on the growth of biotechnology in San Diego in the late 1980s was the decision of Hybritech's board of directors to allow the firm to be acquired by the pharmaceutical giant Eli Lilly in 1986 for about $413 million in stock and cash, the largest corporate acquisition of a biotechnology company at the time (Johnson, 1986). This acquisition had the immediate effect of transforming Hybritech's top management team, all of whom owned shares in the company, into wealthy individuals. As part of the acquisition, the top management team was encouraged to remain, but Hybritech became a subsidiary of a large Indiana-based pharmaceutical company with a relatively conservative managerial ethos that contrasted with the free-flowing, informal corporate culture at Hybritech. Contrasting cultures created immediate clashes between Hybritech and Lilly managers. Tina Nova, one of the senior scientists at Hybritech, reflects that "it was like 'Animal House' meets 'The Waltons'" (Fikes, 1999). Lilly was ultimately unable to integrate

Hybritech's management and scientific team into its corporate culture; in the years immediately following the acquisition, most of the former Hybritech senior managers left.

This cadre of former Hybritech managers is widely credited within San Diego for "seeding" the region's biotechnology industry. This group of managers served as a reliable and trusted referral network that venture capitalists could tap into to incubate new firms, and their credibility as successful biotech entrepreneurs aided the recruitment of skilled individuals to join San Diego start-ups linked to former Hybritech managers. The rise in entrepreneurial activity created significant demand for inventions that could be commercialized, leading an increase in the number of new companies being formed with ties to UCSD and other San Diego–area research institutes. Managers from Hybritech founded or assumed senior management position in at least twelve companies formed between 1986 and 1990 (Casper, 2007). A study conducted in 2002 found over forty biotechnology companies in San Diego employing a senior manager or board advisor linked to Hybritech (Lee and Walshok, 2002).

Many of the new start-ups could be traced to two groups with links to Hybritech (Casper, 2009). The first includes the scientific founders of Hybritech, senior members of the firm's research team, and Kleiner Perkins. From 1986 to 1993 members of this group participated in the founding of Gensia, Nanogen, Genta, Ligand, and the Immune Response Corporation. With the exception of Genta, a firm incubated by Thomas Adams using technology from Johns Hopkins, each of these firms coupled science from UCSD or the Salk Institute with management talent from Hybritech. The second group is centered around former members of Hybritech's commercial management team. After leaving Hybritech in 1986, Ted Greene cofounded with Tim Wollaeger (one of the former Baxter execs from Hybritech) a short-lived venture capital seed investment company called Biovest that invested in six San Diego biotech start-ups, all founded or managed by former Hybritech employees. Greene and Wollaeger did not rely on ties to local scientists in organizing their new investments, and only one of the new start-ups, Vical, was founded in 1987 by a UCSD scientist, Douglas Richman. Greene financed and oversaw two companies drawing on technology sourced from outside the region, Cytel and Amylin, the latter of which he led as long-term CEO. Wollaeger oversaw the founding (in 1988) and served as the CEO of Biosite, another monoclonal antibodies diagnostics company drawing on technology developed by Gunars Valkirs, a former senior scientist from Hybritech who was well known for developing the firm's popular pregnancy test.

The dissolution of Hybritech led to a wave of new firms founded on the basis of UCSD science, strengthening the university's role as a leading source of founding ideas for biotechnology companies. However, new company formation in the San Diego regional biotechnology industry during the late 1980s also benefited from the experienced, wealthy, and high-status networks of managers and scientists linked to Hybritech. These managers had financial resources, managerial experience, and a reputation for developing one of the biotechnology industry's early and rare success stories. As former senior managers from Hybritech took the helm at these new start-ups, they brought their vision of how a biotechnology company should be organized. For most of the new companies, this meant that the commercially oriented patterns of organization and strategy developed at Hybritech would prevail.

Table 3.2 compares the publication activity of the group of twelve "first-generation" biotechnology firms located in San Diego that were founded in the wake of the Hybritech acquisition by individuals who had previously held senior roles within the company. To facilitate comparison with other cohorts of firms, the number of publications and forward citations for each company is provided for the ten years following each firm's founding. Although all firms have published, very few appear to have followed the open-science strategy that is prominent in San Francisco. The companies closely linked to Hybritech alums did not publish high-profile articles, presumably following Hybritech's commercially oriented strategy and using publications primarily to document clinical progress of products in development.

Three companies linked to Hybritech alumni do appear to have embraced more of an open science policy: Cytel, Ligand Pharmaceuticals, and Vical Pharmaceuticals (each founded in 1987). The foundation of each of these firms was based on research advances from high-profile scientists (located respectively at the National Jewish Center for Immunology and Respiratory Medicine in Denver, the Salk Institute, and UCSD) and used publications to attract corporate partnerships. Vical, for example, published a high-profile article in *Science* reporting a fundamental discovery in gene therapy that helped solidify a funding relationship with Burroughs Wellcome (Monroe, 1990). Ligand Pharmaceuticals commercialized discoveries of Salk Institute scientist Ronald Evans pertaining to the biological pathway surrounding intracellular receptors linked to hormones. Intracellular receptors became one of the most important biological pathways for the development of new medicines. Six compounds discovered by Ligand have become medicines, and at least fifteen others are in development

TABLE 3.2. Publication activity of first-generation San Diego biotech firms with links to Hybritech.

Firm	Year of founding	Source of founding science	Total publications (first 10 years)	Total citations (first 10 years)	Papers in Science or Nature
Hybritech	1978	UCSD	141	2,287	1
Gen-Probe	1983	Center for Neurological Research	17	375	0
IDEC	1985	Hybritech/ UCSD	113	4,419	1
Gensia	1986	UCSD	138	3,545	1
Amylin	1986	Oxford University	81	2,180	2
Cytel	1987	National Jewish Center for Immunology and Respiratory Medicine, Denver	312	28,030	9
Immune Response	1987	Salk Institute	84	2,932	1
Vical	1987	UCSD and Scripps	106	10,998	4
Viagene	1987	UCSD	62	1,889	0
Biosite	1988	Individual	5	165	0
Ligand	1988	Salk Institute	231	17,556	5
Genta	1989	Johns Hopkins	48	1,901	0
Nanogen	1993	UCSD	48	2,222	0

(Funding Universe, 2012). Ligand used these early publications to highlight the importance of intracellular receptors in producing drug targets, which helped attract Pfizer as the firm's initial corporate partner.

Embracing open science is a strategic choice taken by biotechnology companies and is not necessarily dictated by the strength of a firm's founding science or the scientific reputation of key founders. A striking example is the relatively low publication profile during its early history of the Immune Response Corporation, a firm managed by former Hybritech managers but founded in 1986 by Jonas Salk, one of the most famous scientists in the world. Other San Diego biotechnology companies that did not follow the open-science model also had extremely strong scientific credentials. Idec, for example, was a pioneer in developing targeted cancer therapies using antibodies, which has become a dominant approach to treating cancer. The firm published much less than most San Francisco–based therapeutics firms, with only one publication in *Science* or *Nature* during its first decade. Another example is Gen-Probe, which has used its research in nucleic acid–based diagnostics to become a major firm in molecular diagnostics. Gen-Probe has also adopted a strongly commercial stance, with very few publications. Although it is most clearly seen within the San Diego biotechnology companies that were founded and managed by former senior managers from Hybritech, the "proprietary science" orientation thus also is apparent in firms with weaker ties to former Hybritech employees.

From the late 1980s through the 1990s, the success of the San Diego biotechnology cluster began to attract venture capitalists into the area. One of the first major venture capital companies to be established in San Diego was Avalon Ventures, founded by Kevin Kinsella in 1983. Kinsella became a major player within the San Diego biotechnology industry, launching a series of prominent local companies in the early 1990s that included Idun, Neurocrine Bioscience, Sequana Therapeutics, CombiChem, and Aurora Biosciences. Avalon Ventures was followed in the early 1990s by the establishment of Forward Ventures, launched in 1993 by Hybritech founder Ivor Royston, and Kingsbury Capital Partners, founded in 1994 by Tim Wollaeger (see Casper, 2009).

Table 3.3 surveys the publication activity of prominent companies established in the San Diego from the mid-1980s to mid-1990s that had no direct senior management or founder ties to Hybritech alumni. Three companies, Agouron Pharmaceuticals, Neurocrine Biosciences, and Idun Pharmaceuticals (founded respectively in 1984, 1992, and 1993), adopted an open-science strategy. Agouron, as mentioned earlier, was a pioneer in the development of protease inhibitors as a drug against HIV/AIDS, and its scientists produced a series of high-profile publications in *Nature* and *Science*. Idun Pharmaceuticals and Neurocrine Biosciences were founded on the basis of basic research discoveries in the area of neuroscience and cell death, respectively, and each published basic research findings in its area of expertise.

The majority of prominent San Diego bioscience companies without links to the Hybritech network appear to have adopted the commercial

TABLE 3.3. Publication activity of prominent San Diego biotechs outside Hybritech network, 1984–1995.

Firm	Year of founding	Source of founding science	Total publications (first 10 years)	Total citations (first 10 years)	Papers in Science or Nature
Agouron Pharmaceuticals	1984	UCSD	192	11,245	11
Advanced Tissue Science	1987	New York University	101	1,851	0
Depotech	1989	UCSD	17	158	0
Sequana Therapeutics	1993	Individuals	88	5,131	5
Immusol	1992	UCSD	26	702	0
Idun Pharmaceuticals	1992	Burnham Institute and MIT	111	12,626	1
Neurocrine Biosciences	1992	Salk Institute	230	13,088	4
Signal Pharmaceuticals	1993	Salk Institute and UCSD	40	4,089	4
Diversa	1994	Individual	88	4,525	3
Collateral Therapeutics	1995	UCSD	31	451	0
Aurora Biosciences	1995	UCSD	48	2,867	4
CombiChem	1995	Scripps Research Institute	58	1,461	0

orientation established by Hybritech. This includes companies with ties to high-profile university scientists. Aurora Biosciences, for example, was launched in 1996 by UCSD scientist and future Nobel Laureate Roger Tsien to commercialize advances in the creation of biological assays that could improve the reliability of drug discovery screening processes. The company did not publish intensively, instead focusing on the development of partnerships with pharmaceutical firms, and was acquired by Vertex Pharmaceuticals in 2001. To take other examples, Advanced Tissue Sciences (founded in 1987) was one of the first tissue engineering companies to be launched; though the firm ultimately failed, it helped pioneer the field of regenerative medicines. CombiChem (founded in 1994), a firm linked to several Scripps Institute founders, was one of the early firms active in the field of combinatorial chemistry. Despite being at the forefront of their respective scientific fields, neither Advanced Tissue Sciences nor CombiChem emphasized scientific publication as a core technology strategy.

REGIONAL VARIATION IN THE ORIENTATION OF BIOTECHNOLOGY CLUSTERS: AGGREGATE EVIDENCE

The historical analysis suggests that the majority of San Francisco biotechnology companies adopted a propublication model that reflected the regional influence of the technology strategy adopted by Genentech. By contrast, many of the key San Diego firms followed the strategy of Hybritech and adopted a more inward-looking proprietary-science model that did not emphasize publishing. Although this historical discussion has emphasized the contrasting evolution of a small number of leading firms in each region, during 1976–2005 at least 208 independent biotechnology firms were active at some point within the San Francisco region and 186 firms in San Diego. How does the publication and patenting behavior of biotechnology firms in these two regions compare at an aggregate level? These aggregate bibliometric and patent data suggest that the early patterns of university–industry interaction discussed in this chapter have affected the development of the two regional clusters.

Turning first to bibliometric evidence, Figure 3.1 displays the total number of publications by all active biotechnology firms in the San Francisco and San Diego regions for the 1980–2005 time period, highlighting a striking contrast. Overall, San Francisco biotechnology firms published 23,317 articles, compared to 7,606 for San Diego firms during this period. The threefold difference in publication output is heavily affected by Genentech, which averaged about 300 publications a year from 1995 through 2005. Nevertheless, a sizable gap remains (16,465 versus 7,606 publications) if Genentech's 6,853 publications are removed from this comparison.

Within the life sciences, publications frequently include authors from multiple organizations, a signal of interorganizational collaboration. A hallmark of the open-science strategy is collaboration between researchers in companies and universities. Data on the extent to which companies collaborate with universities are compiled in Tables 3.4 and 3.5, summarizing the publication activities of the ten most prolific biotechnology corporate

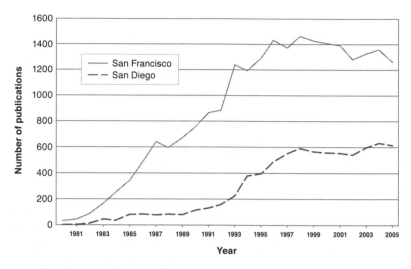

FIGURE 3.1. Aggregate publications by San Francisco and San Diego
biotechnology companies, 1976–2005.
SOURCE: ISI Web of Knowledge.

publishers in each region.[8] The results again illustrate that San Francisco
biotech companies publish far more than San Diego companies—the top
publishers in San Francisco have nearly five times as many publications
overall. This finding is striking, as it focuses on the San Diego companies
that have been most active in publishing.

Tables 3.4 and 3.5 also include information on the number of publications involving corporate researchers and researchers in local universities,
an indicator of the breadth of collaborative networks linking firms and
universities. San Francisco biotech firms have published about five times
as many papers (2,163) with local university coauthors as have San Diego
firms (408).[9] Note also that UCSF scientists are coauthors on over 1,100
publications, more than five times as many co-authored publications as
UC Berkeley (183) and more than 50 percent higher than Stanford (675).
These data suggest that scientists from UCSF, and slightly less so at Stanford, are unusually deeply embedded in the scientific networks linking
regional biotechnology firms to academic research. Indeed, the number
of UCSD scientists listed as coauthors on papers published by San Diego
biotechnology firms, which is three to four times as large as the number of
Scripps Institute or Salk Institute coauthored papers, is less than one-half

TABLE 3.4. Top ten San Francisco companies by frequency of academic publications and collaborations with local universities, 1980–2005.

Company	Founding university	Total publications	Average publications per year	Publications with UC San Francisco	Publications with Stanford University	Publications with UC Berkeley	Publications with UC Davis
Genentech	UCSF	6,847	263.35	539	267	46	57
Chiron	UCSF	2,407	96.28	258	54	62	54
DNAX Research Institute	Stanford	2,334	89.77	88	158	17	13
Cetus Corporation	UC Berkeley	984	37.85	65	78	35	30
Gilead Sciences	None	734	66.73	43	19	4	18
Scios Inc.	UCSF	450	19.17	46	10	0	3
SUGEN	NYU School of Medicine	409	31.46	15	14	3	6
COR Therapeutics	UCSF	376	25.07	6	16	12	1
Onyx Pharmaceuticals	UCSF	357	17.00	31	13	4	2
GeneLabs	Stanford and Yale	330	23.57	29	46	0	1
Total		**15,219**		**1,120**	**675**	**183**	**185**

TABLE 3.5. Top ten San Diego companies by frequency of academic publications and collaborations with local universities.

Company	Founding university	Total publications	Average publications per year	Publications with UCSD	Publications with the Salk Institute	Publications with Scripps Research Institute
Neurocrine Biosciences	Salk Institute and Stanford University	582	32.3	25	18	13
Ligand	Salk Institute	566	27.0	11	12	8
Amylin	Oxford University	513	24.4	10	2	5
Agouron	UCSD and Caltech	385	13.8	80	10	20
Gen-Probe	Center for Neurological Study, La Jolla	262	10.1	6	1	4
Vical	UCSD	258	11.7	26	2	5
PharMingen	None; founder trained in Taiwan	227	10.3	66	0	10
Alliance Pharmaceuticals	None; product of merger	223	13.1	44	0	3
Molecular Simulations	Caltech	218	36.3	5	0	6
Hybritech	UCSD	144	18	61	2	2
Total		3,730	14.7	278	48	80

the number of Stanford scientists collaborating with Bay Area biotechnology firms.

Data on university patenting highlight similar contrasts. Table 3.6 contains information on university patents in technological classes related to biotechnology within the San Francisco and San Diego regions (see Casper, 2013, for the methodology used). It is important to note that patent counts are an imperfect indicator of a university's inventiveness or technology transfer capability because the decision to patent a faculty invention is itself a matter of considerable discretion for the university, and many university patents are never licensed to com-

TABLE 3.6. University patents, San Francisco and San Diego, 1980–2005.

	Total patents	Linked scientists
UC San Francisco	621	117
Stanford	411	131
UC Berkeley	371	52
UC Davis	185	29
UC San Diego	415	27
Salk Institute	266	29
The Scripps Research Institute	418	21

SOURCE: USPTO data compiled by the author. The San Francisco data have been previously published in Casper, 2013.

panies (see Association of University Technology Managers [AUTM], 2010). Moreover, the data in Table 3.6 do not control for the number of faculty involved in biomedical research across universities (or regions), or the level of biomedical research funding at the various universities that are included. Overall, the four universities in the San Francisco region (Stanford, UCB, UCD, and UCSF) received nearly 1,600 biotechnology patents during this period, compared with roughly 1,100 biotechnology patents assigned to the three leading biomedical research organizations (UCSD, Salk Institute, and Scripps) in the San Diego region. These data show that UCSF researchers have received nearly 50 percent more biotechnology patents (621) than UCSD (418). These contrasts between UCSD and UCSF in patenting, as well as the contrasting numbers of overall university and research institute patenting in the two regions, are consistent with the overall discussion of the contrasts between the Bay Area biotechnology industry, which historically has relied more heavily on licensed technology, and the San Diego biotechnology industry, which (at least in its earlier phases of development) relied less heavily on university intellectual property.

Table 3.6 also contains data on a second patent-related indicator, the number of "linked" scientists in each region (see Lam, 2007, and Casper, 2013). Linked scientists are defined as scientists who are listed as inventors on at least one patent assigned to the university and one patent assigned to a corporation. Such ties are typically formed when a university scientist moves to a company, establishing ties between the firm and university through patenting with scientists at both organizations. This often occurs as PhD students or postdoctoral fellows move into industry, but it sometimes develops when more senior professors take sabbaticals at companies or, rarely, decide to move more permanently to companies. The data in Table 3.6 show that UCSF has four times as many linked scientists as UCSD (117 compared to twenty-seven) and that the San Francisco region has about three times as many (229 to seventy-seven). This finding is hardly definitive, but it is consistent with the hypothesis that more academic scientists (including university postdocs or graduate students) have moved to regional biotechnology jobs in San Francisco than is the case in San Diego and also is consistent with the more general argument that university–industry collaborations are much more common in the San Francisco biotech cluster than in San Diego.

CONCLUSION

UCSD and UCSF occupy anchor positions within their respective regional biotechnology clusters. This chapter has argued that differences in the processes through which science from the two universities was commercialized led to the adoption of different technology strategies within firms in the two regions. Although variation across firms does exist within each region, a key finding from this chapter is that the general characteristics of biotechnology clusters, in terms of both the broad technology strategy of firms and the resulting pattern by which universities develop ties with firms, can differ.

San Diego biotechnology firms have succeeded with their more commercial strategy despite the absence of strong inventor networks in the region, largely by exploiting strong regional entrepreneurial networks forged in the aftermath of Lilly's acquisition of Hybritech. While the core competency of most San Francisco biotechnology firms is science, most San Diego companies developed strong capabilities in the area of technology management and commercialization. The entrepreneurs founding these firms often "pulled in" science, frequently from UCSD, Salk, or Scripps but occasionally from elsewhere, and then focused on its commercialization.

The success of a large number of San Diego firms suggests an alternative theory of the role of regional networks in firm performance—access to strong entrepreneurially focused managers early in a firm's development may lead to competitive success for many firms. This conclusion may be important for thinking about public policy toward cluster development.

The inventor network theory of cluster success, which privileges scientific spillovers and thus investment primarily into creating world-class research, may not be the only way to promote cluster formation. While access to a strong science base remains important, policies emphasizing entrepreneurial network formation may also promote regional economic development.

A similar set of conclusions surrounds the role of universities within regional technology clusters. Much recent public policy discussion surrounding universities has emphasized commercialization as part of a "third mission" to promoting economic development (see, for example, Etzkowitz, 2002; Florax, 1992). UCSF and UCSD both occupy anchor positions within their respective biotechnology clusters and are thus highly salient examples of universities supporting economic development. As seen from the data in Table 3.4, the frequent engagement of university scientists within local inventor networks at UCSF (and Stanford) is particularly attractive from a public policy perspective, as such networks represent channels by which university research may have a direct impact on regional economic development. Through becoming embedded within local innovation networks, UCSF scientists appear to have created a pattern of organization—mixing basic and applied research at the level of practice—that contrasts with conventional portrayals of university–industry relationships that emphasize the licensing, or transfer, of scientific discoveries from academic laboratories to firms within a more linear process.

The dramatic success of the San Francisco region, including Silicon Valley, not just in biotechnology but in many other new technology industries, and the role of UCSF, UC Berkeley, and Stanford within the formation of these industries, demonstrates the power of the "inventor network" model of cluster development (see, for example, Kenney, 2000) that emphasizes the central role of academic scientists. The comparison of UCSD and the San Diego biotechnology cluster, however, provides an important counterexample. UCSD has developed a world-class infrastructure for biomedical science research, including the country's top-ranked biological sciences department, while relying on a much more traditional, less collaborative model of commercializing research, although nonetheless serving as an anchor for a top-tier biotechnology cluster. Entrepreneurial networks have, in a sense, served as a substitute for the inventor networks that appear to drive success in the San Francisco region. Nonetheless, the success of biotechnology in San Diego suggests that regions and universities can have different commercialization "recipes." This is not to say that one approach is superior to the other, but the success of both UCSF and UCSD in serving as anchors to regional biotechnology clusters suggests that alternative recipes can emerge even within roughly similar scientific fields.

NOTES

I thank Martin Kenney, David Mowery, and Mary Walshok for useful comments and editorial help on the development of this chapter. Funding supporting this research was provided by the Joseph Randolph Haynes Foundation.

1. Though referred to as Kleiner Perkins throughout the chapter, their formal name was changed to Kleiner Perkins Caufield and Byers (KPCB) in 1978.

2. The human growth hormone project also led to protracted litigation between UCSF and Genentech, precipitated by Seeburg transferring biological materials from his UCSF research to Genentech when joining the firm without securing prior permission from the university (see discussion in Hughes, 2011, and Hall, 2002). Genentech eventually settled the lawsuit and paid $200 million to UCSF in 1999. This and other examples of litigation involving UCSF and local biotechnology companies point to a more general issue: Blurred organizational boundaries created by collaborative R&D projects can create legal challenges that may not exist in situations when university–industry relationships are more transactional in nature.

3. All bibliometric data cited in this article is from the ISI Web of Knowledge, accessed on-line in February and March 2012.

4. Research on the Silicon Valley electronics industry has highlighted interfirm mobility as a key mechanism behind the development of technical communities in the region (Saxenian, 1994; Almeida and Kogut, 1999).

5. In a subsequent review of UCSD's Biology Department, in 1981, the ACE wrote that it was "astonished" that such as excellent program had been built so quickly (Anderson, 1993, ch. 7).

6. Biology has long been one of the largest departments at UCSD, responsible for about 30 percent of the overall UCSD science budget by the late 1970s (Anderson, 1993: ch. 7). During this same period the department had forty-five faculty positions, the majority of which were full professors (Ibid.).

7. As helpfully pointed out by David Mowery.

8. The data in Tables 3.4 and 3.5 are drawn from a database of all firms existing in each region between 1978 and 2010.

9. One surprising result of this analysis is that only 15 percent of San Francisco firm publications and 10 percent of San Diego publications have a local university coauthor. Two factors driving this are the existence of articles in which all authors are from the biotechnology company and the widespread publishing of data from clinical trials, which are often geographically dispersed.

CHAPTER FOUR

Electrical Engineering and Computer Science at UC Berkeley and in the Silicon Valley

Modes of Regional Engagement

MARTIN KENNEY, DAVID C. MOWERY,
AND DONALD PATTON

It is widely accepted that research universities provide substantial knowledge spillovers to local firms (for a review, see Feldman, 2000). Knowledge transfer occurs through a diversity of channels including publishing, students, sponsored research, licenses, consulting, and spin-off firms. Much of this literature has focused on the transfer of technology from the university to industry, but university–industry interactions are more accurately described as involving a two-way flow of people and knowledge (Lenoir, 1997: chapter 9; Mansfield, 1991; Mansfield and Lee, 1996; see also Chapter Six in this volume, by Mody).[1] University researchers absorb knowledge from industry through many of the same mechanisms that transfer knowledge from the university to industry. Proximity and face-to-face interaction (including the movement of academic researchers to permanent or temporary positions in industry and vice versa) are important facilitators of knowledge transfers. Reflecting links with industry that date back to the late nineteenth and early twentieth centuries (Noble, 1977), many U.S. university electrical engineering departments have hired corporate scientists as professors; industry researchers have held temporary fellowships and other research positions; and a number of academic researchers have worked in industry for a portion of their careers. Leading electrical engineering departments have also benefited from expanded industry research support in the form of funding and state-of-the-art equipment donated by the firms with which they have collaborated.

Postwar academic research in electrical engineering and computer science has yielded technologies in semiconductors, computer networking, computer software and hardware, and other areas that have had massive economic and social impacts. This chapter explores some of the pathways through which the Department of Electrical Engineering (which later merged with the Computer Science Department) at the University of California, Berkeley, contributed to the growth of information technology industries in the San Francisco Bay Area. Since the 1980s, firms such as Cadence Design Systems, Google, Silicon Graphics, Sun Microsystems, Sybase, and Yahoo!, all of which had university researchers, students, or faculty among their founders, have become major employers in the San Francisco Bay Area. Remarkably, there have been few studies of how the technologies developed in the EE&CS departments of UC Berkeley or other U.S. research universities diffused to either the general economy or their respective regional economies.[2]

This chapter does not attempt to compare the mechanisms of technology transfer and industry–university collaboration at the UC Berkeley EE&CS Department with those associated with similar departments elsewhere in the region or the United States, nor does it address the much larger topic of the emergence of Silicon Valley.[3] Instead, we discuss the paths through which important technical contributions made by UCB's Department of EE&CS diffused into the economy and supported the growth of the San Francisco Bay Area's high-technology economy. This chapter's discussion of the overall development and research agenda of the UCB EE&CS Department thus complements Lécuyer's comparison of the Berkeley department's role with that of UCLA and UCSB in their respective regional semiconductor industries (see Chapter Two in this volume).

UNIVERSITY–INDUSTRY RELATIONSHIPS IN EE&CS

The regional economic and technological contributions of UCB EE&CS are rooted in the post–World War II transformation of electrical engineering from a largely practice-based study of electrical power generation and transmission to a research-based discipline spanning a broader and more diverse field of inquiry.[4] As with its departmental counterparts at other U.S. research universities, the transformation of research in electrical engineering and computer science at UC Berkeley is linked to the expansion of research funding from the Department of Defense, which sought to sustain the science-based engineering capabilities it had supported during World War II for the Cold War. The Defense Department supported applied and fundamental research at a few universities, led by the California Institute of Technology, Johns Hopkins University, MIT, Stanford, and UC Berkeley and, as the other chapters show, expanded its research support within California to include UCLA, UCSD, and UCSB. As we discuss in the following pages, DoD funding strategies affected the types of research projects undertaken and indirectly influenced the regional economic effects of this research.[5]

MIT was the national leader in shifting electrical engineering away from power engineering toward electronics (Wildes and Lindgren, 1985; Terman, 1976).[6] After World War II, the armed services offices of research, especially the Office of Naval Research, supported specific universities and departments in creating institutional centers of excellence in desired fields of research (Barus, 1987; Sapolsky, 1990). Program officers in the emerging information technology research program of the Defense Advanced Research Project Administration (DARPA) during the 1950s and 1960s, for example, focused on building academic "centers of excellence" through multiyear awards of funding to selected U.S. universities (National Research Council, 1999: 100). The evolution of policy governing the allocation of Department of Defense funding of academic research also differed somewhat from procedures followed by NSF and NIH. For example, a significant portion of DoD funding was not allocated through peer-review processes. DoD-funded university research often drew on, competed with, and contributed to parallel developments in the commercial sector, especially research underway at AT&T Bell Laboratories and IBM's laboratories (Flamm, 1988: Chapters 2–4; National Research Council, 1999). The DoD and the National Science Foundation also funded the purchase by academic departments of expensive equipment such as computers; this was particularly important in the 1960s and 1970s.

The Department of Defense adopted a liberal policy toward intellectual property rights to DoD-funded research in both industry and academia (National Research Council, 1999: 119–120; Wells, 1978: 244), supporting the patenting of research results by federal contractors as long as a royalty-free license to any patents was granted to the DoD. Not only were many new firms in the early computer industry founded to commercialize DoD-funded research, but, in many cases, the DoD purchased their products. Further, the military (and other parts of the national security system) was a price-insensitive customer, supporting high profit margins on military sales that could support further product development (National Research Council, 1999: 165); a feature of particular importance to small research-based startups.[7]

THE UNIVERSITY OF CALIFORNIA, BERKELEY, AND EE&CS

In 1868 the College of California, a liberal arts college incorporated in 1855, and the Agricultural, Mining, and Mechanical Arts College formed in 1866 under the aegis of the 1862 Morrill Act were merged to form the University of California in Berkeley.[8] UCB soon adopted the German research university model first imported by Johns Hopkins University.[9] Because of the difficulties of competing with the established East Coast private universities in terms of salary and prestige, from the 1890s onwards UCB pioneered a strategy to attract promising young scientists by providing financial support for their research (Matkin, 1990: 29).

In 1892 the hiring of the first faculty member specifically dedicated to electrical engineering within the "College of Mechanics" initiated the development of the discipline of electrical engineering at UC Berkeley. In 1930, the College of Engineering was created by merging the Colleges of Mechanics and Civil Engineering with a Department of Civil Engineering and a Department of Mechanical and Electrical Engineering. In 1942, the Colleges of Engineering and Mining merged to form a single administrative unit, the College of Engineering, with a Department of Engineering that included electrical engineering as a "Division." In 1958, the Division of Electrical Engineering was renamed the Department of Electrical Engineering (Torous, 2006). In 1968, a group of faculty left the Department of Electrical Engineering to form a Department of Computer Sciences in the College of Letters and Sciences, but in 1973 Computer Sciences merged with Electrical Engineering to form the Department of Electrical Engineering and Computer Sciences (EE&CS) within the College of Engineering. This chapter refers to the department throughout its existence as EE&CS.

The transformation of EE&CS is illustrated by the changing educational attainment of its faculty. In 1945, approximately 20 percent of the EE professors had doctorates, but by the mid-1970s virtually the entire faculty had doctorates.[10] Further evidence of the growth of research within the department can be seen by the fact that UCB moved from a position of national insignificance during the early postwar years in graduate training of electrical engineers to one of national leadership by the late 1960s, rivaling MIT and Stanford and surpassing Cal Tech and Cornell in advanced degree production (Terman, 1976: 1796).[11] According to the ex-Department Chair and Dean John Whinnery, EEC&CS went from being

> . . . a sound but little known department in the prewar and immediate post-war period [to one that] was ranked third after MIT and Stanford in the 1966 Carter Report and in the 1970 Roose and Anderson report. The standing was maintained in a National Academy of Sciences ranking of graduate programs in 1982, with Berkeley tied with Stanford as close seconds to MIT. (Whinnery, 1994: 223)

UCB electrical engineering faculty had initiated research on radio waves and electronics prior to 1940, but American entry into World War II dramatically expanded federal funding for a new research agenda focused on radio waves, electronics, and computation. Although little of this funding supported engineering research on the UCB campus during wartime (in contrast to the Manhattan Project in physics), with the return of peace the Navy approached the UCB Dean of Engineering Morrough P. O'Brien (1988: 117) with the idea of relocating a naval electronics laboratory from San Diego to UC Berkeley.[12] According to O'Brien, the officers encouraged him to submit a contract proposal and assisted in writing the proposal for an unrestricted research contract that initially provided $500,000 per year. These funds and the naval laboratory were the genesis of the UCB Electronics Research Laboratory (ERL). The U.S. Navy research contract and subsequent federal research support were critical in the subsequent transformation of the research activities and faculty composition of EE&CS.

KEY RESEARCH PROJECTS: BUILDING THE DEPARTMENT AND LOCAL INDUSTRY

This section discusses six EE&CS research projects to highlight the operation of the channels of interaction between UCB research and industrial innovation already discussed.[13] These multiyear projects involved teams of faculty and graduate students and focused on developing new hardware or software. Nearly all of the project results were published and placed in the public domain; in some cases, new firms based on the research were founded as vehicles for technology commercialization. The commercial and financial success of these new firms was mixed; the graduate students supported and educated through these research projects almost certainly proved to be the most important long-term contribution from UCB to the regional economy.

The selection of case studies discussed in this section is dictated in part by the availability of primary and secondary information on their development and significance, meaning that all of these projects were relatively large academic research undertakings that each influenced the course of industrial innovation in IT and electronics. We cannot claim that these cases and their associated effects on regional and national innovation are representative of all of the research projects undertaken during this period at EE&CS. Research failures, uninfluential results, and "dead ends" are common in all areas of academic activity, and EE&CS is no different in this respect. The results of these six research projects within industry also proved to be significant, something that may not apply to other EE&CS research activities (for a summary of the projects discussed, see Table 4.1). Rather than arguing that these projects are in some sense typical of all EECS research projects, we instead use them to highlight the varied channels of interaction between academic and industrial research and innovation, as well as noting the channels that appear to have been of little importance. The projects span nearly fifty years, enabling us to observe the emergence of new forms of interaction between UCB researchers and industry during the period.

CALDIC: The California Digital Computer Project, 1948–1954

In the immediate aftermath of World War II, the nascent West Coast computer industry was concentrated in Los Angeles. A number of Southern California aerospace firms received military funding to develop computers, many of which were meant to support aircraft design and research (Eckdahl, Reed, and Sarkissian, 2003; Norberg, 1976). The CALDIC (California Digital Computer) built at UC Berkeley in 1954 was the first computer developed in the Bay Area and the first computer developed at a West Coast university. Supported by the Office of Naval Research, in 1948 Professors Paul Morton (EE), Leland Cunningham (astronomy), and Richard Lehmer (mathematics) began building the CALDIC, which was meant to be an intermediate-size computer (Hoagland, 2010: 15). Like many university-developed computers during this period, the CALDIC was not commercialized, nor were any patents issued on the results of the work. Instead, the project's main contribution to the local economy was the graduate students supported by the project, several of whom later became industry leaders.

TABLE 4.1. Summary of characteristics of major EE&CS projects.

Projects	Funding	Technology	Dates	UCB-related individuals[1]	Major technology or student destination	Start-ups
Caldic	ONR	Digital computer	1948–1954	A. Hoagland, J. Haanstra, and L. Stevens	IBM San Jose Laboratories	
				D. Englebart	SRI	Digital Techniques (1956–1957)
Project Genie	DARPA	Time sharing	1964–1968	**M. Pirtle, W. Lichtenberger**	Various	Berkeley Computer Corporation
				B. Lampson, C. Thacker, and L. P. Deutsch	Xerox PARC	Berkeley Computer Corporation
				N/A	N/A	Tymshare
Ingres	DARPA	Relational Database SW	1973–mid-1980s	**M. Stonebraker, E. Wong, L. Rowe**	N/A	Ingres
				R. Epstein, M. Ubell , P. Hawthorn	N/A	Britton Lee
				G. Held	Tandem	N/A
Postgres	Unknown	Relational Database SW	Mid 1990s	**M. Stonebraker, L. Rowe**, P. Hawthorn M. Ubell	N/A	Illustra
RISC	DARPA	RISC	Late 1970s–mid-1980s	**D. Patterson**	Sun Microsystems	N/A
RAID	DARPA	Storage	1987	**D. Patterson, R. Katz**	Many	Various
BSD Unix	DARPA	Operating System SW	1973–1995	**R. Fabry**, William Joy	Many	Sun Microsystems

[1] Professors' names are boldfaced; the remainder were graduate students.

For example, Albert Hoagland, Roy Houg, and Louis Stevens worked on CALDIC's magnetic data storage system and on graduation joined the newly formed IBM research laboratory that had been established in San Jose in 1956 (Flamm, 1988: 20ff).[14] Drawing on their CALDIC experience, they became the key engineers in designing the moving-head hard disk drive used in IBM's 305 RAMAC mainframe computer released in 1956, which proved to be an enormous financial success (Flamm, 1988: 20). IBM's San Jose Laboratory soon became a global center for digital magnetic storage innovation. Beginning in the 1970s, the laboratory spawned a number of merchant disk drive startups that concentrated in Silicon Valley (McKendrick, Doner, and Haggard, 2000: 80).[15] Another CALDIC PhD student, Douglas Engelbart, went to the Stanford Research Institute and developed some of the cornerstones of personal computing such as the mouse, "windowed" user interfaces, and hypertext (Bardini, 2000). Students trained through the CALDIC project thus emerged as leading industrial researchers in the Bay Area computer industry of the 1960s.

Project Genie and Commercial Time Sharing, 1964–1968

By the early 1960s, large mainframe computers had been adopted by many larger firms, but, for smaller firms and university research groups, computing resources were difficult to access. State-of-the-art mainframe computers relied on batch processes requiring punch cards to be read into the computer, a tedious and inconvenient method of data entry and program operation. In the 1960s, DARPA funded the development of technologies allowing the remote sharing of computer processing power through what came to be known as "time-sharing systems." MIT researchers developed time sharing for IBM mainframes, while DARPA funded UC Berkeley researchers to develop a system that could be used on a new class of smaller machines that came to be known as "minicomputers."

The UC Berkeley team developed their time-sharing program, GENIE, on a new scientific computer produced by a Los Angeles–based start-up, Scientific Data Systems (SDS). The UCB researchers purchased an SDS 930, modified its software so that it functioned as a time-sharing machine, and, with the encouragement of their DARPA program officer, gave the modified software to SDS. In fact, DARPA is said to have helped sell the first SDS 940s, which were SDS 930s outfitted with the UCB software (Taylor, 1989; Hiltzik, 1999). The SDS 940 with UCB software was an enormous success, and Xerox purchased the firm in 1969 for $1 billion.[16]

The success of the SDS 940 resulted in the establishment of a number of firms that purchased or leased SDS 940s and sold computing time to organizations that could not afford a computer.[17] One of the time-sharing pioneers using the SDS940 was Cupertino-based venture capital–financed Tymshare, Inc.[18] According to the founder of Tymshare, Tom O'Rourke (2002), the firm was established in 1964 and its programmers "wrote the whole operating system on the basis of the work at Berkeley." The closeness of the relationship between the firm and the UCB research team is illustrated by the fact that, prior to receiving its own machine, Tymshare used the UCB SDS 930 computer.

The success of Tymshare was not lost on UCB faculty. In 1968 EE&CS Professors Mel Pirtle and Wayne Lichtenberger left UCB to establish the Berkeley Computer Corporation (BCC) to sell commercial time-sharing services using the GENIE software (Ranelletti, 2001). The University of California system invested $1 million in BCC (Hiltzik, 1999: 74; Matkin, 1990: 164), but the venture failed and the university's investment was lost. Three of the students affiliated with Project GENIE, Butler Lampson, Charles Thacker, and L. Peter Deutsch, left BCC in 1970 to become the core of Xerox PARC's computer research group, which went on to develop the first computer workstation (Hiltzik, 1999).[19]

The free availability of the GENIE software contributed to the success of SDS and Tymshare and influenced the decision of Tymshare to locate in Northern California (O'Rourke, 2002). The initially strong position within the time-sharing industry held by SDS computers, Tymshare, and the GENIE software subsequently was eroded by the Massachusetts-based DEC minicomputer. Although Tymshare became one of the largest U.S. timesharing firms, no regional concentration of time-sharing firms in the Bay Area developed around it. The UC system's investment in BCC was a failure, but the students who worked on the project became important innovators in the regional computer industry.

INGRES: The Interactive Graphics and Retrieval System Project and the Relational Database Industry, 1973–1980s

The San Francisco Bay Area is the center of the relational database software industry, a dominance that is based on research performed during the 1970s at IBM's San Jose Laboratory and at UCB. Prior to the important innovations produced by IBM-San Jose and UCB EE&CS, the database software industry was concentrated on the East Coast. For example, in the

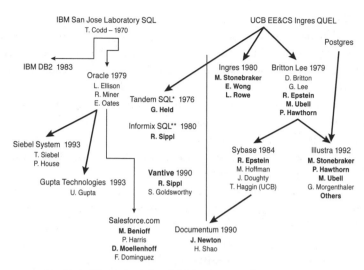

FIGURE 4.1. Selected Bay Area relational database/CRM software firms, founders, and spin-offs.

1970s IBM's database operations were located on the East Coast, and two of the most important independent firms, Cullinane and Applied Data Research, were headquartered in Massachusetts and New Jersey, respectively. This regional landscape was transformed, however, as pioneering work by IBM San Jose and UCB unleashed a cascade of firm foundings that were concentrated in the Bay Area (for the most important of these, see Figure 4.1).

The concept of a relational database was first articulated in an article published in 1970 by Ted Codd, a researcher at IBM San Jose (Computer History Museum, 2007a). Inspired by Codd's work, in 1973, two UCB EE&CS professors, Michael Stonebraker and Eugene Wong, submitted proposals to the Department of Defense and NSF for support to build a relational database software program (Computer History Museum, 2007b). The ensuing competition between IBM and UCB resulted in two different relational database software systems, IBM's SQL and UCB's QUEL. Both IBM and UCB published their research findings, and UCB offered the software to all interested parties.

SQL was introduced commercially in 1979 and marketed by IBM and Oracle. In 1979, some members of the UCB Ingres team, including Robert

Epstein, Paula Hawthorn, and Michael Ubell, left UCB to form Britton Lee, Inc., which developed a computer dedicated to database processing. QUEL, introduced in 1980, was commercialized by Relational Technology, Inc., a new firm founded by Stonebraker, Wong, and another EE&CS professor, Lawrence Rowe. Relational Technology later was renamed Ingres Corporation (Rowe and Stonebraker, 1984). In November 1990, Ingres Corp was acquired by another Bay Area firm, ASK Corporation, and in 1990 Britton Lee was acquired by Teradata. Later, Ingres employees Howard Shao and John Newton (a UCB EE&CS undergraduate) established Documentum, which became an important Bay Area software corporation that grew to nearly 1,200 employees in 2002 prior to being acquired by Massachusetts-based EMC. Finally, in 1984 one of Britton-Lee's founders, Robert Epstein, and another employee, Mark Hoffman, left to establish Sybase, which grew rapidly and for a time was the second largest independent database vendor, based on global sales revenues, after Oracle.[20] In 1985, Stonebraker returned to UCB and, with Professor Lawrence Rowe, developed Postgres, which was commercialized by the Illustra, a firm established in 1992 and purchased by Informix in 1996. IBM's SQL software ultimately dominated commercial applications, but the growth of a Bay Area cohort of relational database software vendors shifted the locus of the database software industry to the Bay Area.

The other important Bay Area relational database firm established by a UCB EE&CS graduate was Informix (later purchased by IBM). Although the founder, Roger Sippl, received his undergraduate degree from EE&CS, at the time of the firm's founding he was unaware of the UCB relational database software research, so Informix cannot be described as a direct result of the INGRES research (Computer History Museum, 2007c). The only Bay Area relational database firm from this period that remains independent is Oracle, a firm whose initial product offerings were based on the IBM SQL software, which now accounts for nearly 40 percent of overall industry revenues.[21] IBM's main relational database product, DB2, is also based on the San Jose SQL work.

This brief discussion of the relational database industry highlights the contributions of UCB, many of which relied on formal and informal interactions between UCB faculty and the regional industry. Equally important to the dominance of Bay Area firms in relational database software is the fact that many other firms such as Documentum, PeopleSoft, Salesforce. com, and Siebel Systems were founded by individuals from the pioneering firms (look again at Figure 4.1). Although UCB's QUEL software ultimately failed in the marketplace, individuals trained in the INGRES program contributed to the concentration of relational database expertise in the Bay Area. For example, of the thirty-two students acknowledged in Michael Stonebraker's 1984 book on the development of Ingres, twenty-two remained in the Bay Area as of 2011, two were in Massachusetts, one was in Florida, two were in Southern California, and the location of five could not be ascertained.

As was true for CALDIC and GENIE, UCB research contributed to the development of a regional relational database software industry by producing trained personnel and freely distributed software. But in this case the contribution went a step further, as several start-ups directly commercialized the university research.[22] As a result, Silicon Valley came to dominate a key technology in organizing, storing, and making large amounts of data accessible, skills that proved invaluable to later generations of firms.

Reduced Instruction Set Computing (RISC), Late 1970s–mid-1980s

In the late 1970s, researchers at IBM, Stanford, and UCB began considering ways to accelerate integrated circuits' processing speed. IBM pioneered the idea of "reduced instruction set computing" (RISC), but Professors David Patterson at UCB and John Hennessey at Stanford, both funded by DARPA, independently improved the technology and transferred it to local start-ups (Joy, 1995; Khazam and Mowery, 1994). The RISC semiconductor architecture optimized the use of microprocessor processing power to speed data-intensive functions such as engineering graphics. The early adopters of RISC technology were computer workstation firms that provided desktop computers for engineers and designers with computing-intensive needs that benefited from faster processing speeds.

The RISC microprocessor architecture developed at UCB, which was published and available to all interested parties, was the basis for the Sun Microsystems SPARC microprocessor (Markoff, 1991).[23] The RISC microprocessor developed by John Hennessey's team at Stanford was commercialized by MIPS Computer, whose chip became the heart of the workstations introduced by the Stanford spin-off, Silicon Graphics.

UCB researchers facilitated the transfer of RISC technologies to industry through their relationships with firms. For example, David Patterson of UCB convinced Sun Microsystems to adopt his design, which evolved into the SPARC (Scalable Processor Architecture) processors. Although still relatively small in 1984, Sun was reaping large profits from sales of workstations using Motorola 68000 microprocessors. In 1984 William Joy, a former UCB EE&CS student, approached Patterson for technical assistance in developing a Sun RISC chip (Patterson, 2007: 11–12). According to Patterson, he was one of the first persons on the project and helped recruit Robert Garner from PARC to manage the project full-time. He and Garner then recruited other SPARC team members (Patterson, 2007: 11–12).

Although both the SPARC and MIPS chips and their associated firms, Sun and Silicon Graphics, eventually failed as the market for workstations was overwhelmed by lower-cost computers based on Intel-designed microprocessors, RISC technology found new applications outside workstations. Arguably the most widely deployed RISC chip is the ARM Corp microprocessor widely used in cell phones, development of which was influenced by UCB research. In 1983, the firm Acorn Computer, a Cambridge University spin-off, was developing a new microprocessor for its personal computers. According to Steve Furber (2011: 38–39), the Acorn engineering team was dissatisfied with existing microprocessors on the market. The solution came when a colleague "dropped a couple [of] papers on our desks, which were RISC papers from Berkeley and Stanford, where a grad class had designed a microprocessor that was competitive with the best industry could offer." The graduate student class that had designed the microprocessor was taught by Professors David Patterson and Carlos Sequin. Acorn Computer did not survive, but the RISC chip designed by an Acorn spin-off, ARM, now powers many handheld devices.

Patterson at UCB and Hennessey at Stanford introduced a new way of thinking about microprocessor design that led to the development of new computer architectures and the formation of initially successful venture capital–funded start-ups. The competition between UCB and Stanford resulted in technological advances that benefited the entire computer industry and the Bay Area's regional industry in particular. As in most projects discussed in this chapter, patents and intellectual property were of minor importance in the transfer of the technology to industry. The two-way exchange of personnel and ideas between firms and academia undergirded the rapid development and widespread adoption of this technology.

Berkeley UNIX Software Distribution (BSD), 1973–1995

As was the case earlier with GENIE, UC professors and students actively developed software programs. UNIX is a multitasking, multiuser computer operating system originally developed in 1969 at AT&T Bell Laboratories by a UCB PhD graduate Kenneth Thompson, who had been exposed to GENIE while he was a graduate student (Salus, 1994: 8), and another researcher, Dennis Ritchie. When UNIX was developed, AT&T was operating under the 1956 consent agreement requiring it to license its nontelephone technology to all parties and prohibiting it from entering the computer business. The terms of the decree prevented AT&T from marketing UNIX commercially (Raymond, 2003). UNIX was a pathbreaking software program whose portability, flexibility, and ease of use, as well as the fact that it permitted a transition from the "batch" processing to an interactive environment, contributed to its rapid adoption by research labs and universities all over the world.

In 1973 Robert Fabry, a UCB EE&CS professor, attended a presentation on UNIX, and soon thereafter the University of California acquired a UNIX license. The licensing agreement drawn up by UCB and AT&T granted enormous freedom to UCB researchers in altering UNIX. UCB researchers modified UNIX to operate on their DEC minicomputer, and the UCB modifications to UNIX initiated an intense interaction between UCB and Bell Labs researchers, facilitated by the fact that Thompson was a UCB alumnus.

Researchers at UCB and elsewhere quickly began modifying and improving UNIX. In 1975 Thompson returned to UCB from Bell Labs for a one-year sabbatical and taught UNIX programming to graduate students. UCB PhD students, including William Joy, released their UNIX improvements as Berkeley Software Distribution UNIX (BSD UNIX) to all interested parties (McKusick, 1999).[24] Other UCB researchers, notably the team developing INGRES, also were attracted to UNIX (McKusick, 1999: 1).

A further impetus to the improvement and adoption of UNIX was provided by DARPA, which in 1979 was planning to upgrade its ARPANET computer network (the architectural foundation and predecessor of the Internet), which was extensively used by academic, industrial, and government researchers. Rather than requiring the purchase of a single computer design to ensure compatibility, DARPA instead mandated that all ARPANET machines run the UNIX operating system, a decision that accelerated the adoption of the operating system within the research community.

DARPA also decided that the TCP/IP Internet protocol underpinning ARPANET should be integrated into UNIX (McKusick, 1999). Based on the expertise UCB had developed through its UNIX work, DARPA gave UCB an eighteen-month contract to integrate UNIX and TCP/IP, a project undertaken by William Joy. The DARPA funds enabled Professor Fabry to establish the Computer Systems Research Group to update and release new versions of BSD UNIX. The successes by the UCB team in the first contract convinced DARPA to provide another two-year contract almost five times larger than the original. Half of the funding in this contract went to the UNIX project and the rest supported other researchers in the department (McKusick, 1999: 5).

Joy's work on UNIX influenced his decision in 1982 to leave UCB to become one of the founders of Sun Microsystems, which adopted BSD as its operating system. BSD had been optimized for operation on expensive DEC VAX minicomputers, but also could be used on Sun machines that cost roughly one-tenth as much (Bechtolsheim, 2006: minute 22:14). BSD contributed to Sun's success in attacking the minicomputer market by offering networked desktop workstations (Baldwin and Clark, 1995).

AT&T was also aware of the value of UNIX; after its settlement of a second federal antitrust suit in 1982, the firm issued a new set of licensing terms for its UNIX System V. AT&T increased UNIX license fees and formed a subsidiary, UNIX System Laboratories (USL), to market its UNIX. In 1991, a number of Computer Systems Research Group members formed Berkeley Software Design Inc. (BSDI) to develop a commercial version of BSD for personal computers. The following year, BSDI released a BSD-based UNIX for $995, undercutting the $20,000 price charged by AT&T for its version of UNIX (McKusick 1999: 12). To protect its market, USL demanded that BSDI separate the networking code, which had no AT&T software code within it, from the UNIX code. In 1992, AT&T's subsidiary USL sued BSDI and the University of California, petitioning the court to prevent distribution of the most recent BSD version. The University of California countersued, stating that USL's UNIX release had incorporated code developed at the University of California without proper attribution. A 1994 settlement of the litigation required the University of California to make some minor changes so that EE&CS researchers could continue to freely distribute the operating system (McKusick, 1999: 13). In 1995, the UC Computer Systems Research Group disbanded, and the final source code was offered to all interested parties at no cost.

Another significant product from the BSD project was the "sendmail" program (originally delivermail), an early implementation of SMTP (Simple Mail Transfer Protocol) for delivering electronic mail between networks (Meagher, 2007). The first version was written in 1979 for the

ARPANET by a UCB student, Eric Allman, who had worked on the INGRES project. Sendmail was included in BSD releases; as late as 2001, Sendmail ran on 42 percent of all SMTP servers (Bernstein, 2001). Eventually, Allman established an independent firm, Sendmail Inc., to provide software services and updates. Sendmail further simplified the first Internet "killer application" (e-mail) for the ARPANET (Abbate, 1999: 106–110; Greenstein, 2010; Mowery and Simcoe, 2002).

The importance of BSD is difficult to overstate, because of its wide adoption and role as a foundation for the Internet. According to a 1996 article in *Information Week*, "The single Greatest Piece of Software Ever, with the broadest impact on the world, was BSD 4.3. Other UNIXs were bigger commercial successes. But as the cumulative accomplishment of the BSD systems, 4.3 represented an unmatched peak of innovation. BSD 4.3 represents the single biggest theoretical undergirder of the Internet" (Babcock, 2006). The quotation underscores the linkage between the development and deployment of BSD and the creation of the Internet (West and Dedrick, 2001).

The BSD story illustrates the dynamics of EE&CS's interactions with industry. Based on software originally developed at AT&T, with further development funded by the Defense Department, it became a central building block of contemporary computing and the Internet. Sun Microsystems was the immediate beneficiary of BSD development and release, but the broad adoption and extensive reuse of BSD were of enormous economic significance. The UC system copyrighted the code it added to BSD but made those advances available to the computing world. When AT&T sued to halt distribution, at considerable cost, the UC system defended and won the right to freely provide the software to the public. Marshall McKusick (1999) describes the UC policy in this way:

> The licensing terms were liberal. A licensee could release the code modified or unmodified in source or binary form with no accounting or royalties to Berkeley. The only requirements were that the copyright notices in the source file be left intact and that products that incorporated the code indicate in their documentation that the product contained code from the University of California and its contributors.

This legal success ensured that BSD Unix stayed in the public domain.

The UC system received no licensing revenues or royalties from BSD, but firms such as Sun provided substantial donations of research funding and equipment. Federal research funding through DARPA supported the development and improvement of BSD and allowed EE&CS to attract and support students such as William Joy, Eric Schmidt, and Eric Allman. These individuals, all of whom remained in the region, became leaders in the Bay Area ICT industry. Today, BSD UNIX, or parts of it, remain important in the operating system software of firms such as Yahoo!, Cisco, Apple, and many other firms.

Redundant Arrays of Inexpensive Disks (RAID), 1987

In 1987, as an outgrowth of the INGRES project, Professors Randy Katz, David Patterson, and Garth Gibson (then a graduate student) began considering the "upper bound on the number of transactions that could be processed" in database systems. In 1988 they published a paper describing "the continuum of performance and capacity trade-offs in making large numbers of small disks a reliable alternative for organizing the storage system" or what they termed "Redundant Arrays of Inexpensive Disks" (Katz, 2010: 82). Although the idea of replacing large expensive magnetic data storage disks with "arrays" of lower-cost, lower-capacity storage drives had attracted experimentation and commercial interest (McKendrick and Carroll, 2001: 669), Patterson, Gibson, and Katz (1988) described in detail a methodology for building superior storage systems. Their key insight was that prices for small hard disks used in personal computers were plummeting and, with the proper software, arrays of these small disks could be coordinated and connected to provide not only cheaper but also more robust (through greater redundancy) data storage. Demonstrating the feasibility of their concept, in 1990 they constructed a 192-disk array.

RAID was commercialized by large existing firms such as IBM, DEC, and EMC, as well as by newly formed startups. According to McKendrick and his coauthors (2003), as of 1998 258 firms had entered the RAID market; of these, forty-five were new firms, a majority of which were located in the San Francisco Bay Area. The UCB research was not directly responsible for the concentration of RAID firms in the Bay Area, but it demonstrated the feasibility of a novel design concept and thereby accelerated the experimentation already underway in the region.

Summary of the Case Studies

Each of the UCB EE&CS projects examined was supported entirely or significantly by the DoD, though DoD support was often supplemented by the NSF, industry, and even state funds (see the following discussion of the MICRO program). New firms were formed to exploit the results of some research projects, but in others, such as CALDIC, the most important contribution was the graduates who later became industrial leaders and innovators. In the cases of INGRES and RISC, UCB's contribution spurred regional competition that led the Bay Area to dominate this economic sector. In some cases, UCB EE&CS research contributed to the formation of entirely new segments of the overall IT industry, with significant economic benefits for the Bay Area. The development of BSD was important to the growth of the commercial Internet that also propelled an economic boom (followed by an epic bust) in the region in the late 1990s.

In many of these cases, research at UCB EE&CS included and benefited from significant interaction with industry, through faculty members transferring technology to industry, as was the case with RISC; through industry members visiting the campus, as was the case with BSD; through appointing professors who had industry experience; or through UCB professors taking sabbaticals in industry. In most of these cases, UCB reaped no direct income from these ventures, though the success of the projects generated additional funds (from government and industry) for EE&CS research. These successful projects generated few university patents, and those that were granted rarely proved to be lucrative, but they all made significant contributions to the growth of Silicon Valley.

PEDAGOGY, INDUSTRIAL RELATIONS, ENTREPRENEURSHIP, AND PATENTS

Although the cases in the previous section highlight channels of interaction with industry that are linked to specific research projects at EE&CS, the department also interacts with regional and global firms through other channels. This section briefly reviews these other modes of interaction.

Attracting Talent to Industry

The role that first-tier universities play in attracting highly capable individuals to a region has been widely recognized but little studied. In the case of EE&CS, this is illustrated by graduates such as Douglas Engelbart (born in Portland, Oregon; undergraduate at Oregon State University), Al Hoagland (undergraduate at UC Berkeley), Butler Lampson (Boston, undergraduate at Harvard), L. Peter Deutsch (Boston, undergraduate at UC Berkeley), Charles P. Thacker (Pasadena, undergraduate at UC Berkeley), and William Joy (Farmington Hills, Michigan; undergraduate at University of Michigan), all of whom later became Bay Area–based information and computer technology industry leaders. In some cases, the entrepreneurial success enjoyed by individual researchers led them to participate as venture capitalists or investors in the foundation of subsequent firms.

Postgraduate Education for Working Professionals

Through mechanisms such as university extension, universities have long assisted industry through the provision of postgraduate education for employed engineers and other professionals. Such postgraduate training is particularly important in fast-changing fields and has proven decisive in the growth of other regional high-technology clusters centered on UC campuses (see the discussion of UCSD in Chapter 5), but EE&CS was relatively inactive in this field for much of the postwar period. Morrough P. O'Brien (1988: 106), the dean of engineering from 1943 to 1958, reflected on his experience in establishing courses for industry:

> We were under pressure to do more for Industry in the way of off campus courses. People like Bill Hewlett of Hewlett-Packard needled me a bit. We did set up some instruction on the [San Francisco] peninsula, in Silicon Valley, a few individual courses. But I said to Hewlett, "Stanford's right there. Let them do it if you want something in the plant."

O'Brien explained his decision by stating that UCB was more interested in "basic" research.

John Whinnery (1994: 151), an EE faculty member and the dean of engineering from 1959 to 1963, remembered that:

> The electronics industry on the peninsula wanted a master's degree program centered there. . . . That was one of the things the Academic Senate had to approve, and there were a number of restrictions that they put on it. One of the major ones, and one we agreed with, was that no student would be able to get a degree from Berkeley without spending at least a term on the campus.
>
> The industry association that requested this program, Western Electronics Manufacturer's Association, WEMA, wasn't too happy with that restriction. But anyway, we decided to start on that basis. We started with good instructors from our own faculty, but it was difficult to service because of the travel. So the program didn't survive in that form. One problem was that we were competing with Stanford on its home ground.

UCB University Extension subsequently established professional development programs and various certificates in EE&CS fields, but it does not grant academic degrees, and, in contrast to the results Walshok and West found at UCSD, these programs do not appear to have been very important for the region.

Professorial Recruitment from Industry

In contrast to the limited department interest in postgraduate professional training, EE&CS has through most of its postwar history enjoyed close research relationships with industry. First and perhaps foremost, as Lécuyer similarly pointed out in Chapter Two for UCSB and UCSD, UCB has a long history of hiring new faculty members from elite industrial research laboratories, notably Bell Laboratories, as well as other industrial research organizations. Many other industrial researchers spent sabbaticals and gave lectures in the department, and UCB faculty took sabbaticals at corporate research facilities. These personnel exchanges facilitated the transfer of knowledge and identification of research challenges, and they create employment opportunities for graduate students and faculty.

Entrepreneurship

Tabulating the number of EE&CS graduates who have established new firms is not feasible, nor is it possible to claim that their UCB educational experience somehow "caused" the formation of their firms. Nonetheless, new-firm formation has been an important source of economic dynamism and growth in the Bay Area, and we summarize the limited evidence available on this topic.

Building on information assembled from the EE&CS website and our own data, we identified fifty-three new firms formed by EE&CS faculty and students while in residence or immediately on graduation from UCB.[25] EE&CS faculty served as advisors or in management for at least seventy-eight other firms (Kenney and Goe, 2004). Only two of the new firms established by faculty and students were located outside the Bay Area (one in San Diego and one in Ann Arbor, Michigan) and only thirteen of the firms for which faculty served as advisors were located outside the region. As might be expected from the projects described earlier, this advisory and entrepreneurial activity has been concentrated in the CAD, fabless semiconductor, semiconductor design software, relational database, and, most recently, Internet fields. The most dynamic single field of firm formation was the semiconductor design software field, which Lécuyer describes in greater detail in Chapter Two of this volume. Our database suggests EE&CS professors were involved in forming or advising at least eighteen

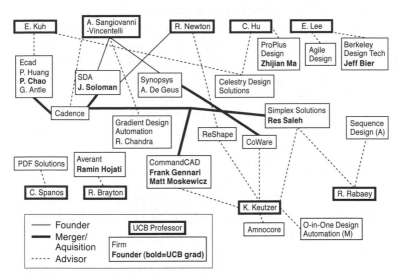

FIGURE 4.2. UC Berkeley professors and their relationships to the EDA industry.

SOURCE: Author's compilation and Lebret 2007.

different firms, a number of which also had UCB EE&CS graduates as founders (see Figure 4.2). Overall, the pattern of new-firm formation and relatively formal channels of faculty interaction with industry captured in these data strongly supports a "localized" characterization of these links with industry.

Patents

UCB EE&CS professors have not filed large numbers of patents through the university,[26] and few of the UCB EE&CS professors responsible for the research described in the cases discussed in the previous pages secured patents. For example, David Patterson (2007: 17), a central figure in both the RISC and RAID projects, reminisced that he "probably never filed a single patent at Berkeley." As Lécuyer discusses in Chapter Two, the University of California did file for patents on mixed-signal MOS capacitors developed by Professor David A. Hodges and colleagues, patents that earned the UC system approximately $2 million (Hodges, 2012b). Despite this success, Professor Hodges, a former dean of the College of Engineering, remains skeptical about faculty patenting, stating that "faculty wants to publish and then they [the university] can't force you [the faculty member] to patent. So it is the faculty decision. An engineering professor can say this is not an invention, and therefore it is not an invention." By choosing not to disclose a research result as a potentially patentable invention, a professor can limit the ability of the university to patent. Faculty participation is nearly always essential for a successful university patent application, and if anything is even more important for the licensing of such intellectual property (see Jensen and Thursby, 2001).

Although many have argued that patenting is necessary for technology transfer, David Hodges (2008–2010: 34) believed that forbearance regarding patenting was beneficial to interacting with and learning from industry because "if they're thinking you're going to go off and patent it, they're not going to talk to you, but if you tell them what you're doing and they're confident that you're not going to steal their stuff and write a patent, they'll tell you more about their stuff." This philosophy was especially important in the cases of BSD and, as Lécuyer shows in Chapter Two, SPICE, where interaction with industry was critical to campus research advances.

Although UCB licensing royalties from the inventions developed by EE&CS through much of the postwar period rarely have been substantial, EE&CS has reaped important benefits through other channels, primarily industry support for faculty research and industry philanthropy (see the following discussion). The modest role of patenting within the commercialization of EE&CS research results may reflect the characteristics of the key technologies in semiconductor electronics and IT, where the technological and commercial value of individual patents typically is far smaller than is true in fields such as biomedical innovation. There is little evidence that a lack of IP protection has inhibited the flow and adoption by industry of the knowledge created within the UCB EE&CS Department. Indeed, a policy that relied on patenting and licensing the results of EE&CS research might have yielded modest revenues while limiting the interactions with industry that proved intellectually stimulating, technologically fruitful, and financially beneficial for the department.

THE GROWTH OF INDUSTRY-FUNDED RESEARCH WITHIN EE&CS AND INDUSTRIAL LIAISON

As we have noted throughout this chapter, the rise to academic excellence of UCB's EE&CS Department was aided significantly during the early

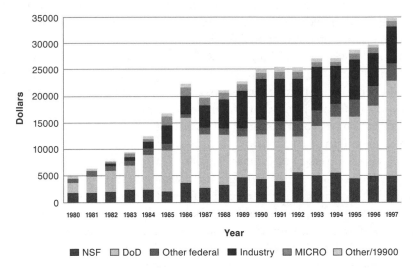

FIGURE 4.3. Electronics Research Laboratory, UC Berkeley, expenditures by source ($1,000), 1980–1997.
SOURCE: Hodges 1998.

postwar years by federal funding, much of which flowed from the Defense Department. Although still significant, DoD research support has been supplemented in recent decades by industry-funded research, as well as research funding from other federal agencies. Unfortunately, comprehensive longitudinal data on sources of research funding for UCB's EE&CS Department that would enable a more precise description of these changing sources of support are not available. David Hodges assembled data regarding the research funding sources for a key period in the department's development, 1980–1997.[27] These data, which form the basis for Figure 4.3, depict research funding sources for the Electronics Research Laboratory (ERL), the single largest research unit within the department and a source for the majority of extramurally funded research. The figure demonstrates the importance of research funding from the Defense Department, which accounted for the largest single share of ERL research funding throughout the period. Industry-supported research grew considerably, however, and by the 1990s industry's share of EE&CS research support was second only to that of the DoD.

Another significant factor in the expansion of industry-funded research within the ERL was the MICRO program established in 1981 by the state of California (Lécuyer, Chapter Two in this book; Hodges, 2008–2010). MICRO (Microelectronics Innovation and Computer Research Opportunities) initially provided annual funding of $4 million from state sources to support University of California EE&CS research that "may lead to products in the mid- to long-term" so that the California electronics industry could continue to remain competitive. MICRO required that California firms provide matching contributions on at least a one-to-one basis in the form of cash or "contributions in the form of state-of-the-art NEW [emphasis in original] equipment, which is an integral part of the proposed research" (University of California, 1985). An important objective of the MICRO Program was to train graduate students who "will upon graduation help to transfer the research results to California industry, become leaders in established companies, and become the entrepreneurs who form new companies that stimulate the State economy" (University of California, 1985). Although MICRO funding tapered off after 1985, according to David Hodges (2008–2010) the program helped increase interactions with industry and triggered a significant expansion of industry-funded research at the ERL.

Although industry funding of EE&CS research was important, especially after the 1980s, David Hodges (2012b) considered equipment donations from HP, DEC, IBM, Applied Materials, and the like to be nearly as important stating that "the industry support came as gifts, not via contracts, including the first 10+ years of Semiconductor Research Corporation support."[28] For the $18 million building expansion mentioned earlier, "the largest donor was DEC, which gave many VAXes. AMD and Intel and many others made cash donations of $500K or less."[29] In addition, of course, the willingness of private firms to support their employees' temporary research residences in EE&CS represented a substantial in-kind contribution of well-compensated talent, albeit one that often yielded significant near-term benefits to the sponsor firms.

Another successful method of securing funding and building bridges to industry was through the EE&CS industrial liaison program (ILP), established in 1982 to provide industrial firms with access to research and students in return for membership fees. Well before the creation of the ILP, however, institutional channels for interactions with industry had been developed. For example, in the late 1960s EE&CS established a "University–Industry Committee charged with exploring how our Department and the industries that hire our students might interact more effectively" (Everhart, 1971). In 1970, a University–Industry Conference was introduced, which became an annual event. By 2012, the ILP had grown to seventy-six members contributing at least $3.1 million annually to EE&CS research (Electrical Engineering and Computer Sciences [EE&CS] website, 2012).

Needless to say, leading regional and national IT and electronics firms often maintained a complex array of relationships with EE&CS faculty and the overall department. For example, Thomas Haycock (1989: 28) described Harris's interaction with EE&CS in this way: "Key individuals at Harris and Berkeley were responsible for most of the early activity that included industrial residents, participation on advisory boards, faculty and student visits of varying lengths, and investment in the CAD startups, SDA and Synopsys." Sending industry researchers to the university provides "free" research assistance for faculty, student and faculty visits to firms are very often compensated, and participation in advisory boards is often accompanied by a commitment of tangible resources such as contributions of funds or equipment. Finally, Harris, along with other firms, frequently invested in the UCB-linked startups. The complexity and variety of industry connections a top-tier university engineering department has make a comprehensive evaluation of its role so difficult to capture in the types of "metrics" (for example, counts of patents, licenses, "spin-off" firms) that are often employed by academic administrators, policy makers, or researchers.

CONCLUSION

Just as the U.S. Defense Department played a catalytic role at Stanford, MIT, and other U.S. research universities after 1945, its importance in the postwar emergence of UC Berkeley as a leader in electronics and IT research cannot be overstated. Defense-related funding provided the resources to transform a relatively undistinguished unit of the College of Engineering into a national leader. As a result, even as the UCB College of Engineering grew, EE&CS grew more rapidly. In 1946, EE&CS accounted for approximately 20 percent of the entire engineering faculty, while in 2012 it had 39 percent of a much larger faculty.

Although this chapter does not directly compare the electrical engineering and computer science departments at UCB and Stanford, the rise to excellence of electrical engineering and computer science at both universities contributed in significant ways to the parallel rise of Silicon Valley. The regional benefits of academic research strength for high-technology development were compounded further by the location of major research facilities of IBM and later, Xerox, in the area, drawn in part by the research excellence of these local universities. Although both of these corporate laboratories were located nearer to Stanford, UCB contributed a number of their key researchers. These corporate laboratories were themselves major sources of technological innovation that were exploited by new firms in the region and fertilized the local universities. For example, the competition between UCB and IBM San Jose to develop relational database software undoubtedly spurred both institutions.

We noted earlier that the DoD emphasized funding of team projects, and their success can be seen in Professor Patterson's observation that

> . . . projects like Genie have both a technical piece and a people piece . . . If you look over the years at the projects Berkeley is famous for, they share this component of a group of talented grad students and a set of faculty working together to build things—as opposed to making theoretical contributions—to create an exciting new prototype that has an effect on industry. (Spinrad and Meagher, n.d.)

The role of students, and particularly graduate students, in transferring technology and providing a trained cadre for industry has long been recognized. The UCB contribution has not been confined to students, however, inasmuch as faculty also advised and interacted with firms in the region and globally and some faculty resigned to join firms. These multifaceted contributions added to the fertility and diversity of the regional innovation ecosystem.

Contemporary academic research on technology transfer often uses the number and importance of patents as a metric of performance. But, as we have shown in this chapter, few if any of the important research projects through which UCB EE&CS made major technological and economic contributions to the global and regional economies involved patenting. Indeed, merely counting patents could lead one to overlook these research projects entirely in assessing the contributions of this group of researchers to the regional or national economy. Measures of the research output of EE&CS faculty, including citations from industry-linked publications or patents to EE&CS faculty publications, yields a more accurate (albeit still incomplete) portrait of the importance of EE&CS contributions to industrial innovation. Measures of EE&CS spin-offs would capture a portion of the contributions of more of the projects, particularly INGRES and, as Lécuyer shows in his chapter, SPICE, but the most far reaching of all, BSD, would be missed entirely. The flow of students and researchers from UCB to industry clearly is among the most important measures of interaction, but it is among the most difficult to track over time and to properly weigh.

The impact of these projects on the regional economy benefited from interactions between EE&CS faculty and industry. Repeatedly, in the chapter, we found that research success involved a two-way flow of researchers and ideas. For example, a number of EE&CS professors had industrial and startup experience. In the case of BSD, one of the AT&T authors came to UCB on a sabbatical and taught a graduate course on UNIX, transferring his programming knowledge to UCB students and researchers. In the case of relational database software, although IBM and UCB researchers were competitors, they also exchanged seminars and some of the key IBM researchers were UCB graduates (McJones, 1997). In semiconductors and, in particular, SPICE, the relationships included faculty taking sabbaticals in industry, industry members in residence in the department for prolonged periods, joint research projects, and numerous other forms on interaction. Many of these interactions were strengthened further when UCB graduate students left to become industry employees and often research leaders. In each case, the specifics of the interactions differ, but they were continuous and complex. The intensity of this knowledge sharing and creation, which we believe is quite characteristic of those in a top-flight engineering department, are impossible to capture through studies of technology licensing offices or joint patenting.

The technological and economic impact of these projects also varied. Many contributed to the accumulation of regional knowledge and the development of new firms or specialized research units within established firms. For example, CALDIC produced an important group of industry leaders and influenced the emergence of the IBM San Jose Laboratory as the center of the magnetic data storage industry that, a few decades later, would be the source of the entrepreneurs that created the merchant disk drive industry. The competition between UCB and Stanford in the RISC research and between UCB and IBM in relational databases increased regional innovation and dynamism. In the GENIE project, both SDS and Tymshare commercialized the software developed at UCB. For RAID, the seminal work at UCB articulated a trajectory that was developing within the industry, laying out a roadmap that facilitated additional entry and intense competition, spurring industrial innovation.

When considering the impact of university knowledge creation, BSD UNIX is possibly the most interesting project of all because its economic effects are so vast and so difficult to capture. Although UNIX originated in industry, its UCB refinement resulted in code that diffused to a plethora of operating systems, but neither the industrial nor the academic leader in developing the software reaped significant financial gains from it. Nonetheless, by linking UNIX with TCP/IP, BSD became the operating system for Internet servers and thus made possible the growth of the Internet, a development that provided significant economic benefits to the regional Bay Area economy. As so much of the world's UNIX expertise was concentrated in the Bay Area, the region was ideally placed to become the leader in commercializing UNIX-based applications and innovations. The continued vibrancy of the Bay Area as a center of innovation in new computing software, hardware, and architectures cannot be attributed to any single factor or local university, but the intellectual contributions of the UCB EE&CS Department should not be underestimated even though most of them were disseminated to local and global economic actors through "public," nonproprietary channels.

NOTES

The authors acknowledge David A. Hodges's consistent willingness to assist by reading versions and giving advice. Michelle Gittelman, Richard Nelson, and Joel West provided valuable comments on an earlier version. The authors thank Ronda K. Britt of the National Science Foundation for providing data from WebCASPAR.

1. For a practitioner's perspectives, see Mimura (2010).

2. There are exceptions to this generalization. For example, in a study of the MIT EE&CS Department Ajay Agarwal and Rebecca Henderson (2002: 45) found that "only about 10–20% of the faculty patented in any given year, and nearly half of the faculty in our sample never filed a patent during the 15-year period under investigation." According to one MIT EE&CS professor they interviewed, there was not a very strict patenting culture (Ibid.: 50). Similarly, Paula Stephan et al. (2007) found that computer scientists were least likely to patent of all engineering professors. In a study of microelectronics researchers in Italian universities, Balconi and Laboranti (2006) found that the universities having the best scientific performance were those with professors most closely connected to industry. These studies suggest that EE&CS faculty derive significant benefits from interacting with industry, but that patenting and licensing historically have not been salient modes of interaction.

3. For discussions of these topics, see, for example, Kenney, 2000; Gillmor, 2004; Lécuyer, 2005a; Lowen, 1997; Saxenian, 1994; and Sturgeon, 2000, among others.

4. For a detailed discussion of the transformation of electronics engineering into a science-based discipline, see McMahon (1984) and Kline (1988).

5. The three universities with the leading EE&CS departments—MIT, UCB, and Stanford—are located in and contributed to the growth of the two most celebrated hotbeds for IT entrepreneurship, Silicon Valley and Greater Boston.

6. According to William Aspray (2000: 46), the federally funded radiation laboratory at MIT

> . . . had established a model during World War II for the future of engineering at MIT, which called for science-based engineering instead of a practical, experienced-based discipline. MIT's administration believed in this model, and perhaps more importantly, so did the government officials who funded so much of MIT's postwar computing work.

7. Many early U.S. high-technology firms in industries ranging from semiconductor components to computers benefited from the demand for their products from the U.S. armed services (Leslie, 1993). Military procurement policy also had significant implications for the evolution of industry structure in these sectors, which naturally influenced the development of the emergent San Francisco Bay Area electronics industry.

8. Although the University of California has grown to include ten campuses, this chapter examines only the original Berkeley campus.

9. For a detailed examination of the influence of Johns Hopkins on U.S. research universities, see Geiger (1986) and Veysey (1970).

10. This was ascertained by examining UCB course catalogs, which list the faculty members' highest degree, for each year from 1946 to 1981, after which all faculty had doctorates.

11. For example, UCB had awarded a cumulative total of only eight EE PhDs by 1950, while MIT and Stanford had awarded fifty-two and sixty-nine, respectively. By 2010, according to the NRC rankings, the Electrical Engineering and Computer Science Departments at both UCB and Stanford were roughly comparable.

12. As the war was ending and reconversion was being pursued, the Office of Scientific Research and Development transferred various laboratories and activities to the respective services, but they did not want to retain all of the laboratories and therefore encouraged universities to accept them (Stewart, 1948; see also Sapolsky, 1990: 40–45).

13. Christophe Lécuyer's Chapter Two in this book discusses the development of semiconductor design automation software by UCB faculty and students.

14. John Haanstra was another UC Berkeley PhD graduate who joined the IBM laboratory at the same time, but he had been only peripherally involved in the CALDIC project (Flamm, 1998: 20ff).

15. This regional concentration prompted Albert Hoagland (1998) to quip that San Jose should have been called "Iron Oxide Valley."

16. SDS's success was an important event for the growth of the Silicon Valley venture capital industry. It received funding from the second venture capital partnership formed in Silicon Valley, Davis and Rock, named for Thomas Davis and Arthur Rock, the investment banker who arranged the funding of Fairchild. Their investment of $257,000 in SDS reaped a large payoff when Xerox purchased the firm. D&R was liquidated in 1970 after disbursing $94.5 million to its investors for an approximately 60 percent compound annual rate of return (Kenney, 2011: 1699).

17. For a discussion of the time-sharing business, see Campbell-Kelley and Garcia-Swartz (2008).

18. Tymshare was funded by George Quist, who at the time was a venture capitalist at the Bank of America Small Business Investment Corporation. Quist joined William Hambrecht to establish Hambrecht and Quist, which became a leading Bay Area investment banking/venture capital firm.

19. The noted software engineer Charles Simonyi (2008) worked at BCC during its short existence and then also moved to Xerox PARC. According to Simonyi, after BCC Lichtenberger became a professor at the University of Hawaii, where he participated in the development of the ALOHANet radio communication network whose packet collision detection schema was the inspiration for the Ethernet network software that Robert Metcalfe, then at Xerox PARC, developed. Lichtenberger later became a senior executive at the Ethernet-based startup Ungermann-Bass and then at Cisco Systems (Simonyi, 2008).

20. They were immediately joined by Jane Doughty and Tom Hagen, who were both UCB graduates and key in building the new software (Hoffman, 2007: 26).

21. In an odd twist of fate, Oracle briefly used UCB's VAX computer to rewrite its software for the newly introduced DEC VAX computers in 1979 (Wilson, 1997: 80–81).

22. The other global giant in this field is the German firm SAP, which employs 1,500 persons in the Bay Area.

23. Sun Microsystems was named after *Stanford University Network* and was founded by three Stanford students, who were immediately joined by the fourth founder, UCB PhD student William Joy, who brought the Berkeley Unix release with him.

24. Eric Schmidt, who took leadership positions at Sun Microsystems, Novell, and then finally Google, was also a PhD student developing software (BerkNet) for the campus network during this period.

25. Our definition of service on advisory boards or a firm's founding team, and so on, required that the faculty member or student be affiliated with the university at the time or, in the case of founding a firm, that he or she directly left the university to establish the firm. This strict definition eliminates ambiguity. The data are available on request.

26. Google patent searches found patents that listed EE&CS professors as inventors on patents filed by firms. For example, two patents listing Alberto Sangiovanni-Vincentelli are assigned to Cadence.

27. We are indebted to Professor and former Dean of the College of Engineering David A. Hodges for making these data available to us.

28. The Semiconductor Research Corporation, which was an industry consortium supporting university research, helped fund the development of IC design automation (Cavin, Sumney, and Burger, 1989).

29. See also Matkin (1990).

CHAPTER FIVE

Serendipity and Symbiosis
UCSD and the Local Wireless Industry

MARY WALSHOK AND JOEL WEST

This chapter considers the evolution of the relationship between a young research university—the University of California, San Diego—and what has become one of the premier global centers of technological development in the wireless industry. San Diego's wireless industry emerged and grew out of a long history of military-related communications R&D in the region that began with the Navy's earliest radio communication experiments with aircraft and was institutionalized through sizable federal investments during World War II that set the pattern for ongoing Department of Defense funding in the Cold War era.

The seeds for the wireless cluster came from the University of California's 1912 acquisition of a nonprofit marine research station, the Scripps Institution of Oceanography (SIO), which during the 1920s and 1930s became a key marine research lab for UC faculty and graduate students, including Roger Revelle. As part of the war effort, in the 1940s SIO became the Southern California base for the University of California's Department of War Research, and some key SIO employees joined with the Navy to found its West Coast sonar lab. In the 1950s and 1960s, Revelle used the now influential and well-funded SIO scientists as the nucleus for founding the basic research-focused UCSD campus on city and federal land adjacent to SIO.

The UC San Diego campus was strongly influenced by the national trend toward expanding basic science R&D in the 1950s and 1960s, especially science-driven engineering and technology development, particularly for defense and aerospace applications. Its early leaders, like so many university scientists of the time, were shaped by wartime and postwar experiences in efforts such as the Manhattan Project, the Office of Naval Research, and the Lawrence Livermore Laboratory. Revelle organized local support for the new campus, rallying defense contractors and civic boosters eager for basic science in the region. The early UCSD research programs in turn benefited from the tight links the founding faculty had to the Department of Defense and the numerous federal agencies that were providing research funds for basic science in the postwar era. And, as a greenfield institution, the nascent engineering programs rejected the craft-like approach that had characterized engineering education during the preceding seventy-five years, instead embracing the new model of engineering as applied science pioneered at MIT and strongly supported by national engineering leaders such as Frederick Terman at Stanford—a model that later resulted in the transformation of communications engineering from analog to digital communications.

Another factor was that—unlike its contemporaries UC Irvine and UC Santa Cruz—from the start UCSD was expected to become "another Berkeley." Building on the long relationship Scripps had with the national science and technology community and its success in attracting major federal funding, its leaders strove to achieve what was described by Nancy Scott Anderson (1993) as "instant greatness." The campus strategy was to build world-class science programs in biology, chemistry, mathematics, and physics by recruiting senior scientists who were among the best researchers in their fields. Many of the early elite UCSD hires had experience in securing Defense Department–funded research, and they brought these contacts with them. What attracted them was the opportunity to create a first-class, science-driven university from the ground up. From its inception, UCSD focused on hiring renowned researchers from established elite research institutions such as Chicago, Cornell, MIT, and Princeton.

Among these early hires was Henry Booker, a physicist from Cornell's School of Electrical Engineering, to be the founder of what eventually became the Electrical Engineering and Computer Science Department. For our story, in turn, Booker's most important hire may have been his former student, Irwin Jacobs, from a similar position at MIT. Jacobs later cofounded two of the region's most influential communications companies, Linkabit and Qualcomm. After his enormous success with these two business ventures, he went on to become the university's most generous donor.

The San Diego wireless communications companies founded by Jacobs were not university spinouts in the usual sense. Rather than being formed to commercialize university intellectual property (IP), they benefited from the highly trained scientists and engineers that UCSD attracted to the region. These science-based engineering companies coevolved in a symbiotic relationship with UCSD and its education and training programs. In particular, the firms benefited from University Extension as well as UCSD's early applied science departments, which, by the 1990s, were reorganized to form the School of Engineering. During this evolutionary process, the firms provided resources to the university by hiring its graduates, sponsoring its researchers, and collaborating in developing new cutting-edge communications technologies. This was most pronounced after 1990 as wireless communications expanded dramatically, and the San Diego firms were perfectly positioned to benefit.

This chapter documents how UC San Diego serendipitously provided the seeds of the regional telecommunications cluster and symbiotically evolved with it. It also shows the extent to which a developing university worked closely with a developing wireless industry to build curricula, research, and PhD programs that have brought distinction to the UCSD campus as well as much-needed talent to the industry, as part of a mutually beneficial symbiotic relationship. The success of this collaboration is measured not only by the emergence of Qualcomm as one of the largest and most successful communications firms in the world, or by the attraction to the region of other global wireless telecommunication firms' R&D operations, but also by what *Forbes* magazine concluded was the highest per capita concentration of wireless employees in the United States (Fidelman, 2012).

SIO, DEFENSE RESEARCH, AND THE BIRTH OF UCSD

Scripps and Navy Research

Founded in 1903 as a local nonprofit association and funded during its early years by the Scripps family, as mentioned earlier, the Scripps Institution of Oceanography was acquired by the University of California in 1912. During World War II, SIO helped launch the Navy's West Coast sonar research lab in San Diego (Raitt & Moulton, 1967; Shor, 1978; Naval Ocean Systems Center [NOSC], 1990). The SIO collaboration with the Navy's Point Loma Station and the Radio and Sound Laboratory during World War II gave rise to significant connections in Washington, D.C., and meant San Diego was well positioned to take advantage of the continuing growth in defense-related R&D funding in the postwar era (Walshok & Shragge, 2013).

Throughout the 1930s, 1940s, and 1950s, in addition to the active duty naval forces and defense contracting building up in the region, San Diego became a major site for military-related R&D. In addition to the Navy's sponsorship of sonar and other oceanographic research at SIO, the Navy sponsored local research on communications, building on San Diego's unique location in the continental United States and its proximity to deep ocean waters. The links were strengthened by the concentration of facilities at the tip of Point Loma.

During the war, Vannevar Bush and the National Defense Research Council (NDRC) mobilized universities to conduct basic and applied research developing technology for the war effort. As one part of this massive mobilization, the NDRC and University of California teamed up to establish a Navy sonar research and training facility. With this, the UC Division of War Research was established by UC President Robert Gordon Sproul in 1941 in Point Loma, adjacent to the NRSL; it was initially staffed by SIO employees. After the end of the war, the Navy combined these labs into a single Naval Electronics Lab, which remains active to this day (Raitt & Moulton, 1967; NOSC, 1990). Throughout the 1940s and 1950s, the Navy and Scripps collaborated on multiple forms of research funded by substantial sums of federal money. This contributed to an increased appreciation among San Diego elites of the role of the Navy and technology-related R&D in the region's growth and prosperity.

Creating a New UC Campus

The defense contractors in San Diego were eager in the postwar era to advance technology development through science, in large part because of the role science played in winning the war. In the 1950s, SIO director Roger Revelle argued for a UC graduate institute of science in San Diego that built on SIO's substantial research base. Significant industry lobbying and local community mobilization resulted in the 1957 approval of the UC San Diego campus and the unique Cold War science-oriented research culture that shaped its formation and founding values.

Revelle leveraged both Scripps's existing resources and the expansion goals of two UC presidents, Robert Gordon Sproul and Clark Kerr, to attract the resources necessary to create a UC campus in San Diego. He drew on his wartime and postwar ties to defense funders as well as local industries. All were eager to have an advanced science campus. Revelle's (1985) goal was to create "a publicly supported Caltech." Leaders of the local defense firms, such as General Atomic, Convair, Solar, Rohr, Cubic, and Ryan, were great supporters. General Atomic, a spin-off of Convair dedicated to the study of atomic energy, was a particularly strong supporter and pledged $1 million in startup support at the time when the UC regents were deliberating on whether to establish a new campus. The campus was poised to ride the postwar funding wave that had been unleashed by Vannevar Bush's influential *Science: The Endless Frontier* (Bush, 1945).

The founding members of the UC San Diego campus spoke euphorically about the opportunity to create a completely new kind of modern research university. This can be seen in a 1999 interview with Sol Penner, head of UCSD's first engineering department. Penner described what attracted him to the campus in the 1960s, as well as the approach to faculty recruitment that shaped the early culture of the campus:

> Our focus was an exceptional person rather than a particular subject . . . [Harold] Booker, for example, was a physicist in Systems and Control, and we brought him to the campus in order to build an applied physics and information sciences program. He built the nucleus of the department. I was Vice Chancellor for Academic Affairs when [Irwin] Jacobs was hired [by Booker]. (Penner, 1999)

Penner also believed that, during this postwar era, basic and applied science—rather than traditional engineering—had become the focus of the federal government and the defense establishment. He described:

> In the early '60s, the Cold War was the driver of basic research and engineering companies. Engineering was becoming indistinguishable from physics . . . like at Cal Tech, where 70 engineers and scientists might be working together all in one group. (Ibid.)

The importance of these social and cultural dynamics to the efforts that created the UCSD campus in the decade from the mid-1950s to the mid-1960s is that (1) the Cold War research funding linked many of the early UCSD scientists to entities interested in "applying" science to new technology solutions simultaneously with (2) enabling the campus to rapidly achieve a national reputation for its research programs. For example, UCSD gained admission into the prestigious American Association of Universities (AAU) in 1982, less than twenty years after its founding. Building on the research dollars and the reputation SIO had already established, senior-level professors arrived with and then attracted to UCSD the major grants, graduate students, and postdoctoral students that enabled the young campus to realize its aspirations to rapidly become a first-rank scientific institution. The young university's faculty, research output, extramural funding, and concomitant rise in reputation also eventually allowed it to contribute in diverse ways to the region's growth of highly robust clusters of commercially oriented R&D companies, initially in the defense contracting sector and subsequently in commercial sectors such as wireless. It is important to underscore that local industry actively supported this strategy by UCSD. Primarily engaged in defense, space, and security issues, their technology development was informed by the basic and applied science to which the campus was committed.

In his 1999 interview, Penner noted the extent to which most of the early hires at UC San Diego were people who had worked on the Manhattan Project and other war-related research programs at institutions such as Princeton, Chicago, and Berkeley (see Table 5.1). He referred to many of them as the postwar-era McNamara "whiz kids," reflecting back on the Kennedy era of space exploration and expanding Cold War tensions. In other words, the establishment of UCSD significantly contributed to the growth in the region's general intellectual capital.

Communications Engineering as Applied Science

In the early twentieth century, communications engineering was a series of loosely related arts, organized around disparate communication technologies such as telephony, radio, and acoustics. The transformation of communications from craft to applied science—and later from analog to digital—was led by MIT researchers in radar and radio communications from the 1920s through the 1960s, funded by the federal government to address military and space applications. The theoretical foundations of this transformation were provided by the information theory of Claude Shannon, who joined MIT in 1956 (Wildes and Lindgren, 1985; Pang, 1990; West, 2008).

Reflecting the school's initial emphasis on science—both in its leadership and their research—UCSD did not have a single engineering department until 1964. As the first dean of Revelle College, Keith Brueckner (1994) put it: "In engineering I felt that UCSD in the beginning should concentrate on applied science rather than conventional engineering." In doing so, UCSD bypassed the early-twentieth-century conception of engineering as craftwork and instead reflected the postwar paradigm of engineering as building on advances in math, physics, and other basic sciences.[1]

Perhaps influenced by the strength of San Diego's local aerospace industry, the first engineering department was Aerospace and Mechanical Engineering Sciences, created in April 1964 and headed by Sol Penner. Communications research was housed in a second department, termed "Applied Electrophysics," which covered what elsewhere would be considered the radio engineering component of electrical engineering and would soon include the nascent field of computer science. The department would not be renamed "Electrical Engineering" for more than a decade.[2]

Following the launch pattern of UCSD as a whole, the Applied Electrophysics Department was inaugurated with graduate courses but soon added undergraduate courses that came to account for the bulk of enrollment. Brueckner hired Henry Booker as one of two faculty to launch the department in July 1965, and Booker served as chair from 1965 to 1971.[3] Booker exemplified the university and department's view of communications as being applied physics.

Born in England, Booker earned his PhD from Cambridge, where he did seminal work on the physics of radio wave propagation in the ionosphere. He headed theoretical communications research for the English air ministry during World War II, where he "was involved in development of new ideas on antennas, electromagnetic wave propagation, and radar systems, all of which were critical to the defense of Britain" (Gordon, 2001). He was recruited to Cornell's Electrical Engineering Department in 1948, where his 1952 paper (Bailey et al., 1952) provided the science necessary to implement the Defense Early Warning System (DEWS), a series of Cold War forward-scatter radar stations that searched for incoming Soviet ICBMs (Gillmor, 1986).

Not surprisingly, Booker repeatedly sought to push engineering education away from application skills and toward a strong theoretical understanding. In 1954, he suggested that the goal of undergraduate engineering education is to teach what is known, while graduate education should emphasize research and creating novel ideas (Booker, 1954). In a 1963 letter to *Science*, he argued that for university education, "even in an engineering department, the objective of the operation is mental development" (Booker, 1963: 488).

The research of many early faculty related directly or indirectly to radio communications. For example, Carl Helstrom was a former Navy radio technician and prominent information theorist; J. Pieter M. Schalkwijk was a leader in information theory; Elias Masry did research in remote signal processing; Victor Rumsey was an expert in radio antennas; and

TABLE 5.1. Early UCSD leaders.[1]

Name	PhD	Earlier positions	Honors	UCSD positions
Roger Revelle	Geology, UC Berkeley, 1936	U.S. Navy: Sonar officer, 1941–1942; Bureau of Ships, 1942–1946; Office of Naval Research, 1946–1948 SIO: researcher, 1931–1941; associate director, 1948–1950; Director, 1950–1958	Member, National Academy of Sciences, 1957 President, AAAS, 1974 National Medal of Science, 1991	Director, Institute of Technology and Engineering 1958–1960 Chief administrative officer, 1960–1961
Herbert York	Physics, UC Berkeley, 1949	UC Berkeley: Physicist, Manhattan Project, 1943–1945; assistant professor, 1941–1954 Lawrence Livermore Laboratory: **Director**, 1952–1958 Department of Defense: **Chief scientist**, ARPA, 1958; **director**, Defense Research and Engineering, 1958–1961		Professor, physics, 1961–1988 **Chancellor**, 1961–1964; acting chancellor, 1970–1972 Dean of graduate studies, 1969–1970 **Director**, Institute on Global Conflict and Cooperation, 1983–1988
Keith Brueckner	Physics, UC Berkeley, 1950	Institute for Advanced Study, Member, 1950–1951 Indiana University: Assistant professor, 1951–1955 Brookhaven National Laboratory: Physicist, 1955–1956 University of Pennsylvania: Endowed chair, 1956–1959	Member, National Academy of Sciences, 1969	Professor, physics, 1959–1991 **Chairman**, Department of physics, 1959–1961 **Dean**, School of Engineering, 1963 **Dean**, Letters and Sciences, 1963–1965
Harold Urey	Chemistry, UC Berkeley, 1923	Johns Hopkins: 1924–1929 Columbia: Associate professor, 1929–1934; professor, 1934–1945; project leader, Manhattan Project, 1942–1945 University of Chicago: Chaired professor, 1945–1958	Nobel Prize, Chemistry, 1934 Member, National Academy of Sciences, 1935 Medal of Merit, 1946 National Medal of Science, 1964	Professor, chemistry, 1958–1970

James R. Arnold	Chemistry, Princeton, 1946	University of Chicago: Postdoc, 1946–1947; research associate, 1948–1950; assistant professor, 1950–1955 Princeton: Manhattan Project, 1943–1945; assistant professor, 1955–1957; associate professor, 1957–1958	Member, National Academy of Sciences, 1964 NASA Exceptional Scientific Achievement Medal, 1970	Associate Professor, Chemistry, 1958–1960; professor, chemistry, 1960–1983; Urey Chair in Chemistry, 1983–1993 **Chairman**, department of chemistry, 1960–onward
Stanford (Sol) Penner	Chemistry, Wisconsin, 1946	U.S. Army Allegany Ballistics Laboratory, 1944–1945 Caltech: Research engineer, Jet Propulsion Laboratory, 1947–1950; professor, 1950–1962 Institute for Defense Analyses: 1962–1964	Member, National Academy of Engineering, 1977 NAE Founders Award, 2007	Professor, engineering physics, 1964–1991 **Chairman**, department of aerospace and mechanical engineering sciences, 1964–1968 Vice chancellor, academic affairs, 1968–1969
Henry Booker	Physics, Cambridge, 1936	Cambridge University: Fellow, 1935–1948 U.K. Ministry of Aircraft Production: Principal scientist, Telecommunications Research Establishment, 1940–1945 Cornell: Professor of electrical engineering and engineering physics, 1948–1965; director, School of Electrical Engineering, 1959–1963	Member, National Academy of Sciences, 1960	Professor of applied physics, 1965–1988 **Chairman**, department of applied electrophysics, 1965–1971

[1] *Note*: Founding administrators listed in boldface type.

Jules Fejer, like Booker, pioneered research on radio propagation in the ionosphere.

It was not surprising that on arriving at UCSD in 1965, Booker sought to hire thirty-two-year-old Irwin Mark Jacobs, then an associate professor at MIT. In the 1950s and early 1960s, MIT had created and led the efforts to develop a probabilistic approach to communications based on Shannon's theory of information. Jacobs was among seven MIT graduate students who turned the graduate lectures of famed mathematician Norbert Wiener into a monograph. He had also coauthored the first undergraduate textbook on digital communications (Wiener, 1958; Wagner, 2005; West, 2008). Jacobs later recalled:

> At Cornell, I had taken electromagnetic theory courses from Henry Booker and antenna courses from William Gordon and was leaning towards graduate work in that area. . . . The fact that it [UCSD] was a public university meant a broader selection of students, and the opportunity to form a new curriculum was a challenge. (Morton, 1999)

Jacobs chaired three computer science dissertations at UCSD and served on two information theory PhD committees while there.[4] He began to do consulting with the Navy on its important fundamental problems of communications research. Although he spent only five years in the department, his impact on the regional economy and on UCSD spanned the following five decades.

BIRTH OF THE LOCAL TELECOM INDUSTRY

UCSD's Serendipitous Role

Jacobs joined the Applied Electrophysics Department in the fall of 1966 as one of eight new faculty. More important, two years later he cofounded Linkabit Corporation to pool his consulting efforts with those of two UCLA engineering colleagues. One of the UCLA professors, Leonard Kleinrock, had completed his doctorate at MIT in 1963—four years after Jacobs—and had shared the same dissertation advisor. The other, Andrew Viterbi, earned a master's at MIT and then took a job at JPL in 1957—so he could support his wife and immigrant parents—and, while working, completed his PhD at USC before joining UCLA with Kleinrock in 1963.[5]

Linkabit's first offices were in Los Angeles, near UCLA. Kleinrock soon left the company but later would become one of the pioneers of the

ARPANET, which evolved into the Internet (Leiner et al., 2009). Jacobs became the natural administrative leader of the firm, based on his two years of business courses in Cornell's hotel school before switching to engineering. In 1971–1972, he took a leave of absence from UCSD to straighten out the company's finances. Facing exploding demand for computer science classes, in December 1970 Booker wrote a memo to the chancellor and provost complaining about budget cuts to the department and a shortage of qualified CS faculty, correctly predicting that Jacobs would never return to UCSD:

> The senior professor in computer science desires to go on unpaid leave of absence next year. This is to look after his prospering business instead of spending time on a UCSD computer science program whose status is becoming absurd. He may never return to the campus. I have no current reason to believe that the campus would replace him either temporarily or permanently. (Booker, 1970)

Jacobs later recalled, "Running Linkabit turned out to be challenging and fun, so I resigned from academia after thirteen years to continue full time, and I have been in industry ever since" (Morton, 1999).

One of Jacobs's first acts was to move the company and its employees (except Viterbi) to light industrial space in the Sorrento Valley near the intersection of two Interstates, 5 and 805, approximately four miles from his UCSD office. The company eventually expanded to other rented space throughout the Sorrento Valley, setting the pattern for the development of San Diego's telecom industry in the valley and Sorrento Mesa on the east side of I-805, where Qualcomm is headquartered today.

Linkabit hired Jacobs's and Viterbi's students from MIT, UCSD, and UCLA, and later aggressively sought MIT graduates with ads promising "seventy miles of beaches." In interviews with the second author, Linkabit hiring managers said that recruiting electrical engineers from Stanford and Berkeley proved largely unsuccessful during the 1970s and 1980s due to the abundant job opportunities in Silicon Valley. Eventually UCSD was to become a valuable source of talent for the growing wireless cluster and most especially Qualcomm throughout the 1990s.

Spin-Off and Cluster Formation

From 1984 to 1990, at least ten companies were founded by Linkabit employees.[6] All told, from 1984 to 2004 more than 200 communications companies were founded in San Diego—some created by employees of existing firms and later others by entrepreneurs seeking access to the region's infrastructure for communications startups (Simard, 2004). In some cases, employees of these spin-offs formed yet other spin-offs. This explosive growth in companies was less the result of UCSD faculty or patenting than the effect of UCSD-educated scientists and engineers choosing to work for local companies, whether Linkabit in the 1970s or the dozens of companies formed after its eventual sale. These applied-science companies both developed their own IP and (as discussed in the following pages) built on talent and IP developed by UCSD.

The first round of startups tended to be variations of Linkabit's approach to technologies, markets, and competencies in digital communications. This included satellite communications for the government (ViaSat) and communications chips for cellular phones (PCSI). The best known was Qualcomm, founded in 1985 by Jacobs, Viterbi, and five Linkabit colleagues, which grew rapidly and had an initial public offering in 1991; in 1999, it joined the *Fortune* 500.

Extending the probabilistic communications theory first used with NASA, in the 1990s Qualcomm introduced its Code Division Multiple Access (CDMA), which promised higher capacity than the European-developed Groupe Spécial Mobile (GSM) and other digital ("2G") cellular standards and was quickly adopted as the sole 2G technology by South Korea. Although CDMA won a narrow majority of U.S. carriers, such as Verizon Wireless, Sprint, MetroPCS, and Leap Wireless—and had market wins with selected carriers in Japan, Hong Kong, and Latin America—it never achieved more than 20 percent of the global market share among 2G subscribers. However, the CDMA approach (and Qualcomm's CDMA-related patents) was incorporated in the world's major 3G cellular standards, cdma2000 and the GSM-derived W-CDMA (Mock, 2005; Bekkers and West, 2009).

In addition to patent licensing, Qualcomm also developed a successful business selling mobile communications semiconductors, which by 2001 made it the world's largest "fabless" semiconductor vendor. To help promote adoption of 3G data services, it created the BREW software platform, which made it easier for software developers to write applications for all 3G phones sold for use on the Verizon (United States) and KDDI (Japan) networks.

The success of Qualcomm's various technologies attracted other firms to the region. In addition to startups, this also included branch offices of major cellular manufacturers such as Nokia, Sony, and Ericsson—some of which had unsuccessfully fought against adoption of Qualcomm's 2G and 3G technologies (Simard, 2004). The region demonstrated all the normal characteristics of a cluster: a common supplier base, buyer–seller relationships among the firms, opportunities to found firms that provided third-party complements (such as software or training), and high labor mobility among regional firms. Many firms exited by being sold, whether to local companies (notably Qualcomm) or to out-of-town firms seeking their technology (as with TI's $475 million purchase of Qualcomm spin-off Dot Wireless).

As the industry grew, so did UCSD's communications capabilities and the ties between the wireless industry and the university. The original collection of engineering sciences departments became the "Division of Engineering" in 1982 and was organized as the School of Engineering in 1993. With a $15 million donation by Irwin and Joan Jacobs, in 1998 it was renamed the Jacobs School of Engineering. In the 1990s, UCSD created an industry-funded research center in the Division of Engineering while UCSD Extension trained hundreds of already credentialed engineers in CDMA and other emerging wireless technologies.

COEVOLUTION OF UNIVERSITY AND INDUSTRY

Linkabit seeded San Diego's communications industry in the 1980s, and from then on, the industry and UCSD grew together in a mutually beneficial relationship. The university has become a home for multiple forms of research important to the wireless industry (that is, in science, engineering, and public policy vital to the industry's competitiveness) and has been a continuing source of talent. The industry in turn has contributed equipment; helped fund facilities; provided matching funds for collaborative research, including state and federal grant proposals; and endowed professorial chairs and graduate fellowships, as well as participating in a variety of general support, corporate affiliate programs.

From UCSD to Industry

UCSD had an impact on the wireless telecom industry in San Diego in three distinct ways over four decades: (1) indirect support for Linkabit in the 1970s; (2) direct and significant support of talent development for the startup companies after 1985; and (3) strategic R&D partnerships for Qualcomm's CDMA ecosystem after the mid-1990s.

Linkabit Era

UCSD's promise of doing basic science to further new technology applications attracted Henry Booker and brought Irwin Jacobs to San Diego. Jacobs moved Linkabit to San Diego in 1971. Linkabit was enormously innovative, designing a variety of radio-related products, and proceeded to grow very rapidly. Perhaps, even more important, it was the nucleus for the region's telecom cluster.

Although we lack the personnel records of Linkabit that would enable us to measure the number of UCSD graduates employed by the company, there are other measures of the impact of UCSD alumni on Linkabit and its spin-offs. For example, according to the Simard (2004) database of San Diego–area telecom startups, thirteen of the sixteen local telecom start-ups formed by UCSD graduates included at least one Linkabit alumnus among the founders. Although interviews of Linkabit executives from the 1970s emphasized the importance of initially hiring from MIT, two Southern California universities—USC and UCSD—became central to Linkabit and the local industry in the late 1970s and early 1980s (Simard and West, 2003; West, 2009).

As has been the case in other high-technology regions, the rapidly growing Linkabit hired summer interns and other part-time employees from UCSD. After graduation, many of these became permanent employees.[7] The earliest UCSD graduate to join Linkabit was Jim Dunn (2004), who had taken a course from Jacobs at UCSD and joined Linkabit as their tenth employee on graduating from the now renamed Department of Applied Physics and Information Science in December 1970.

In another example, in the early 1980s Ladd Wardani (2005), a UCSD undergraduate student in communications engineering, was among about twenty students who were employed by Linkabit as summer interns. On graduation, Wardani joined Linkabit full time and remained until 1991, when he left to join ComStream, a Linkabit spin-off company. As Linkabit grew, it hired an increasing number of UCSD students, graduate and undergraduate.

Linkabit's Spin-Offs

Direct involvement of UCSD faculty in founding local telecom companies was minimal. Beyond Irwin Jacobs, Simard's (2004) data on local telecom

TABLE 5.2. San Diego telecommunications companies founded by UCSD alumni, 1985–2001.

Organization	Date founded	UCSD alumnus
Qualcomm[1]	1985	Franklin Antonio[2]
ViaSat [a]	1986	Steven Hart [b], Mark Miller [b]
Primary Access	1988	Jim Dunn[b]
Tiernan Communications	1988	James Tiernan (PhD)[b]
Peregrine Semiconductor	1989	Ronald Reedy (PhD), Mark Burgener (PhD)
Broadband Innovations	1990	Ron Katznelson (PhD)[b]
CommQuest	1991	Mark Lindsey [b]
VIA Telecom	1995	Mark Davis (PhD)[b]
ComCore	1996	Sreen Raghavan (PhD)
Dot Wireless	1997	Rick Kornfeld [b]
Path1 Networks	1998	Doug Palmer [b]
AirFiber	1998	Jim Dunn[b]
RF Magic	2000	Dale Hancock[b]
La Jolla Networks	2001	James Tiernan (PhD)[b]
Entropic Communications[a]	2001	Ladd Wardani [b], Anton Monk (PhD)
Vativ Technologies	2001	Sreen Raghavan (PhD)

[1] Went public via IPO.
[2] Employee of Linkabit or M/A-Com Linkabit prior to 1985.
SOURCE: Adapted from Simard (2004).

startups identify only one other UCSD professor who started a local telecommunications company: Ronald Fellman, a professor of electrical and computer engineering from 1988 through 1996 who in 1998 founded Path 1 Networks. Of course, faculty also worked on consulting and sponsored research for industry clients; for example, UCSD Professor Jack Keil Wolf, who like Viterbi was awarded the IEEE Information Theory Society's top research prize, was a consultant to Qualcomm for more than a decade.

The Simard (2004) database of San Diego telecom company founders identifies eighteen local telecom companies with UCSD alumni among the founders—the best known of which is Qualcomm (Table 5.2).

The earliest UCSD graduate at Linkabit, Jim Dunn, later cofounded two local start-ups: Primary Access (1989) and AirFiber (1998). The next early UCSD graduate to become a local telecom entrepreneur was James Tiernan, who finished his UCSD PhD in 1972 with Jacobs as a committee member and after working at Linkabit founded two companies: Tiernan Communications (1988) and La Jolla Networks (2001).

However, Dunn and Tiernan were not the earliest UCSD alumni to become founders of Linkabit spin-off companies. The first was Franklin Antonio, an engineer who was one of the seven ex–Linkabit employees to found Qualcomm in 1985.[8] Next came Mark Miller and Steven Hart, two of the three founders of ViaSat (1986), which went public in 1996. Two members of the UCSD class of 1982 later founded companies with successful exits: Rick Kornfeld with Dot Wireless (1997), which was acquired by Texas Instruments for $475 million in 2000; and Ladd Wardani, cofounder of Entropic (2001), which went public in 2007.

Other UCSD alumni founded local companies without working at Linkabit. For example, Ronald Reedy (PhD, electrical engineering, 1983) and Mark Burgener (PhD, physics, 1989) joined in 1989 to form Peregrine Semiconductor, a radio frequency semiconductor design firm.

Talent Synergies

The spin-offs and other local telecom companies benefited not only from UCSD's engineering programs but also its programs in management education. By the early 1980s, the university's extension program offered a variety of technology management, project management curricula that engineers working in the growing industry took advantage of on a course-by-course basis. UCSD Extension also organized two executive education programs after Richard C. Atkinson became UCSD chancellor in 1980. One program, known as the Executive Program for Scientists and Engineers (EPSE) targeted master's- and PhD-level engineers who needed to hone their management skills. The other was the Leadership and Management Program (LAMP), which targeted bachelor's-level engineers working in local industry. Over a twenty-five-year period (1985–2010), these programs have graduated approximately 1,500 scientists and engineers from local industry, and they continue to be fully enrolled today. During this same period, William Decker of UCSD's Office of Technology Transfer reported licensing agreements with "more than two dozen wireless companies" representing in the neighborhood of thirty to forty individual licenses, modest numbers compared to the thousands of extension enrollments and hundreds of master's and PhD students during this same period.

Extension Support for the CDMA Ecosystem

As Qualcomm grew in size, wealth, and importance to the telecom industry, it worked with UCSD to strengthen its teaching and research related to the company's wireless communications needs. From the beginnings of its efforts to promulgate CDMA adoption, Qualcomm worked directly with UCSD to address the shortage of engineers competent in the new CDMA technology. UCSD alleviated the education gap that Qualcomm faced in disseminating its complex and little-understood CDMA technology. Although the company was able to demonstrate technical performance that was superior to the European GSM and U.S. D-AMPS[9] technologies that were closer to market release, if hardware manufacturers and network operators were unable to build and install the necessary systems, the technology would have little practical value. Qualcomm thus needed new CDMA-specific training to support its ecosystem of suppliers and partners and to train its ever-increasing roster of engineers. The UCSD Extension division thus became an important partner of Qualcomm in enabling communications engineers to develop their capabilities in working with CDMA in systems design and integration.

In 1991 Qualcomm approached University Extension and offered their senior-level R&D people, as well as their facilities and computing capabilities, to work collaboratively to develop a CDMA curriculum that could be made available locally and online. In fact, Qualcomm scientists and engineers developed the curriculum, served as instructors, and helped the University Extension division at that time to launch its first online learning provision, thanks to their advanced skill in building web-based learning programs.

All told, UCSD Extension developed and offered more than a dozen certificate programs to serve the local wireless telecommunications industry, including programs in CDMA engineering fundamentals, digital signal processing, and wireless engineering (Table 5.3). Enrollments grew dramatically in the 1990s, then declined after the burst of the telecom bubble in 2001, but have recently recovered to approach the earlier levels (Table 5.4).

The curriculum developed by Qualcomm has been updated over time and is still available online. Fourteen years later, the extension's online courses enroll more than 21,000 students in a wide variety of programs that began with the courses initially developed collaboratively with Qualcomm.

TABLE 5.3. UCSD extension certificate programs serving the local telecommunications industry.

Certificate	Certificate name	First course offered[1]	Total enrollment	Total graduates
EMHA	Embedded Computer Hardware	1995	51	29
EMSE	Embedded Computer Systems Engineering	1995	22	6
EMSO	Embedded Computer Software	1995	224	105
MENG	Embedded Computer Engineering	1995	311	50
SYSE	Systems Engineering	1995	534	272
CPMA	CDMA/WCDMA Engineering	1998	378	218
VLSI	VLSI Digital Design	2002	23	4
BBMWE	Broadband Mobile Wireless Engineering	2003	8	4
CMENG	Communications Engineering	2003	37	19
DSPR	Digital Signal Processing	2003	42	21
RFENG	RF Engineering	2003	122	41
CDMA	CDMA Engineering Fund.	2004	0	0
ICDE	Integrated Circuit Design Engineering	2006	8	0
ICDSG	Integrated Circuit Design Engineering	2008	15	3
WLENG	Wireless Engineering	2009	35	8
MADVL	Mobile Applications Development	2011	11	0
MDPRG	Mobile Device Programming	2011	31	2
	Grand total		**1,852**	**782**

[1] Totals may vary slightly due to changes in data gathering systems between the 1990s and 2010.

Communications-Related Research and Graduate Education

The research areas and courses offered by the faculty and staff of UCSD's School of Engineering also evolved in conjunction with the specialization of the local industry in CDMA and other areas of communications engi-

TABLE 5.4. Telecommunications-related
extension enrollment by year.

Year	Program enrollment
1995	46
1996	43
1997	50
1998	74
1999	103
2000	90
2001	105
2002	104
2003	160
2004	200
2005	109
2006	96
2007	100
2008	114
2009	110
2010	113
2011	142
2012	93
Grand Total	**1,852**

NOTE: Total enrollments in certificate programs are listed in Table 5.3.

neering. For example, graduate degrees in communications awarded annually by the School of Engineering have grown from fewer than fifty in the
early 1990s to more than 250 in 2011 (Figure 5.1).

The audience for UCSD's expertise in wireless technology extended
beyond Qualcomm and the other local start-ups, attracting leading foreign wireless firms. As Qualcomm and CDMA grew in importance in the
wireless industry, major electronics companies such as Sony, Nokia, Ericsson, and Texas Instruments established R&D operations in the region to
gain access to the knowledge from UCSD, Qualcomm, and the other local
wireless communications firms (Simard, 2004). These firms joined Qualcomm in supporting wireless research efforts at UCSD.

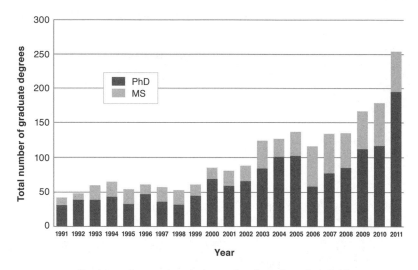

FIGURE 5.1. Graduate degrees in wireless-related engineering fields, 1991–2011.

An important advance in these collaborative research efforts was the establishment of the Center for Wireless Communications within the Jacobs School of Engineering in 1995. The Center enlists member companies such as Ericsson, LG, Qualcomm, Mitsubishi, and Nokia Siemens Networks to invest annually in research projects that are of equal interest to the companies and faculty/graduate students at UCSD. Research areas range from wireless applications to digital communication systems to high-speed integrated circuits. The corporate members work with UCSD researchers to identify research priorities and participate in a variety of monthly seminars and networking events.

A second and larger effort came with the establishment of the California Institute for Telecommunications and Information (Calit2), an ambitious public–private partnership and one of four California Institutes for Science and Innovation at UC campuses. The program was part of an initiative announced by Governor Gray Davis and UC President Richard Atkinson[10] in December 2000—a time when the state enjoyed abundant tax revenues generated by the capital gains of the dot.com bubble.

Calit2 was funded as a collaboration of UCSD and UC Irvine, with UCSD as the lead partner. As with other institutes, state funding of $100 million was conditioned on industry pledges of $200 million. Among the initial pledges were $15 million each from Qualcomm and Swedish tele-communications giant Ericsson. More than a decade after its founding, Calit2 represents a major hub of research programs involving academia, government, and industry. Its website is explicit about its commitment to contributing to the economic competitiveness of the state and the nation:

> Calit2 is taking ideas beyond theory into practice, accelerating innovation and shortening the time to product development and job creation. Where the university has traditionally focused on education and research, Calit2 extends the focus to include development and deployment of prototype infrastructure for testing new solutions in a real world context. (Calit2, 2012)

Calit2's members include many of the leading firms in the telecommunications equipment and software industries, including AMCC, AT&T, Broadcom, Ericsson, Fujitsu, Hughes, Intel, IBM, Microsoft, Nokia, Oracle, Qualcomm, Samsung, Sun Microsystems, and Texas Instruments. Calit2 receives millions of dollars in funding every year for research intended to be of direct interest to industry. However, in acknowledgment of its primary source of industry funds, in the spring of 2013 the UCSD branch of Calit2 was renamed the Qualcomm Institute for Telecommunications and Information Technology (or Qualcomm Institute, for short).

From Industry to UCSD

In recognition of the value of UCSD's research and education to the local telecommunications cluster, the local wireless firms have provided significant resources to support UCSD, especially in engineering. In addition to resources, industry demand for engineering students increased the legitimacy of the engineering programs within UCSD; industry also worked to encourage interaction and linkages with faculty and students.

As was previously noted, the UCSD School of Engineering was renamed the "Irwin and Joan Jacobs School of Engineering" on their gift of $15 million in 1998. In 2003, the couple pledged another $110 million: $10 million over five years, and a $100 million bequest—the largest gift in the university's history. Commemorating Jacobs's original faculty role, the couple endowed a chair of information and computer science in the Jacobs School. Qualcomm also endowed a chair in communications and technology policy at the Graduate School of International Relations and Pacific Studies. Many related chairs in engineering were endowed during this period, thanks to the growth of this sector. As of early 2012, the School of Engineering had four chairs endowed by Qualcomm, one endowed by

Ericsson, and a communications industry professorship funded through CWC member companies.

Other local executives made contributions to UCSD's new business school, including a founding gift in 1993 of $5 million from Bill Stensrud (former CEO of Primary Access) and an endowed chair funded by Harvey White, cofounder and former president of Qualcomm, who later became CEO of Leap Wireless.

The growing telecommunications cluster provided an important source of employment for UCSD graduates, which was no small concern during the 1970s and 1980s, before the region's high-tech employment in other sectors began to grow. The local firms also brought national engineering and communications conferences to the region, such as those sponsored by the Cellular Telecommunications Industry Association. These events provide visibility and access for faculty and students.

The shared growth and success of UCSD and the San Diego economy were summed up in a June 2012 column in *Forbes* (Fidelman, 2012), which described San Diego as the "World's Wireless City":

> "The San Diego community is not only the largest wireless community but is also the origin of the wireless industry with Qualcomm at the center of it all. Even beyond the traditional uses of wireless technologies, research institutes like West Wireless are helping to usher healthcare into the wireless age to cut costs and provide whenever, wherever health care support," Dexcom's CEO Terry Gregg told me when explaining why the company is located in San Diego. As it turns out, Gregg believes it's a competitive advantage to be located at the convergence of wireless technology and healthcare—and there's no better place than San Diego.

Forbes calculated per capita employment in wireless-related industries to illustrate San Diego's strength:

> The concentration of wireless employees in San Diego is 484 per 100,000 residents, compared to Silicon Valley's 375 per 100,000 and Los Angeles's 141. San Diego also boasts the fastest growth in wireless employment (275%) and in payroll (371%) in the last decade. While the City declares it's America's Finest, the local economy suggests it's America's most Wireless.

UCSD's centrality to the San Diego wireless industry can be illustrated geographically (see Map 5.1). The largest concentration of IT and communications jobs in the county are found in an area located ten miles to the north and east of UCSD—an area that includes both Linkabit's original 1970s location underneath the I-5/I-805 interchange, as well the more than dozen buildings that comprise the Qualcomm campus today east of Interstate 805.

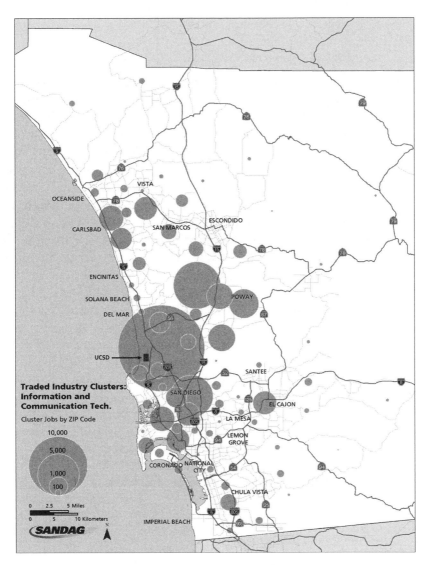

MAP 5.1. Information and communication technologies (ICT) jobs in San Diego County.

SOURCE: Sandag 2012.

CONCLUSIONS

The Symbiosis of UCSD and the Wireless Industry

The growth of UCSD and rise to excellence of its engineering programs enabled and later was enabled by the rise of the wireless telecom industry. UCSD's early focus on basic science attracted a number of eminent researchers in radio-related fields to the region. They were enormously successful in attracting research funding from the Department of Defense, and some of these projects developed technology that would be commercially valuable. In the case of Irwin Jacobs, his expertise was such that he was able to establish a firm, Linkabit, which eventually begat dozens of new firms, including Qualcomm. In the 1960s and 1970s these small but rapidly growing firms had to rely almost exclusively on skilled engineers and scientists recruited from outside the region. However, by the 1980s and 1990s UCSD had become a major source of highly trained personnel, particularly for Qualcomm and the wireless industry. In the last decade, the relationship between UCSD and the wireless sector deepened, as demonstrated by the increase in industry research partnerships through such mechanisms as the Center for Wireless Communications and Calit2. The development of San Diego's wireless industry was seeded by the presence of the University of California, and the relationship between UCSD and this regional industry seems likely to remain strong in the century ahead. This is in large part due to the continuing alignment between the values and practices that animate UCSD and those at the heart of the telecom cluster's success; a belief in the industrial value of basic science, aspirations to be the best, effectively garnering resources, attracting (and retaining) exceptional talent, and using those resources and talent to deploy cutting edge technologies.

Implications beyond San Diego

Policy makers and researchers have gone to considerable lengths to document the role of Frederick Terman and Stanford University in the success of Silicon Valley. Despite the latter's unique characteristics, it is important to consider the parallels (and differences) in the shared development of UCSD and the local tech industry. As in the Bay Area, universities were essential in training workers to provide the human capital necessary to support local high-growth technology companies. San Diego was similar to the Santa Clara Valley two decades earlier, in that it first relied on out-of-town sources of technical talent (notably MIT) but gradually strengthened its support for and use of the hometown engineering school (Stanford and UCSD, respectively).

However, the outcomes differed considerably in scale. The Bay Area built a highly diversified technology cluster that (at various times) included semiconductors, hard disks, personal computers, Unix workstations, software, Internet services, computer networking, biotechnology, and clean technologies. San Diego's clusters are dominated by telecom and biotechnology (Chapter Three) companies, but, particularly in electronics, the San Diego firms are smaller, and there are fewer of them than in the Bay Area. Nonetheless, UCSD has played a subtle but critical role in the growth of the local wireless industry. The San Diego case suggests that the potential contributions of research universities to regional growth include more than star researchers or patented intellectual property. The regional wireless cluster in San Diego has benefited from UCSD's role (a) in educating and training the engineers and scientists who are building the emerging cluster and (b) in collaborative research activities that contribute to the sector's growth and sustainability. UCSD's role in the growth of the wireless cluster has some parallels with the role of UC Berkeley in the growth of the semiconductor industry in the Silicon Valley described in Chapter Two of this volume. Both the regional economy and a UC campus have benefited from this symbiosis.

NOTES

We thank Nathan Owens and Josh Shapiro for their assistance in compiling UCSD data for this chapter and Caroline Simard for generous use of her database on San Diego wireless startups.

1. Wildes and Lindgren (1985) document how this paradigm shift from craftwork to applied science was implemented at MIT's largest academic department, the Department of Electrical Engineering (later Electrical Engineering & Computer Science).

2. The Applied Electrophysics department was renamed Applied Physics and Information Systems in 1969 and then Electrical Engineering and Computer Sciences in 1978. In 1987 it was divided largely along hardware/software lines into its current configuration, with separate departments of Electrical and Computer Engineering and Computer Science and Engineering.

3. The other faculty member hired in 1965 was Ken Bowles, a former Booker student who in the 1970s headed the campus computing center and created UCSD Pascal (Bowles, 2003). In 1979, those efforts were spun off to create San Diego–based SofTech Microsystems, a new division of Boston-based SofTech Inc.

4. James Tiernan completed his PhD in 1972 under Schalkwijk and later worked for Jacobs at Linkabit before starting two companies on his own. Jacobs also served on the USC PhD committee of Bob Gray, who later joined Stanford's faculty and became a top information theorist.

5. This discussion of how Linkabit was founded and its growth from 1968 through 1985 is adapted from West (2009) and is based on interviews with all three Linkabit founders and various other primary and secondary sources.

6. Data for this section are adapted from Simard and West (2003), Simard (2004), and West (2009), as well as from unpublished databases of San Diego telecommunications firms provided by Martha Dennis and Caroline Simard.

7. Linkabit's first employee, Jerry Heller, visited UCSD for a year to finish the MIT PhD that he had started under Jacobs.

8. In addition to UCSD alumnus Antonio, the other Qualcomm founders were two former University of California professors (Jacobs of UCSD and Viterbi of UCLA), two other engineers—Andrew Cohen (an MIT grad) and Klein Gilhousen (a UCLA grad)—and two finance executives, Harvey White and Dee Coffman. UCSD Chancellor Richard Atkinson was an early member of Qualcomm's board of directors.

9. D-AMPS was the first U.S. digital cellular standard, based on the Advanced Mobile Phone System used for all U.S. analog cellular calls. Through mergers of U.S. cellular carriers, D-AMPS was gradually replaced by GSM to allow for access to the global GSM equipment market.

10. Prior to becoming president of the University of California System, Atkinson had been the chancellor at UCSD and was a founding board member and major shareholder in Qualcomm (Potter, 2001; Ainsworth, 2002).

CHAPTER SIX

University in a Garage

Instrumentation and Innovation in and around UC Santa Barbara

CYRUS C. M. MODY

On June 4, 2007, UC Santa Barbara announced "a $12.5 million gift . . . to support pioneering research at the California NanoSystems Institute" from two local philanthropists, Virgil Elings and his former wife, Betty Elings Wells. Elings and Wells's gift boosted UCSB's already high profile in nanotechnology research by helping fund a new building, Elings Hall, to house specialized equipment and clean rooms needed to make and characterize nanomaterials (UCSB Office of Public Affairs, 2007). Up to that point, UCSB's reputation in nanotechnology was based largely in nanoelectronics and materials research led by former IBM and Bell Labs physicists such as Evelyn Hu and David Awschalom, who had moved to academia in the late 1980s and early 1990s (Lécuyer, Chapter Two in this volume; McCray, 2009). Yet UCSB's strength in nanoscience was also a product of Virgil Elings's own move *away* from the university in the late 1980s to run a local start-up, Digital Instruments (DI).

This chapter examines the fraught but fruitful relationship between Elings and UCSB that enabled DI to dominate sales of one of the most important classes of instruments used in nanotechnology research and development: scanning probe microscopes, especially the scanning tunneling microscope (STM), atomic force microscope (AFM), magnetic force microscope (MFM), and other variants. In the 1990s, DI's reputation rose in tandem with that of UCSB scientists who were developing and using probe microscopes, especially Paul and Helen Hansma in the Physics Department. After DI merged with a Long Island semiconductor process equipment company, Veeco, in 1998, many DI employees left to found a series of local nanoinstrumentation firms in partnership with

UCSB researchers. Thus, where Elings's move out of the university had been unusual and contentious in the late 1980s, the model set by DI and other early firms helped make Santa Barbara one of the leading sites for start-up formation in the UC system.

Given the timing of its founding in 1986, DI might at first glance appear to have been a product of the institutional, economic, and legislative changes of the late 1970s and early 1980s that were intended to stimulate "technology transfer" out of universities: for example, the Bayh-Dole Act, the widespread establishment of university technology transfer offices, and the routinization of venture capital financing of faculty start-ups. Yet DI was not founded with venture capital money, its licensing of UC patents was intended as much to forestall oversight by the university as to gain competitive advantage, and there was as much technology transfer from DI into UCSB as vice versa. While explicitly procommercialization developments such as Bayh-Dole no doubt fostered the growth of an instrumentation cluster in Santa Barbara, they were not factors in DI's founding and initial growth and were equivocal contributors to its later success.

This chapter will argue, instead, that DI's corporate culture and its employees' approach to technology were shaped much more by the dire conditions of the late 1960s and early 1970s that demanded significant institutional innovation from American academic scientists and engineers. In the UC Santa Barbara Physics Department, *pedagogical* innovation—particularly an unorthodox master's of scientific instrumentation (MSI) program—was one tool for overcoming budgetary and demographic problems at an institutional level. At the same time, some UCSB physicists turned to entrepreneurship and interdisciplinary collaboration, partly to overcome budget shortfalls at the individual level. By the 1980s, the combination of increasing entrepreneurial activity, interdisciplinary collaboration, and a cadre of MSI graduates gave rise to a cluster of scientific instrumentation companies that have enriched UCSB and the Santa Barbara economy in a variety of ways.

MOMENT OF CRISIS FOR UCSB PHYSICS IN THE LATE 1960S

When budgetary and cultural crisis engulfed American academic physical and engineering science disciplines in the late 1960s and 1970s, the UCSB Physics Department was still climbing toward top-tier status, largely by mirroring peers at Stanford, MIT, and elsewhere who had successfully adapted to the postwar funding landscape. Those departments prioritized training PhD (rather than undergraduate and especially terminal master's-degree) students in a narrow set of basic research fields that were highly valued by federal funders (Leslie, 1993; Lowen, 1997). Prestige subfields such as high-energy physics that could attract the best PhD students and generate large grants from the Atomic Energy Commission and other national security funders were an obvious stepping-stone into the top tier. Hence, UCSB embarked on a long-term strategy to build clusters in high-energy research (Barrett, 1987: 1–7) and other basic research fields linked to the military-industrial complex (particularly experimental high-energy physics, theoretical particle physics, condensed matter theory, and relativistic astrophysics) to better compete for students and federal grants.

Several trends combined in the late 1960s to undermine that strategy. First, federal defense and space (closely related to defense) R&D began dropping as a percentage of total U.S. R&D in 1965 and only began rising again in 1981 (National Science Foundation [NSF], 1994). Total federal R&D (defense and nondefense) funding reached a peak of 3 percent of GDP in 1964 and declined steadily until the 1980s (Neal, Smith, and McCormick, 2008). During that period, Congress and both the Johnson and Nixon administrations shifted away from the early Cold War funding model and toward research that was deemed "relevant" to civilian social problems. For example, the Mansfield Amendment curtailed the ability of military funding agencies to sponsor basic research (such as most academic high-energy physics) that was not directly applicable to battlefield technologies, while the National Science Foundation dramatically expanded and began placing much more emphasis on engineering and "research applied to national needs" (Belanger, 1998). Perhaps most important, though not easily foreseeable at the time, federal funding for the life sciences began a steady upward climb (in constant dollars) while funding for the physical sciences remained flat for almost three decades. According to the NSF (2004), in 1971 federal funding for the life sciences barely surpassed that for the physical sciences; by 1998, the life sciences were attracting more than twice as much federal funding as the physical sciences.

The second trend affecting physics departments was the souring job market. In 1970 alone, "sixteen-thousand scientists and engineers, each holding advanced degrees, lost their aerospace-industry jobs. . . . The number of academic [physics] jobs on offer at the [April American Physical Society] meeting dropped . . . [by] a factor of four" from 1968 to 1971

(Kaiser, 2002: 152). With fewer grants to support stipends, and dimmer job prospects for graduates, enrollment in physics PhD programs waned. As David Kaiser has shown, the number of physics doctorates awarded annually by American universities dropped from a high in 1971 by a quarter to 1974, and by more than a third by 1978.

These trends significantly hindered the UCSB Physics Department's move toward the top tier. As a UCSB research administrator complained (Reese, 1972), the department's postwar strategy focusing on basic research fields was increasingly out of touch with federal priorities:

> Shortly after World War II, basic research flourished, however, in recent years a new emphasis has evolved toward applied research. In fact, there is a growing concern that even the National Science Foundation may be failing in its original mission and may in fact assume the role of directing instead of supporting research. This change in trend for NSF is evident in its RANN program (Research Applied to National Needs) and in other new approaches that are in their proposed budget. On this campus over 90% of the 313 active projects continue to be directed toward the study of basic research. The increased competition for the shrinking basic research funds has undoubtedly contributed to the 22% decrease in the value of awards and an 8% decrease in the number of awards recorded for this reporting period.

In tandem with that funding shortfall, PhD enrollments in UCSB Physics dropped precipitously between 1969 and 1970 (see Figure 6.1).

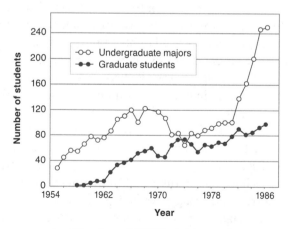

FIGURE 6.1. Number of UCSB physics graduate and undergraduate students, 1955–1986.

SOURCE: Barrett 1987.

Figure 6.1 also offers evidence of a third, related, trend affecting academic physics departments in the Vietnam era: disaffection arising from the war and other cultural changes. The department's undergraduate enrollments, according to former Department Chair Paul Barrett (1987), "peaked at 2.35% [of total UCSB undergraduate population] in 1959 (the post-Sputnik bulge), fell to a low of 0.64% in 1976 (post-Vietnam reaction), and rose to only 0.74% in 1981." According to Barrett, the recovery after 1981 was more an artifact of UCSB's Engineering Departments raising their standards than of physics overcoming its legitimacy deficit.

As Stuart W. Leslie (1993, 2010), Matthew Wisnioski (2003, 2005), and others have documented, student disaffection stemmed from the perception that physical and engineering science departments were too narrowly focused on research funded by national security agencies, too technocratic and elitist, and thereby too insulated from civil society's concerns. Student activists at schools not only opposed applied, defense-oriented research but also basic research on the grounds that both did little to solve problems such as pollution. I have explained elsewhere (Mody, 2012; Mody and Nelson, 2013) that campus activists believed that applied, defense-related research tended to be more interdisciplinary than basic, and therefore argued that research applied to civilian issues should also be interdisciplinary. At the same time, budgetary pressures encouraged university researchers to cross disciplinary lines to find new sources of research funding. Thus, many academic physical and engineering scientists in the early 1970s forged wider-ranging collaborations than was typical in the early Cold War, especially with life science and medical school departments and with humanistic disciplines such as philosophy and music.

Members of the UCSB physics faculty were keenly aware that students wanted them to move toward civilian, applied topics and a more interdisciplinary, humanistic outlook. Department brochures from the 1970s complained of popular perceptions of physics as oblivious to "human concerns" and countered that physics was "practical. It serves as a fundamental science in preparing the base for all technological advances. . . . The influence and interconnections physics has had on our history, on our religions, on our philosophies, on our languages and literatures are deep and broad" (UCSB Physics, n.d.).

Of course, brochures are one thing; most physics faculty members remained focused on basic, relatively monodisciplinary research. Still, the department experimented with various ways to address physics' budgetary and legitimacy crises. A lecturer, Mel Manalis, started a course on "environmental physics" intended to show that "physics is very relevant to modern environmental topics" (UCSB Physics, 1976). The Physics Learning Center made experimental equipment available to "students from all disciplines. With hundreds of demonstrations maintained in an atmosphere of free investigation, the PLC has established itself . . . in the service to local schools and the community" (UCSB Physics, n.d.). (One of the recurring demands of student protestors was that science departments become more involved in their local communities.) Finally, Herbert Broida—for whom the current physics building is named—created a Quantum Institute in 1969 to serve as "a problem oriented, interdisciplinary research unit . . . designed to respond rapidly to requests for assistance in the solution of problems important to governmental agencies, private industry, and research foundations" (UCSB Office of Research and Development, 1973).

PEDAGOGICAL INNOVATION AS CRISIS RESPONSE: FOUNDATION OF THE MSI PROGRAM AT UCSB IN THE 1970S

The department's most unorthodox response to the Vietnam-era crises was a master's of scientific instrumentation (MSI) degree program introduced in 1970. Although others had a hand in it, the MSI program's leading light was an assistant professor, Virgil Elings, who came to UCSB as one of the first hires in the department's high-energy cluster in 1966. As an external review committee (Fatt, Hahn, and Jackson, 1974) put it, the MSI program's

> . . . major strength is clearly the interest and dedication of its faculty director, Dr. Virgil Elings. . . . Herein, however, lies the major weakness of the program. It is entirely dependent upon the continued interest and activity of Dr. Elings. If he should become disabled, find another position, or take a sabbatical leave there is no one to continue the necessary leadership.

According to the review committee, other tenure-track faculty took little interest in the program, even though the whole department benefited from it: "The other 19 ladder [tenure-track] faculty members [besides Elings] supervise 26 graduate students. The Physics Department is being credited for 20 graduate students (MSI) who are being handled by one ladder faculty member [Elings], thereby giving the other faculty members an exceptionally light load."

Those twenty MSI students were a much-needed boon to the department, because without them the department's graduate enrollments would have flatlined for almost at a decade at about two-thirds of their 1969 peak. Indeed, Elings today indicates that the MSI program was created "because we thought the Ph.D. program was going to die" (UCSB Technology Management Program 2008; also Elings, 2012). Yet in leaving the basic, high-energy research cluster (and the PhD students it attracted) to run a terminal master's program focused on applied topics, Elings risked lowering himself in his colleagues' eyes. The 1974 external review expressed alarm about "the serious threat to [Elings's] career in academic physics if he stays with the MSI program for more than just a few years . . . [rather than] go back to the mainstream of physics" (Fatt, Hahn, and Jackson, 1974). The warning was well-taken; where Elings spent the full eight years moving from the assistant to associate rank, and another eight moving from associate to full, junior colleagues who worked with PhD students were promoted much faster. For instance, Paul Hansma, an electron tunneling spectroscopist hired in 1974 whose fortunes would later be closely tied to those of Elings, spent three years as an assistant and three as an associate.

Yet if the MSI program was, at the time, out of keeping with most of Elings's colleagues' vision for their discipline, it successfully attracted students because it was fully in keeping with young people's aspirations both for jobs and for a different kind of physics. Almost all documents relating to the MSI program from the early 1970s portrayed it as an interdisciplinary, problem-oriented, civilian-minded enterprise. As ads told potential applicants:

> The UCSB Master's Program in Scientific Instrumentation is looking for Creative, Hardworking Bachelor's Degree Scientists who want to Solve Real Problems. . . . The one-year program, supported by the National Science Foundation, provides opportunity and experience in interdisciplinary problem solving. . . . on campus and in nearby hospitals and industrial laboratories. (Elings, n.d.)

Or, as Elings put it in a newspaper article, the MSI program was to be "a leader in the growing movement to involve students directly in interdisciplinary research by tackling problems in areas outside their formal training" (*Santa Barbara News-Press*, n.d.).

The topics that early MSI students worked on, too, indicate their interest in interdisciplinary, civilian, problem-oriented research. Early projects included "an image stabilizer to aid in early detection of cancer in internal organs; a color television speech display system to teach the deaf to speak" (English, 1972); "medical physics aimed at determining properties of human arteries, physiology studies at the [UCSB] Institute of Environmental Stress, design of instrumentation for molecular beam studies in chemistry, bioluminescence studies in marine biology and computer assisted optical spectroscopy" (UCSB Physics, 1975); a tactile sound mixer built for a blind audiophile undergraduate (*Santa Barbara News-Press*, 1975); ocean monitoring instrumentation packages (English, n.d.); and "a portable device to detect and measure the quantity of lead in gasoline" (UCSB Office of Public Information 1973).

Such projects no doubt spoke to baby boomer idealism; but, as *Physics Today* noted, the MSI program was also "preparing students for physics-related jobs" (Strassenburg, 1973). Indeed, pragmatic and idealistic aims were entirely compatible. As Mike Buchin, a mid-1970s MSI student, put it:

> I got involved in this project mainly out of my own interest in medically-oriented projects. Also, I like getting involved with projects that will help people—*applied project work*. In the long run, my work has paid off tangibly as well as esoterically (?). I am going to be working as a Research Physicist for Searle Analytical and Radiographics, a firm in Des Plaines, Illinois deeply involved in nuclear medicine. (Buchin, 1974; emphasis and punctuation as in original)

Or, as the UCSB Office of Public Information trumpeted, "In contrast to the experiences of students in some other scientific fields, every one of the program's continuing students found employment in instrumentation last year" (English, 1972).

Students were not the only ones benefiting from the program. Off-campus organizations such as local hospitals worked with MSI students to develop technologies for in-house use. This kind of technology transfer "provides the widest possible experience for the students and stimulates the flow of ideas between the University and the community" (English, 1972). Students were responsible for considerable internal technology transfer as well because they built free experimental apparatus for researchers in many UCSB science departments, especially physics. In lean budgetary times, free equipment must have been highly desirable; during the first year of the program "the number of cooperating labs on campus increased and soon there were more labs requesting students than there were students" (Elings and Phillips, 1973).

The program also had a lasting impact on Elings himself. Almost immediately on starting the program, Elings (and Phillips, 1973) saw that traditional lectures would neither hold MSI students' attention nor help them with their projects: "The too familiar pattern of factual presentations of material chosen by the instructor was more tolerated than appreciated. . . . One year's experience indicates that experimental science students learn more from doing their 'own problem' than from passive reading and exercises." The most successful MSI students learned more from each other and from plunging into projects for which they had no training than they did from lectures.

UNIVERSITY IN A GARAGE: MSI-BASED ENTREPRENEURSHIP DURING THE 1970S

At almost the same time that the MSI program started, Elings became one of the first entrepreneurs in the UCSB Physics Department. Starting with a small garage start-up called Santa Barbara Technology (SBT), Elings began packaging the same electronics and machine-shop know-how that was the basis for the MSI program into a series of sometimes offbeat commercial products. One of SBT's first products, for instance, was the Tobiscope, a transistorized pen used to locate acupuncture points (Rainbow Enterprises, 1973). SBT was perhaps best known for a toy consisting of two parabolic mirrors stacked with their concave sides facing each other, such that an object placed on the bottom mirror appears to be floating above a hole in the top one.[1] Elings and John Landry (1972), a PhD student in electrical engineering, patented the device together (but did not assign the patent to the University of California). Eventually, Elings licensed the patent to another start-up, Opti-Gone, which makes most of the versions of this product that are sold in science museum gift shops today.

Soon, Elings was selling products derived from MSI students' projects. For instance, Santa Barbara Technology (1973) marketed the SPOT (Speech-Optical Translator) to speech therapists, schools for the deaf, and foreign language instructors after Mike Buchin and other MSI students developed it from an idea suggested by UCSB computer scientist Glen Culler (English, 1973). As an aside, it should be noted that Culler also embarked on an entrepreneurial career in the late 1960s and early 1970s. As Roger Wood, Culler's departmental colleague, put it in 2000, "Out of his lab came more than 20 high-tech companies. And 30 years later, students of his are still starting companies" (Estrada, 2000).

In addition to SPOT, Santa Barbara Technology sold a thermodilution cardiac computer that was also based on one of Buchin's MSI projects.

Elings's later detractors and competitors sometimes cite this as an early example of his allegedly shady approach to intellectual property. That is a reasonable interpretation because Elings and his MSI teaching partner David Phillips (1977) took out a patent for the cardiac computer without acknowledging Buchin (much less including him as a coinventor). However, it is important to note that one of critical components of Buchin's version of the cardiac computer was a Wheatstone bridge (a Victorian-era device for measuring electrical resistance), whereas Elings and Phillips's patent ostentatiously states that "a Wheatstone bridge is not used."

That is, Elings and Phillips's invention differed substantially enough from prior art (including Buchin's) to secure the novelty and therefore validity of the patent—or, to put it more cynically, the exclusion of the Wheatstone bridge from their patent raised the legal barriers high enough to withstand any challenge Buchin might mount given the resources available to him. The ethics of such maneuvering are gray, at best. On the one hand, Buchin and other MSI students were no doubt entitled to some share of any intellectual property derived from anything they invented in the course of their master's projects. On the other hand, the products based on MSI projects that Elings and Phillips (who left the UCSB physics tenure track in 1971 and who also had a garage start-up) marketed to organizations such as hospitals and schools for the deaf contained innovations that went significantly beyond the prototypes that their students had created.

The cardiac computer marked a new phase in Elings's career in which the MSI program, his own on-campus research, and his off-campus entrepreneurship began to converge. As Elings's departmental biography noted, once he began directing the MSI program "he shifted his research interest to medical instrumentation. Many MSI students gained valuable experience working on some of these projects. Among them was a lung water measurement system, and a light-scattering immunoassay instrument" (Barrett, 1987, 28–29). Today, Elings (2012) ascribes this shift to dissatisfaction with the anonymous teamwork typical of high-energy physics—a reason given by other high-energy physicists who moved toward biomedical entrepreneurship in the 1970s, such as Cetus cofounder Donald Glaser (Vettel, 2006; Galison, 1997).

Of course, Elings may also have seen that turning toward biomedical research allowed him to solicit funding from sources that were not available to his departmental colleagues. For example, Elings secured a grant from the American Heart Association for a project that he struck up with

George Jahn, an MSI student who left UCSB to become a cardiologist, and John Vogel, a doctor at the Santa Barbara Heart and Lung Institute who had previously mentored MSI students such as Mike Buchin. Together, Elings, Jahn, and Vogel developed a "dermofluorometer," an instrument for determining whether injured skin flaps were healing properly, which they described in a few scholarly publications (for example, Elings, Jahn, and Vogel, 1977). Elings then sold dermofluorometers to biomedical researchers through Santa Barbara Technology for a few years before spinning off the product line as a separate business owned by his son Mike and based in Boulder, Colorado.

About the same time, Elings also began collaborating on biomedical instrumentation with a new UCSB assistant physics professor, David Nicoli. On joining the Physics Department in late 1976 or early 1977, Nicoli seems to have taken over David Phillips's role as junior partner in the MSI program. In 1978, Elings and Nicoli formed a start-up company, Nicomp, to sell a light-scattering instrument that they developed on campus. It is perhaps notable that only one of Elings and Nicoli's five patents related to this technology was assigned to the regents of the University of California (none of Elings's earlier patents for the dermofluorometer, parabolic mirror gadget, or cardiac output computer were assigned to the regents either).

Nicomp's instruments were used for determining the size and morphology of particles suspended in solution, with specific application as an assay for detecting antigen–antibody complexes. In fact, Nicomp could perhaps claim to be the first Santa Barbara nanoinstrumentation company, because its products were measuring between twenty-five and thirty nanometer particles in the early 1980s (Kuczynski and Thomas 1983), at a time when nanoparticle research was quickly evolving into "nanotechnology" (Nordmann 2009). Unlike Elings, though, Nicoli did not participate in the Santa Barbara nano boom because he left UCSB to run Nicomp in 1984.

THE END OF THE MSI PROGRAM AND THE FORMATION OF DIGITAL INSTRUMENTATION DURING THE 1980S

In the early 1980s, the MSI program continued to average about ten new students per year, although it drew considerably less publicity and constituted a smaller part of the Physics Department's offerings than it had in the early 1970s. The crisis conditions that had contributed to the creation of the program in the Vietnam era had disappeared by the early 1980s. Undergraduate enrollments in UCSB physics skyrocketed from fewer than a hundred to almost 250 between 1981 and 1985; PhD enrollments also grew in the same period, though less rapidly (Barrett, 1987). As federal research budgets rebounded, too, the MSI program's free labor was less valuable to faculty members in need of laboratory equipment.

With the rationale for the program fading, a new department chair abruptly canceled it in 1986. Given his emotional and intellectual investment in the MSI program, Elings now had little to keep him on campus. At the same time, he chanced on a technology, the scanning tunneling microscope (STM), that eventually led to a new life off campus. The STM is an atomic-resolution technique invented at IBM in 1981, for which its inventors won the Nobel Prize in Physics five years later.[2] Elings's departmental colleague Paul Hansma was already one of the few researchers outside IBM to have built an STM, having been recruited early on because one of the inventors, Heinrich Rohrer, knew him from a sabbatical at UCSB in the late 1970s. Recognizing that the cheap, simple STMs that Hansma was building resembled the do-it-yourself devices that he and his MSI students had been making for fifteen years, Elings approached Hansma with an offer to form a start-up to sell STMs.

Hansma had no experience with start-ups and, as he remembers it (Hansma, 2006), his colleague at UC San Diego (later UCLA), John Wheatley, had warned him that forming a start-up in his own research area might raise legal obstacles to using the start-up's products in his own lab. So, instead, he gave Elings the same kind of advice and schematics that he had previously given to other physicists looking to build their own STMs. At this point, Elings sold his share of Nicomp and invested the proceeds in a new STM company he named Digital Instruments. In early 1987, Elings and one of his best former MSI students, John "Gus" Gurley, incorporated DI, and Gurley began developing the electronics and software for the company's digitally controlled STM, the NanoScope. As DI grew, Elings continued to hire MSI graduates into key positions, including Mark Rodgers (eventually a vice president), Jerome Wiedmann (DI's first head of marketing), and James Massie and Matthew Longmire (designers of DI's most successful product lines).

Elings's experiences with the MSI program and with start-ups in the 1970s gave him the seed money and many of the key personnel with which to build DI. Just as importantly, the MSI program offered a model for both the technology and the business practices that DI developed. From the start, Elings envisioned that *Digital* Instruments would sell STMs with digital controllers that could be easily reprogrammed as the technology evolved. In the MSI program, Elings had learned to push students to build projects with digital circuits because "one exciting aspect of microelectronics is that the resulting 'intelligent' instruments may be easily redesigned to meet altered specifications, often by simple software changes" (Nicoli, Barrett, and Elings, 1978).

In other words, for researchers and students in the MSI program, digital circuits were a universal solution that all students could learn and then apply to their individual projects. Similarly, in the context of DI, digital circuits designed for the company's first STM could easily be modified to accommodate later, often radically different, variants of the STM. Digital circuits also had the advantage that almost anyone could learn to design them: in Elings's (1981) view, "one no longer needs a degree in electrical engineering to design state-of-the-art electronic instruments. . . . It isn't true that one needs a course in differential equations or Fourier analysis in order to design top-notch instruments." In the context of the MSI program, that meant that Elings could, and did, attract students from many different educational backgrounds (not just physicists and engineers). As Elings (1995) put it, "The areas that [MSI] students had done undergraduate work in made little difference in their ability to design instruments."

At DI, Elings applied that lesson from the MSI program by hiring employees even if they weren't trained in the quantum mechanics of electron tunneling. James Massie, for instance, had been a psychology major and an MSI student before Elings hired him, while Matt Thompson, who became one of DI's top applications scientists, had a degree in history and was running a bookstore when he joined the company. Several of DI's longest-serving employees, responsible for some of the firm's most profitable inventions, joined while they were still UCSB undergraduates (for example, Dennis Adderton, Dan Bocek, Kevin Kjoller, and Colby Bowles). Very few DI employees (especially early on) had doctorates.

Elings's strategy of flexibility and digital circuitry—drawn from the MSI program—paid off in the end because the STM was rapidly evolving. Thanks in large part to Paul Hansma's UCSB group and researchers at Stanford and IBM, variants of the STM proliferated after 1985: the atomic force microscope (AFM), the scanning capacitance microscope, the scanning near-field optical microscope (NSOM), the magnetic force microscope (MFM), and so on. Within those variants many different "modes" of operation also emerged. A commission of the International Union of Pure and Applied Chemistry (Friedbacher and Fuchs, 1999) eventually identified more than fifty named variants and modes.

Generically known as "probe microscopes," these techniques allowed for the characterization of a much wider range of samples in a greater variety of conditions than the STM, which can examine only electrically conducting or semiconducting samples and performs best in vacuum or aqueous solution. The AFM, in particular, could image such a broad spectrum of materials that practitioners from many different disciplines and industries began to use it. The management and technology lessons of the MSI program helped DI both to incorporate the proliferating variety of probe microscopes into its products and to adapt to the proliferating variety of customers who wanted to use those products.

Other aspects of the MSI program were also borrowed to foster DI's corporate culture of flexibility. Elings, for instance, would hold lunchtime "inventing sessions" where employees would brainstorm solutions to technical problems that had nothing to do with DI's products (for example, a self-balancing washing machine). The point of such sessions was to train employees in how to be inventive and think up new approaches even to problems that had supposedly already been solved. Back at the bench, engineers were expected to learn by doing on their own with little oversight from management, just as MSI students had. Indeed, until the mid-1990s there was almost no middle management for designers—they all reported directly to Elings or his junior partner (Gurley), just as in the MSI program.

THE LATE 1980S: DI ASCENDANT

"Digital was profitable in its first year of operations and has been profitable in all subsequent years" (Veeco, 1998). By 1990, DI had sold around 300 microscopes and accounted for more than 50 percent of global STM sales. Its STMs, however, could image only a small range of samples, limiting their market. Back at UCSB, though, Paul Hansma's group had developed an AFM that could reliably image a broad range of samples, including materials of interest to the life sciences and the semiconductor industry that could not be imaged with an STM. In 1989, therefore, James Massie (the former psychology major and MSI student) began working with Hansma's technician, Barney Drake, to adapt the Hansma group's AFM as a DI product. Drake and Massie took the UCSB AFM—with its wires hanging off and clumsy controls—and used modern design principles to turn it into a clean, hardened, relatively user-friendly product. As Craig Prater (at the time a Hansma PhD student, later one of DI's vice presidents) recalls, Massie "took an already elegant design and then made it even more elegant, easier to use. Over time he found the things that ended up not being reliable and came up with more elegant, more reliable designs" (Prater, 2001).

Drake remained part of the Hansma group, rather than DI, through the tech transfer process. Indeed, he left for his annual rafting expedition before he and Massie had quite finished. Several years later, though, when Drake founded a one-person custom analytics company to characterize customers' samples on DI machines, he was allowed to run his start-up out of DI's headquarters. Likewise, Hansma's students, who had generally avoided DI before, now began to take jobs there: some temporarily, but some permanently, and one or two rising very high in the organization. Their expertise in AFM, combined with the instrument-building expertise DI had already accrued by hiring MSI graduates and UCSB undergraduates, made Digital Instruments' fortune. More than half of the Nano-Scopes sold in the first fifteen months after the introduction of DI's AFM "add-on" in November 1989 were AFMs. After that, AFM sales eclipsed STM sales; where DI had produced roughly eight NanoScopes a month from 1987 to 1990, from 1990 to 2000 it consistently sold more than nineteen units a month, the overwhelming majority of them used as AFMs (or the closely related magnetic force microscope) rather than STMs (Mody, 2011: 179).

Even as DI's relations with the Hansma group grew warmer, however, Elings's relations with the UCSB Physics Department became frosty. As Elings (2012; UCSB Technology Management Program, 2008) tells it, someone at UCSB accused DI of improperly profiting from its commercialization of Hansma's STM design, leading the university to audit DI's use of intellectual property. As it turned out, Hansma's STM was not patented, and it incorporated ideas (some patented, some not) that had been freely circulating in the probe microscopy community for years. But in commercializing another professor's experiment, Elings had raised red flags that had not gone up when he commercialized MSI students' projects in the 1970s. Though no action was taken against DI, pressure mounted for Elings to sever ties with the company.

Instead, he severed his formal ties with UCSB, resigning in 1990. Nevertheless, DI still depended on the Hansma lab (and vice versa), so both Elings and Hansma became more formal in their approach to intellectual property to avoid another audit. Hansma, who had patented almost nothing before 1987, began patenting his AFM innovations. DI then licensed some of those patents "mainly to get a relationship with the university" (UCSB Technology Management Program, 2008), and was given right of first refusal to exclusively license patents as they came out of the Hansma lab. DI paid royalties on those licenses and also directly funded the Hansma group's "further research in the field of Atomic Force Microscopy" (Digital Instruments, 1989).

DI also supplied the Hansma group with AFMs, spare parts, software, and expertise that no other academic group had access to. Hansma (2006) estimates that close to a million dollars in DI equipment came to his lab. DI also licensed patents from—and gave microscopes to—the other leading academic AFM group, Calvin Quate's at Stanford (Manalis, 1998). As a result of these formal arrangements, both Quate's and Hansma's groups' productivities were boosted. Hansma's students and postdocs, though, also realized more informal benefits from their proximity to DI that gave them an advantage over groups such as Quate's: They could drive over to DI and lobby for a specific change to the NanoScope's software or rummage through spare parts for a particular experiment (Hoh, 2002).

THE GROWTH OF NANO-INSTRUMENTATION COMMERCIAL ACTIVITY AND RESEARCH IN SANTA BARBARA DURING THE 1990S

In the early 1990s, then, DI and UCSB each got a great deal from each other. Hansma's group was a magnet for aspiring probe microscope researchers from around the world on the basis of its high-profile publications, some coauthored with Elings or other DI personnel. A striking example of the early 1990s synergy between UCSB and DI is Digital Instruments' "We Have Science Covered" advertising campaign, which showed a NanoScope surrounded by six editions of *Science* (from 1988 to 1992) with NanoScope images on the front cover (Figure 6.2). Five of the six articles corresponding to those covers came from UCSB, with Elings a coauthor on four of them. Several other probe microscope articles

FIGURE 6.2. An advertisement from Digital Instruments' "We Have Science Covered" campaign. Digital Instruments is now part of Bruker Nano Surfaces Division. This ad was printed in *The Journal of Vacuum Science and Technology* A 11 (1993), no. 3: A7.

SOURCE: Bruker Nano Surfaces.

were featured on the cover of *Science* in this period, which attests to the attention that the general scientific community accorded to the technique. However, the STMs and AFMs used for those other articles were either NanoScopes as well, or they were custom built by their users; no other probe microscope manufacturer could claim to have their products featured in such a prominent place.[3]

Because of Hansma's rising status in probe microscopy (fueled in part by resources from, and collaborations with, DI), many researchers made short visits to UCSB, where they were guaranteed to see DI products in use. Those who brought their own funding and interesting samples might be allowed to join Hansma's group for a year or two, during which time they would adapt probe microscopy for use in a new area, and sometimes in a whole new discipline. Such people provided DI with advice on how to fine-tune its products for their disciplinary colleagues, while at the same time offering those colleagues persuasive evidence of the NanoScope's utility. Eventually, Elings began hiring his own in-house "applications scientists" to refine and advertise the AFM's use in fields such as biology and polymer chemistry. Here, too, Hansma and his then-wife, Helen, were helpful in recommending promising candidates (including their own postdocs) to DI.

In helping to spread AFM into the life sciences and other disciplines, Hansma was able to integrate himself into a much more diverse network of collaborators and funders than in his earlier, more monodisciplinary condensed matter research. Though his own funding came mostly from the NSF's materials research division (supplemented by DI and the Office of Naval Research), Hansma's postdocs and other collaborators in the late 1980s and early 1990s brought funding from the National Institutes of Health, the Lucille P. Markey Foundation, the National Oceanic and Atmospheric Administration, the Deutsche Forschungsgemeinschaft, and elsewhere.

Hansma did not, however, receive corporate funding except from DI. Yet his leadership in the probe microscopy community brought him into frequent contact with corporate probe microscopists, particularly at IBM, in ways that enhanced his research and later spilled over to DI. After all, Hansma's acquaintance with the STM's coinventor, IBM's Heini Rohrer, had led to his being invited to enter into STM in the first place. Later, when Stanford's Quate and two IBM researchers (Gerd Binnig and Christoph Gerber, both members of the original STM team) coinvented the AFM, Hansma was again invited—before news of the AFM was even published—to adopt the new variant. Hansma's articles from the late 1980s frequently thanked—and occasionally were even coauthored with—IBM scientists. In general, Hansma's give-and-take with industry was much more varied than is often acknowledged in scholarly and policy debates about university–industry relations; Hansma himself was no entrepreneur, but his group benefited from (and offered benefits to) industry through many different kinds of exchanges.

DI, too, cultivated a variety of partnerships with other firms that went beyond a simple supplier–customer relationship. High-tech companies, particularly in the semiconductor and data storage industries, were both important potential customers for DI and DI's research peers/rivals. IBM, especially, employed many leaders in fields such as AFM, lateral force microscopy, and magnetic force microscopy where DI was also actively developing products. By playing an active role in the probe microscopy *research* community, and by hiring former UCSB students and postdocs such as Ken Babcock, Jason Cleveland, and Roger Proksch, DI was better able *both* to glean useful information from peer firms and to demonstrate to those firms that it would be a reliable tool supplier.

In a few cases, DI hired engineers from firms such as Intel or Bell Labs. In other cases, DI waited until researchers left those companies for academic jobs, then provided prototypes to their lab groups on, essentially, a beta test basis. More generally, DI successfully made the case that as the dominant supplier of a tool that could be used by the semiconductor industry, what was good for DI would be good for individual semiconductor firms and for the industry as a whole. For instance, in 1995 DI and SEMATECH established a joint project to develop a scanning capacitance microscope that could be sold to SEMATECH's member companies (Digital Instruments , 1996). Similarly, when IBM wanted to have a specialized noncontact AFM for semiconductor metrology, it put money into developing an in-house version known as the SXM but also gave a development contract to DI as a hedge. In the end, IBM went with its own SXM, but DI used IBM's contract to develop an AFM that "allowed the probe to be scanned anywhere on a sample the size of an 8″ semiconductor wafer" (Veeco, 1998).

By the late 1990s, a high-end version of DI's industrial AFM sold for around $700,000. With the ability to command prices like that, DI's profits soared. 1995, for instance, saw "an increase of over 50% in sales over 1994" (Elings, 1996); net sales for the following year were an even $50 million (Veeco, 1998). With expanding profits came growth in personnel; by

1997 it had around 130 full-time employees (Veeco, 1998). That growth led, in turn, to a change in DI's approach to intellectual property. As DI got bigger, it could produce many more innovations and patents than Hansma's group: In the 1990s it was patenting at about three times the rate of Hansma's group.

Nevertheless, Hansma's patents were still basic to DI's technology. As the STM and AFM market expanded, DI's royalties to the University of California grew rapidly as well—into the millions of dollars annually by the mid-1990s. Those heightened stakes led both Elings and the UC Office of Technology Transfer to conclude that the other party was getting too sweet a deal. Elings's relationship with the UC system—already strained because of the circumstances under which he quit his faculty position—deteriorated further as Digital Instruments became significantly more aggressive in its negotiations with the OTT than it had earlier (UCSB Technology Management Program, 2008).

Indeed, at this time Elings became well known in the wider probe microscopy community—not just within the UC system—for his hard-driving approach to intellectual property. Stuart Lindsay of Arizona State, for instance, recalls that the employees at his own start-up company were struck with "terror" at the mere suggestion that Elings would visit to negotiate a patent license and product marketing arrangement with DI (Lindsay, 2003; Mody, 2011: 137–138). The consequences of opposing DI were particularly clear after 1993, when the company opened a lawsuit against Topometrix, one of the few firms that tried to compete with DI across the wide range of probe microscope variants and applications. Significantly, just one of the five patents in the original suit was a Hansma patent assigned to the UC Regents that DI had exclusively licensed; the rest were assigned to DI and coinvented by Elings and other DI employees (*Digital Instruments v. Topometrix*, 1993).

DI's growing profits, IP portfolio, and reputation among probe microscopists also made the company a tempting acquisition target for semiconductor equipment companies hoping to add AFM to their product lines. After an abortive merger with one such company, Zygo, in 1997, DI merged with another semiconductor equipment company, Veeco, in early 1998, reportedly for about $150 million in stock (Fasca, 1998). After a couple of years with the merged company, Elings took his share of that money and "retired" into a new career in philanthropy. Elings's alma maters, Iowa State and MIT, have benefited from multimillion dollar donations (Iowa State University Foundation, 2006; Chadis, 2004). Despite Elings's rollercoaster relationship with the university, UCSB has also received gifts from the Elings family, especially the $12.5 million to build Elings Hall in 2007. It is, of course, not particularly unusual for successful academic entrepreneurs to give money back to the universities with which they were affiliated. Certainly, donations such as Elings and Wells's to UCSB should be included in debates about the pros and cons of faculty members' founding start-up companies. Yet the rocky path to Elings and Wells's gift—which involved periods of intense conflict between Elings and UCSB—is one few university administrators would wish to imitate.

Beyond the university, the Elings family's gifts dot the Santa Barbara area, the most conspicuous being the 230-acre Elings Park, "the largest privately funded public park in America" (Elings Park, 2012). Local museums, health-care facilities, and schools have all also shared in DI's success, for example, in the form of Dos Pueblos High School's (DPHS) Elings Aquatic Center a few miles north of UCSB. Mindful of the lessons of the MSI program, Elings also donated a million dollars for DPHS's Elings Center for Engineering Education to aid the Dos Pueblos Engineering Academy. The Engineering Academy uses a problem-based, learn-by-doing approach that independently recapitulates the pedagogical philosophy of the MSI program (Bascomb, 2011). Again, academic entrepreneurs' philanthropy should be included in any assessment of the value of faculty start-ups. It is important, though, to understand philanthropy such as Elings's in part as an attempt to institutionalize lessons learned in careers that span university and industry. DI gained from Elings's experience in the MSI program; now Elings is using philanthropy to bring insights from DI into universities and even high schools.

THE SANTA BARBARA NANOINSTRUMENTATION CLUSTER IN THE EARLY 21ST CENTURY

Veeco, meanwhile, went on a buying spree after merging with DI, acquiring more than a dozen firms, including DI's closest competitors. Yet Veeco's attempt to consolidate the probe microscopy market led to the creation of new rivals, as veteran DI employees frustrated with Veeco's emphasis on middle management, accountability, and orthodox best practices left to found their own companies (see Casper, Chapter Three in this volume, for a similar dynamic at Hybritech). Several of the firms founded in this exodus, therefore, attempted to recapture aspects of DI's looser culture and, by extension, the culture of the MSI program. The most explicit in this regard has been Asylum Research, formed in 1999 by long-time DI employees and a few Hansma group veterans after a long conspiracy hatched in a former bank vault that had been converted into a pizza parlor. As the double-entendre of the name implies, Asylum's founders saw the firm both as a refuge for those disgruntled with Veeco management and as a place where "crazy"—or at least unorthodox—ideas would receive a fair hearing. Having weathered a potentially crippling, five-year patent infringement suit brought by Veeco in 2003, Asylum is competitive with its parent in many research fields and even some industrial applications. Indeed, Veeco sold off what remained of DI to Bruker in 2010.

If Asylum was an explicit throwback to DI's early years, other DI spin-offs have reconnected more to probe microscopy's academic heritage. In particular, several of these companies have brought DI and Hansma group veterans together with alumni from the Hansma group's closest peer, Calvin Quate's group at Stanford. NanoDevices, for instance, was founded in 1998 by Dennis Adderton from DI and Steve Minne from Quate's group to make specialty AFM cantilevers and other nanoelectromechanical systems. Affinity Biosensors was founded in 2006 by Ken Babcock (a former UCSB postdoc and DI/Veeco executive), John Foster (a former Quate graduate student who had set up a semiconductor foundry down the street from the DI castle in 2001), and Scott Manalis (a former Hansma student as an undergraduate, Quate graduate student, and DI intern, now at the MIT Media Lab). Affinity's main product is Archimedes, a cantilever-based particle sizing instrument that is marketed by Particle Sizing Systems, the same company that bought (and still sells) Elings's and Nicoli's Nicomp line (Livingstone, 2010).

Babcock also sits on the scientific advisory board of Anasys Instruments, another Santa Barbara company with an AFM-based technology. Anasys was founded in 2005 by Craig Prater, a former Hansma graduate student and DI/Veeco executive, and Kevin Kjoller, a long-time DI veteran considered by his colleagues to be one of the most skilled operators of AFMs in the world. Anasys is probably best seen as a DI spin-off, but it might also be lumped with a growing group of start-ups from the Hansma lab and other UCSB physical science groups.

For instance, Hansma's most recent area of research, bone density and fracture measurement, is the basis for Active Life Technologies, a Santa Barbara company founded in 2007 by one of his former graduate students. Similarly, Angela Belcher, a collaborator of Hansma's when she was a graduate student in the UCSB Chemistry Department, cofounded Cambrios in 2002 with Hansma's departmental colleague, Evelyn Hu (now at Harvard). Finally, one of UCSB Physics's Nobel laureates, Alan Heeger, has cofounded five different companies since 1990—though probably inspired less by Elings and Hansma than by Bob Schrieffer (his close friend, fellow laureate, and departmental colleague from both Penn and UCSB), who cofounded Superconductor Technologies, Inc., in 1987 (Heeger, 2006).

Academic start-ups from the UCSB Physics Department are, then, much more common today than they were when Elings founded Santa Barbara Technology in the early 1970s. Several local high-tech clusters are now established enough to facilitate UCSB faculty and students in commercializing their ideas.[4] The largest (perhaps around seventy-five companies) is in computing, networking, and e-commerce; this cluster largely owes its existence to Glen Culler and the ARPANET node founded at UCSB in 1970. About half as large is a cluster in electronics, photonics, and advanced materials, which has drawn on research and students from UCSB's Materials Science, Chemistry, Physics, Electrical Engineering, and other departments. Roughly the same size is a cluster of medical device and biotech firms that formed in the 1960s around old-line medical supply and newer breast implant firms, joined by modern biotech start-ups in the 1990s. Finally, there is a small cluster of companies specializing in environmental technologies.

Then there is the network of firms founded by people associated with Virgil Elings in one way or another. In one sense, these firms should be seen as belonging to a localized industrial cluster similar to the ICT, materials, medical device/biotech, and greentech clusters: Call it the nanoinstrumentation cluster, a grouping that would include a few other companies with connections to UCSB, such as SpectraFluidics, RVM Scientific, and NanoPacific Holdings. As we've seen, this cluster includes some of the oldest high-tech firms founded by UCSB faculty (such as Nicomp), as well as some of the newest.

All of the Santa Barbara high-tech clusters are interconnected to a surprising degree. Many of the IT and advanced materials firms, for instance, specialize in medical or environmental applications. Santa Barbara's nanoinstrumentation firms have been particularly prone to this industrial cross-fertilization. In the very beginning, Santa Barbara Technology and Nicomp attempted to integrate into the medical clusters. More recently, veterans of DI and the MSI program have migrated into firms in the IT (for example, Meta Mesh), materials, and environmental (for example,

Zinc Power Matrix, now ZPower) clusters. DI itself captured the probe microscope market because it continually adapted its products to meet the needs of customers in biomedical and materials research, development, and manufacturing. The DI-Hansma group spin-off firms that utilize probe microscope technology (Asylum, Anasys, Affinity Biosensors, Active Life Technologies, and the like) are strongly oriented to biomedical R&D, even if most of their founders have doctorates in physics.

This cross-sector adaptability is traceable in part to the interdisciplinary pedagogy promulgated in the MSI program and in Paul and Helen Hansma's lab groups. More generally, the interconnections among Santa Barbara's high-tech clusters owe much to the extreme optimism and pessimism that suffused American academic research in the early 1970s. The MSI program and other interdisciplinary experiments of the Vietnam era were initiated partly out of fear of declining research budgets and enrollments and increasingly restive students and citizens. But those experiments were also initiated out of an idealistic view that academic research should benefit civil society (rather than just prop up the national security state or expand fundamental knowledge), even if doing so required novel and contentious new arrangements such as tech transfer offices and professorial start-ups. Obviously, university patent offices and faculty start-ups weren't unknown before the 1970s (see Lécuyer, 2005a, for various examples, mostly associated with Stanford). However, patenting and participation in start-ups was almost absent among physicists at UCSB (and most universities) up to about 1970.

Ultimately, the UCSB Physics Department's increasing entrepreneurship and interdisciplinarity prepared the department well for the federal funding situation at the end of the millennium. On the one hand, federal funding for life sciences accelerated yet again, nearly doubling from 1998 to 2004 (National Science Foundation, 2004), benefiting biomedically oriented academic physicists such as Hansma relative to the rest of their discipline. On the other hand, the creation of the National Nanotechnology Initiative in 2000 mandated that federal research funding across almost two dozen agencies be targeted much more heavily toward interdisciplinary research with clear prospects for translation to the civilian marketplace (McCray, 2005). Neither Elings nor the Hansmas contributed much to the creation of the NNI; as Hansma (2006) says, he is not an institution builder in the same way as colleagues such as Anthony Cheetham (who ran UCSB's Materials Research Lab) or Evelyn Hu (who helped establish UCSB's Nanofabrication Facility). Other probe microscopists did help make the NNI a reality, as did other UCSB researchers (especially Hu), and the NNI's leaders explicitly gestured to probe microscopy as the kind of interdisciplinary, commercialization-ready community that they wanted other nanotech research communities to mimic. Thus, somewhat accidentally, other institution builders at DI were able to use the kind of interdisciplinary, entrepreneurial research that Elings and Hansma had pioneered to draw millions in federal nanotechnology funding to UCSB.

CONCLUSION

Elings's and Hansma's moves toward interdisciplinarity and entrepreneurship were, in many respects, highly idiosyncratic and personal. Hansma's adaptation of the STM and AFM for the life sciences, for instance, was driven initially by hopes of obtaining an appointment at UCSB for his then-wife, Helen (who had a biology degree). Elings's slow drift away from the university was facilitated by his background as a machinist and the dawning realization that he was (in his words) a "mediocre physicist" (UCSB Technology Management Program, 2008). Yet despite these very particular motivations for interdisciplinarity and entrepreneurship, I would suggest that certain aspects of Elings's experiences were typical of early entrepreneurs in academic physics departments and that certain themes from their journey toward entrepreneurship are likely to crop up again as we examine other academic entrepreneurs of the Vietnam era. Two observations are particularly salient from the story just told.

First, Elings is a good example of how the extreme conditions of the early 1970s pushed academic physicists toward a more varied funding stream; toward more applied, interdisciplinary, civilian-oriented projects; and therefore toward the market in one way or another. That move toward the market was sometimes, however, an epiphenomenon of other kinds of crisis response and institutional innovation. The role of the MSI program in this story should especially remind us to pay attention to pedagogical innovation as a possible concomitant, alternative, precursor, or spur to academic entrepreneurship. In particular, we should keep in mind the importance of undergraduate and terminal master's programs in technology transfer out of universities, rather than focusing exclusively on university research conducted by faculty members, postdocs, and PhD students (see also Lapsley and Sumner, Chapter Seven in this volume). Digital Instruments is an especially clear example of a high-tech company where employees with bachelor's and master's degrees (or no degree at all) contributed at least as much as people holding doctorates.

Second, we should keep in mind that "universities" and "firms" can take many different forms, that their boundaries can be extremely porous, that firmlike behavior can be found within universities and university-like behavior within firms, and therefore that university–industry interactions can take an astonishing variety of forms. In the groups surveyed in this chapter we can see master's students learning entrepreneurial skills by working with "clients" both inside and outside the university; faculty members running small lifestyle firms out of their garages; corporate researchers taking sabbaticals at universities and faculty members establishing research units to serve industrial clients; corporate and academic scientists interacting as peers in research communities; PhD students taking temporary jobs at start-ups that bring techniques from the university into the firm but also, when they go back, bring tools from the firm back into the university; start-ups giving equipment to prominent academic groups that boosts those groups' productivity but also serves as advertising for the firm; and so on and so on. Especially when localized high-tech clusters grow up near a university (as with the Santa Barbara nanoinstrumentation cluster), individuals are extremely free to move between academic and industrial organizations, whether for an afternoon or for a few years. In such situations, interactions among personnel who, for the moment, belong to an "academic" or "industrial" organization are likely to be social as much as instrumental. In cases such as the ones surveyed here, ideas about both technology and about the proper management of innovation are often products of the thick, densely inhabited boundaries between academic and industrial spheres rather than of those spheres proper.

NOTES

The author thanks Patrick McCray, Jimmy Schafer, Caleb McDaniel, and Linda and Dan Phillips for helpful suggestions. The research for this chapter was supported by the National Science Foundation through the Center for Nanotechnology in Society at the University of California, Santa Barbara.
    1. According to legend, this effect was discovered by accident by a UCSB student (in some versions, a "janitor" or "maintenance man") doing some housekeeping in a lab (Carter 1992).
    2. The rest of this chapter recapitulates Mody (2011). Readers interested in the sourcing of evidence should look there, particularly Chapters 4, 5, and the first section of 6.

3. The other probe microscope images featured on *Science* covers from 1988 to 1992 correspond to articles by Stuart Lindsay (an important collaborator of Hansma's whose company, Molecular Imaging, later comarketed with DI), June, 1989; Gerd Binnig's IBM group, July, 1989; Charles Lieber's Harvard group, July 1992; and Eric Henderson at Iowa State, September, 1992. Lieber's and Henderson's AFMs were in fact DI NanoScopes, although I have never seen the covers corresponding to their articles included in the "We Have Science Covered" campaign. Lindsay's STM was nominally a prototype of an instrument later marketed by the short-lived Angstrom Technology.

4. This section draws on a database of high-tech firms associated with UCSB compiled by Martin Kenney and his students.

CHAPTER SEVEN

"We Are Both Hosts"
Napa Valley, UC Davis, and the Search for Quality

JAMES LAPSLEY AND DANIEL SUMNER

> Napa Valley's success is synonymous with Davis's success.
>
> —*Andy Hoxsey (2012), Napa grape grower and winery owner*

In the minds of American wine drinkers, the Napa Valley is synonymous with fine wine, an American Burgundy and Bordeaux somehow compressed into a narrow valley about a mile wide and only thirty miles long, stretching from San Pablo Bay and the city of Napa in the south to Calistoga and Mount St. Helena in the north. Here we will use *Napa* to mean both Napa County and the Napa Valley, an American Viticultural Area located within Napa County. Napa's dominance in the image of California wine is confirmed by a variety of statistics reflecting the price premium paid for Napa vineyard land, grapes and wine. Although its approximately 45,000 acres of vineyards account for only 8 percent of California's wine grape acreage, and just 4 percent of the state's wine grape production, Napa vineyards regularly garner over 20 percent of the more than $2 billion dollars of wine grape revenue each year (see Figure 7.1). In the first decade of the twenty-first century, Napa Cabernet Sauvignon has averaged well over $4,000 a ton, more than four times the state average for the variety, and vineyards in the heart of the valley routinely sell for over $200,000 an acre, as compared to $20,000 an acre forty miles away in Lodi. With over 700 wine producers, Napa accounts for approximately 20 percent of California's 3,300 wineries, although responsible for 4 percent of California grape production (Wines and Vines, 2010). Wine grape sales accounted for over 98 percent of all of Napa's $0.5 billion agricultural revenue in 2010 (Napa, 2010). Global retail sales of Napa wines were about $4.4 billion dollars in 2011. Napa wine tourism added an estimated $1 billion (Stonebridge Research Group, 2012).

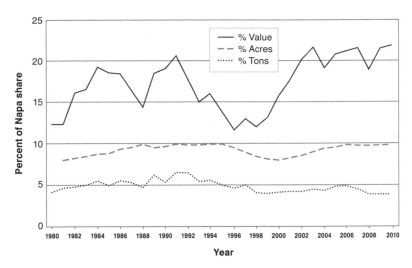

FIGURE 7.1. Napa share of California state total as a percentage.

SOURCE: California Department of Food and Agriculture Grape Crush Report and Grape Acreage Report, Years 1980–2010.

The growth of the wine industry in Napa is a result of many factors, including natural endowments such as soil, climate, and proximity to a major urban center; early and constant promotion by the Napa Valley Vintners' Association; and a competitive commitment to high quality by winery owners that has led to investment in the science of grape growing and winemaking, employment of a trained cadre of progressive winemakers and vineyard managers, and early adoption of innovations. Much of the science, and most of the winemakers and vineyard managers, are the products of the University of California at Davis, located just forty-five miles east of the Napa Valley. This reality was recognized by Robert Mondavi in 2001, when he gifted $25 million to UC Davis to create the Robert Mondavi Institute for Wine and Food Science. Mondavi reminisced that he had gone to Stanford, but that his "bible" had been *Amerine's Principles and Practice of Winemaking*.[1] As he put it, "I learned to make wine only because I followed that book so religiously. I succeeded because of that" (UC Davis News, 2001b). In speaking of his gift he commented: "UC Davis has been a true partner in building the international reputation of the California wine industry . . . We are now leading the way with UC Davis graduates at the helm of many of our finest wineries, Robert Mondavi

Winery included. We are greatly honored to support UC Davis with new facilities that ensure its position as the world's leading educational center for viticulture, enology and food science" (UC Davis News, 2001a).

UC Davis cannot claim credit for the diversity of soils or for the moderate daytime temperatures and cool nights that allow Napa grapes to achieve full varietal intensity and flavor, but application of Davis research both in grape varieties and rootstocks and in canopy and irrigation management has allowed Napa viticulturists to maximize Napa's natural endowments of climate and soil. Nor can Davis take credit for the entrepreneurial and promotional spirit of Napa's vintners and winegrowers, although it is certainly proud that many of the founders of Napa wineries in the 1970s and 1980s traveled to Davis to attend "short courses" on the science of grape and wine production and the economics of small wineries. What Davis can claim is a significant influence on the development of the Napa Valley, and, more broadly, the California wine industry, in four broad areas: research, teaching, viticultural extension, and professional continuing education. This chapter draws on interviews with UC Davis faculty and Napa winemakers, viticulturists, and winery owners to explore the role of the UC Davis in the development of the Napa Valley.

"IT WAS THE WILD WEST": EARLY DAYS AND THE SEARCH FOR QUALITY

Napa has enjoyed a long history of producing quality grapes and wine. *Vitis vinifera*, the European wine grape, was introduced into the Napa Valley before statehood in 1850 and prospered in Napa's Mediterranean climate. By the 1880s, Napa wineries had won major awards at international competitions, and Napa was generally recognized as the producer of California's best dry wines, with well over 100 wineries spread throughout the valley (Lapsley, 1996; Sullivan, 2008; Heintz, 1990). Within a decade, however, an epidemic of phylloxera, an insect that kills *V. vinifera* by feeding on its roots, and the general economic downturn caused by the depression of 1893 combined to reduce dramatically the profitability of grape growing and wine production in Napa and Sonoma. Some vineyard owners went bankrupt; others turned to more profitable crops such as prunes and walnuts.

Prohibition, which ended the commercial production of most wine during the 1920s, actually spurred grape production throughout California, including Napa. Although commercial wine production was curtailed, home wine production was allowed, causing a huge increase in that area. However, the demand was for grapes with thick skins that could survive shipping by rail to the East Coast and for grapes with high levels of tannin and color, such as Petite Sirah and Alicante Bouschet, which could be ameliorated with water to increase volume, rather than for varieties such as Cabernet Sauvignon or Pinot noir. For Napa, the legacy of Prohibition in the 1930s was vineyards grafted to high-yielding but lower-quality varieties and wineries that had not produced wine for over a decade.

Following the repeal of Prohibition in December of 1933, Napa winery owners were surprised and dismayed that commercial demand was for fortified wines, rather than for dry table wines.[2] Fortified wines, such as port and sherry, were manufactured in California's central valley from inexpensive grapes grown in irrigated prolific vineyards yielding eight to ten tons per acre. The main flavors of these fortified wines derived from oxidation, alcohol, and sugar. The varietal characteristics of the grapes used in fortified wine production were relatively unimportant. Located in a cool coastal environment, Napa vineyards produced grapes with higher levels of color, acid, and varietal intensity than did San Joaquin valley vineyards, but Napa's unirrigated vineyards yielded only two to three tons per acre. Without receiving a significant premium for producing higher-quality fruit and wine, Napa growers found it impossible to compete with producers from California's Central Valley. Napa's most famous wineries, such as Beaulieu, Inglenook, Beringer, Larkmead, Martini, and Charles Krug, successfully created niches for themselves by producing and bottling higher-priced table wine in a market dominated by fortified wines. During the decades of the 1940s, 1950s, and 1960s, these wineries produced a disproportionate share of California's higher-quality wines, resulting in an association of Napa with wine quality in the minds of discerning wine drinkers. Yet, despite the commercial success of Napa's quality wine producers, the market for higher-quality wine was still quite small in the United States, and grape and wine production slowly declined in the Napa Valley, reaching its nadir around 1960. Until the wine revival of the late 1960s, most of Napa's grape crop was crushed at the two cooperative wineries in St. Helena and then shipped in bulk to Gallo, which blended the Napa wine with wine from the Central Valley (Lapsley, 1996).

Quality is a difficult concept to define in wine, but because the price differentials received by Napa wineries and growers relative to other regions are predicated on Napa's production of higher-quality grapes and wine, the concept of quality is extremely important to the history of the Napa Valley. In one sense, *quality* means degree of excellence. But as cultural notions of what is "excellent" change over time, so must a notion of quality. A "quality" can also mean an "attribute," and wine quality (excellence) is a result of at least three interactive factors that affect the attributes of grapes and wine. First is environment. Where grapes are grown does affect the attributes of the grapes. Generally speaking, a grape variety such as Cabernet Sauvignon, when grown in a moderately cool area, possesses greater color, acidity, and varietal intensity than does the same variety when grown in a hot area. The Napa Valley is an exceptional place to grow grapes. It is sufficiently warm to ripen grapes fully but cool enough to maintain full varietal flavor. Although there is virtually nothing a grower can do to change the environment, he or she can choose which varieties to plant in a given location as well as deciding on vineyard orientation, trellising systems, and planting density. All of these variables affect grape attributes and resulting wine quality.

If environment is a given, two human factors also effect the attributes of grapes and wine. The first factor is how a grape is grown. Human decisions include crop level (yield), levels of light and air penetration (trellising and canopy management), and amounts and timing of irrigation and fertilization. Each decision can change the attributes of grapes and the resulting wine. The second factor is how the wine is fermented and aged. Processing variables such as fermentation temperature, the amount of contact between skins and juice, whether a wine goes through malolactic fermentation, the level and type of oxygen exposure, and the type of container in which the wine is stored all have a dramatic effect on the attributes of the resulting wine. As the ability to control these variables increased with technology, so did the notion of what constituted "quality" wine. Napa wineries were early adopters of science and technology to improve their wines, but they also discovered that "quality" was a moving target that was defined in the marketplace both by other producers and consumer expectations.

It is a truism that fine wine cannot be made from mediocre grapes. Maynard Amerine and Albert Winkler's pioneering work, "Composition and quality of must and wines of California grapes," published in 1944, identified which varieties would be best for a given climatic region. Wineries focusing on quality table wines thus knew which varieties they should use. Their problem was that available plant material was often diseased or from low-yielding clones, making such plantings uneconomic.[3] In the late 1940s and early 1950s, Dr. Harold Olmo, the Department of Viticulture and Enology's grape breeder, traveled throughout the state and to Europe to acquire improved selections of varieties. In 1952, Olmo, in conjunction with his colleagues, Drs. Curtis Alley, William Hewitt, and Austin Goheen, and in cooperation with the California wine industry, established the California Grape Certification Association, a program designed to eliminate viruses from Olmo's selections by subjecting them to prolonged heat exposure. This program ultimately grew into the present Foundation Plant Services, still located at UC Davis (Alley and Golino, 2000; Walker, 2000). The resulting virus-free selections, when grafted to selected rootstocks, resulted in higher-yielding vines with definite varietal character, thus providing both higher wine quality and improved production economics.

Ultimately, the entire California industry benefited from the UC Davis work on variety improvement, but the Napa Valley had invested early in its relationship with the University of California and enjoyed an advantage of proximity. In 1903 the USDA had established a twenty-acre experimental vineyard in Oakville, adjacent to the ToKalon Vineyard. Research work had ceased at the USDA vineyard with the advent of Prohibition and had remained idle following repeal. Members of the Napa Valley Vintners, an association of Napa Valley winery owners, petitioned Congress to deed the land to the University of California for viticultural research. By 1947, the Vintners had grown tired of waiting for government action and, led by John Daniel Jr. of Inglenook, purchased a twenty-acre vineyard site south of the Oakville Grade road and donated it to the university. Seven years later, in 1954, the USDA Vineyard was made available to the university through an act of Congress. Together the "South Vineyard" and the "Federal Vineyard" comprise forty acres and are collectively referred to as the Department of Viticulture and Enology's Oakville Experimental Vineyard (Wolpert, 2000). Much of Olmo's clonal selection work on Chardonnay was done at the Oakville Station (Kliewer 2012), and Mike Martini, a third-generation Napa Valley winemaker and UC Davis graduate, commented that his father, Louis P. Martini, a 1942 graduate of UC Berkeley, where he had studied winemaking, worked closely with Olmo on variety selections at the Martini vineyard in the Carneros region (Martini, 2012). Napa growers could visit the station, compare selections of the same variety, and, in the early days, acquire bud wood for their own vineyards. Similarly, they could view rootstock trials to compare the effect that different rootstocks had on scion productivity. The presence of a UC station in the heart of the Napa Valley must have encouraged interaction between UC Davis faculty and Napa growers, although the effect can't be quantified. Zach Berkowitz, who received his master's in viticulture from UC Davis and who for many years was director of vineyard operations for Domain Chandon, recalls taking visitors to the station to view vineyard trials in the 1980s and 1990s (Berkowitz, 2012), and Andrew Hoxsey, whose family has grown grapes in the Oakville area since the 1880s, loaned his vineyard workers to the station when it needed viticultural labor. Hoxsey found the relation with the Oakville station to be mutually advantageous. As he put it, "It was a wonderful two-way street. Our crews tried to understand the experiment and always learned something from the trials. There were two plants of most varieties that were available for bud wood, and our Semillon is from the station" (Hoxsey, 2012).

Although these early efforts at quality improvement are now either forgotten or taken for granted by current winemakers and grape growers, the improvements in varietal selection and elimination of plant viruses increased both grape yield and quality. Today Chardonnay and Cabernet Sauvignon are the most widely planted white and red varieties in both Napa and California, but in the 1950s both varieties were rarities. The relative unimportance of varietal grapes is reflected in the lack of information provided in the annual reports of the Napa Agricultural Commissioner prior to 1966. In that year, in response to "the many inquiries," Napa County's Agricultural Commissioner, Albert Delfino, included a listing of Napa's grape acreage by variety in his annual report. In 1966 Napa's vineyards totaled 7,242 bearing acres of red varieties, with Petite Sirah leading the list at 1,650 acres, followed by Zinfandel at 892 acres and Gamay at 819 acres. Cabernet Sauvignon, which forty-five years later in 2010 would account for over 40 percent of Napa's vineyard acreage with over 18,000 bearing acres, was fourth among the red varieties at 682 acres. In 1966, 4,139 acres of Napa's vineyards were devoted to white varieties. French Colombard was the most widely planted white variety at 620 acres, followed by Sauvignon Vert at 453 acres, and such varieties as Burger, Golden Chasselas, and Sauvignon Blanc at just under 300 acres each. A scant 139 acres were planted with Chardonnay, which in 2010, with 6,729 bearing acres, represented over 65 percent of Napa's white variety vineyards (Napa Department of Agriculture, Weights and Measures, 1966 and 2010). Napa's present success is predicated on high-quality Cabernet and Chardonnay, and both became more commercially viable following the Olmo selections and virus eradication.

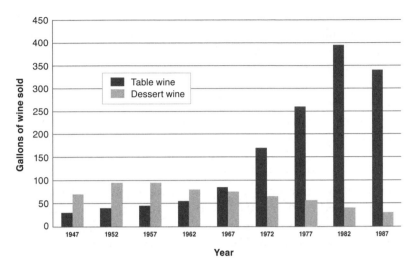

FIGURE 7.2. Thousands of gallons of dessert and table wine sold in the United States in various years.

SOURCE: Lapsley 1996 and other years.

Grapes are the feedstock for wine. In the 1950s professors in enology at UC Davis helped the industry eliminate spoilage and develop a new style of white wine that set the stage for the wine boom of the second half of the 1960s. Quality can be increased both by the addition of positive attributes and the subtraction of negative attributes, and Davis faculty attacked from both directions. Since the repeal of Prohibition, fortified wines had dominated in sales, averaging over two-thirds of U.S. sales by volume (Figure 7.2). These wines were made microbiologically stable by the addition of distilled spirits, and their flavors were the result of controlled oxidation rather than of the grape varieties used in their production. The production of varietal table wines, where the dominant sensory qualities came from the grapes themselves, required a system of production that both emphasized varietal attributes and eliminated characteristics from microbiological spoilage or oxidation. Spoilage was reduced by the use of easily sanitized materials, such as stainless steel, by the measured use of sulfur dioxide, by the use of pure yeast cultures, and later by the introduction of malolactic cultures to conduct the malolactic fermentation, which converts the malic acid in grapes into lactic acid. Varietal characteristics of white grapes were enhanced by cold fermentations through the use of mechanical refrigeration and the resulting varietal aromas were maintained by using inert gas during storage in stainless steel or glass-lined tanks to eliminate oxidation. The marketability of these wines was further enhanced by the use of sterile filtration and bottling, which allowed the wines to be finished with a slight sweetness without risking refermentation in the bottle. Individually, each technology added a bit to the quality equation. Taken in aggregate, these technological breakthroughs allowed the production of a new type of white wine, one that was aromatic of the grape variety (Lapsley, 1996).

The Napa Valley was fertile ground for the processes advocated by the university. Louis P. Martini had studied at UC Berkeley, and Peter Mondavi, the brother of Robert Mondavi, had taken short courses at UC Berkeley following his graduation from Stanford. At Berkeley they were both introduced to the effects of cold fermentation on white wines. On their return from World War II, both were eager to apply their knowledge. In this they were joined by other Napa winemakers. In 1947, Andre Tchelistcheff, the French-trained winemaker at Beaulieu, started an analytical laboratory in St. Helena and organized the Napa Valley Technical Group, a group of Napa winemakers focused on sharing technical information learned from their own experiments (Sullivan, 2008; Lapsley, 1996). The Napa Tech group, which still continues, provided a forum to exchange ideas and applied techniques and certainly was a part of Napa's early adoption of technical information. Ideas that once would have been considered "trade secrets" were openly shared, as winemakers and owners realized that everyone benefited from the enhanced regional reputation associated with higher-quality wines. Clearly, ideas spread and were adopted. By 1949, the California wine industry's trade magazine, *Wines and Vines*, commented that cold fermentation "was almost universal among the leading wineries of the Napa Valley" (Lapsley, 1996: 163), and Napa producers began capturing the majority of awards at the California State Fair.

Peter Mondavi Jr. characterized this early period as "taming the Wild West." In describing his father and other Napa winemakers, he commented that "everyone was learning and self-taught. Europe had generations of tradition, but we were just beginning. We needed an institution like Davis to aggregate information." (P. Mondavi, 2012). The academic side of winemaking was further strengthened in 1950, when the American Society of Enologists was formed, linking Davis faculty with industry members such as Louis P. Martini, who served as president of the society in 1956. Throughout the 1950s and 1960s, Davis faculty interacted regularly with Napa winemakers, sometimes speaking on technical topics at the Napa Tech Group meetings or working on applied technical problems such as malolactic fermentation. Mike Martini remembers that faculty always attended the annual tasting that his father held with the local grape growers, and Dr. Vernon Singleton, who joined the department in 1958, recalled that the faculty sometimes "caught hell" from the larger wineries in the San Joaquin valley for spending so much time in the Napa Valley (Martini, 2012; Singleton, 2012). By the early 1960s, then, winemaking was becoming a science-based profession, the quality Napa producers were investing in education and technology, and a new type of white wine had emerged: one based on varietal characteristics enhanced through processing. All that was missing were consumers.

"THERE'S GOLD IN THEM THAR GRAPES": THE WINE BOOM OF THE 1970S

Sometime in the late 1960s, the world changed for California and Napa producers: American consumers began to consume table wines in increasing quantities. Per capita consumption of table wine doubled in ten years, from 1.2 gallons per adult in 1971 to 2.4 gallons in 1980. Why Americans became interested in wine is unclear, although some part of the explanation is generational and demographic. The first of the baby boomers, that cohort born after the end of WW II, started coming of legal drinking age in 1967, and they adopted wine as an alcoholic beverage at a higher rate than had their parents. For the next eighteen years, approximately 4.5 million baby boomers reached legal drinking age each year, steadily increasing the population base of potential consumers. Total volume consumed is the product of population and per capita rate, and both were rising in the decade of the 1970s. Between 1971 and 1980, total volume of table wine produced in California more than doubled, growing from 109 million gallons in 1971 to 248 million gallons in 1980 (Lapsley, 1996). The wine boom was a sufficient cultural phenomenon that, in its November 27, 1972, edition, *Time* magazine featured Ernest and Julio Gallo on its cover, with an accompanying article entitled "There's Gold in Them Thar Grapes" (Lapsley, 1996).

Increased wine production demanded new vineyards. Approximately 200,000 acres of new vineyards were planted throughout California during the 1970s, more than doubling the 130,000 acres of bearing wine grape acreage that existed at the start of the decade (Garoyan, 1975). Napa vineyards experienced a similar trend, as bearing acres increased from 12,254 in 1970 to 22,456 in 1979, an 83 percent increase (Napa Department of Agriculture, 1970 and 1979). However, this expansion does not tell the entire story. Not only were new vineyards set out, but older vineyards were removed and replaced with what the Aldo Delfino, the Napa agricultural commissioner, described in 1975 as "new, higher quality varietals" (Napa Department of Agriculture, 1975). The trend had begun early. In 1966, the first year that Delfino listed vineyard acreage by variety, he wrote that "grape acreage . . . continues to show a steady climb" and noted that Napa had 11,381 bearing acres of vineyard and 357 acres that were nonbearing. Four years later, in his letter of transmittal in the 1970 annual report, Delfino commented that "wine grape acreage continues to increase substantially in Napa County, as prune orchards are removed and replanted to grapes . . . In 1970, 1200 acres of prunes were removed." He then reported that "1090 acres of vineyards were planted in 1970, 500 of these are new plantings. The remaining 590 acres were replantings of old existing vineyards" (Napa Department of Agriculture, 1966 and 1970). Five years later the trend of replanting old vineyards had accelerated, and Delfino wrote, "Approximately 600 acres of grapes were pulled preparatory to replanting to new, higher yielding, varietals." In that year Napa had 15,725 acres of bearing vineyards but 8,528 acres of nonbearing acres (Napa Department of Agriculture, 1975). Napa growers had seen the future and knew that it would be in grapes. By 1980, wine grapes accounted for 74 percent of all of Napa County's agricultural value, a percentage that would grow to 95 percent by 1990 (Figure 7.3).

The increase in vineyard acreage was paralleled by an increase in the number of Napa wineries. Prior to the emerging interest in table wine, the wine business had been in slow decline in both Napa and the state as a whole, reaching a nadir in Napa in 1960 when Napa counted just twenty-three wineries and California claimed 256. In the decade of the 1960s, the state total continued to decline to 240 wineries by 1970, but Napa increased to thirty-two in 1970. New wineries of the 1960s included Heitz Cellars (1961), started by Joseph Heitz, who had received an MS in enology from Davis; Schramsberg Vineyards (1965); Robert Mondavi Winery (1966); Freemark Abbey and Chappellet (1967); Spring Mountain and Sterling Vineyards (1968); and Chateau Montelena (1969). By the early 1970s, the wine boom was obvious, and during that decade Napa more than tripled its number of wineries. Memorable startups of the early 1970s included Mt. Veeder, Caymus, Diamond Creek, Stag's Leap Wine Cellars (1972), Silver Oak, Joseph Phelps, Cakebread Cellars, and Domaine Chan-

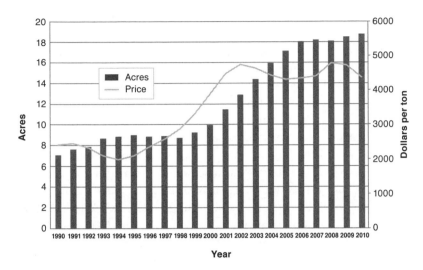

FIGURE 7.3. Napa Cabernet acres and price.

SOURCE: California Department of Food and Agriculture *Grape Crush Report* and *Grape Acreage Report*, 1990–2010.

don (1973), the first foreign-owned investment in the Napa Valley (Sullivan, 2008: 444–445).

For the most part, the new Napa wineries were small operations compared to those in other parts of California. Some of the owners, such as Robert Mondavi of the Robert Mondavi Winery, Charles Carpy of Freemark Abbey, and Justin Meyer of Silver Oak, had long experience with wine production and sales. Some had experience in grape growing. "Chuck" Wagner of Caymus came from a family of Napa grape growers. But most were newcomers who joined the wine business after achieving success and wealth in other businesses. A look at the background of some of the owners of the wineries started in the 1960s and early 1970s reveals a diverse group of individuals. Jack Davies was a Harvard MBA who had worked in the aerospace industry in California prior to buying Schramsberg and producing sparkling wine. Donn Chappellett of Chappellet had founded and run a major food service corporation in Southern California until deciding that growing grapes and making wine in the Napa Valley was a better way to raise a family. James L. Barrett was a successful attorney in Los Angeles before becoming a partner in Chateau Montelena. Michael Robbins, a Southern California real estate investor, had been an investor in the Mayacamas winery and entered the industry as a winery owner when he purchased Spring Mountain vineyards, a historic estate above St. Helena. Peter Newton and Michael Stone were partners in Sterling Paper, a San Francisco paper products company, invested in Napa valley vineyards, and then founded Sterling Vineyards. Al Brounstein owned a pharmaceutical wholesaling firm in Southern California before purchasing vineyard land south of Calistoga and starting Diamond Creek. Warren Winiarski had studied and taught political theory at the University of Chicago until moving to California to become a winemaker. He worked at Souverain and the Robert Mondavi winery prior to founding Stag's Leap winery. Jack Cakebread was a semiprofessional photographer who was working at the family auto repair business in Oakland before purchasing his vineyard in Rutherford and founding Cakebread Cellars. Although different in background and wine experience, all shared a passion for wine and a desire to make the best wine possible (Sullivan, 2008).

Individual motives are difficult to determine, but groups can share traits. Dick Maher, former CEO of Beringer and Christian Brothers who has worked in the Napa Valley for forty years, believes that for most owners of small wineries in the Napa Valley the business is "a hobby, but a competitive hobby" (Maher, 2012). Maher described owners who had excelled in other businesses before starting wineries and who were determined to succeed in creating high-quality wine, with income being a secondary goal. His description aligns with a 1997 study by Morton and Podolny of 184 California winery owners, which divides owners into "profit maximizers" and "utility maximizers" (Morton and Podolny, 2002). Profit maximizers resemble traditional business owners, while utility maximizers are in the winery business primarily for nonmonetary reasons. Thus Morton and Podolny report that

> . . . 78% of owners would be "somewhat" or "very" unlikely to sell their winery if they could get a higher return in the stock market. Almost 40% of respondents would lose over $10,000 to improve the quality of their wines. Although almost all respondents aim to cover costs and earn some profit, less than half have a specific target rate of return in mind. (Morton and Polodny, 2002).

It would seem that most of the individuals starting wineries in the Napa Valley in the late 1960s and early 1970s were "utility maximizers" and, although not immune to financial constraints, were driven to excel in quality.

It was "utility maximizers" such as these who led to Napa's stunning breakthrough in 1976 when Napa wines "beat" the French at an unofficial tasting in Paris. Steven Spurrier, an English owner of a wine shop in Paris,

TABLE 7.1. The Paris tasting.

White	Red
1. Chateau Montelena,* 1973	1. Stag's Leap Wine Cellars,* 1973
2. Domaine Roulot, 1973	2. Chateau Mouton Rothschild, 1970
3. Chalone Vineyard, 1974	3. Chateau Haut-Brion, 1970
4. Spring Mountain Vineyards,* 1973	4. Chateau Montrose, 1970
5. Joseph Druhin, 1973	5. Ridge Vineyards, 1971
6. Freemark Abbey,* 1972	6. Chateau Leoville-Las-Cases, 1971
7. Ramonet-Prudhon, 1973	7. Mayacamas Vineyards,* 1971
8. Domaine Leflaive, 1972	8. Clos du Val,* 1972
9. Veedercrest Vineyards,* 1972	9. Heitz Cellars,* 1970
10. David Bruce, 1973	10. Freemark Abbey,* 1969

* Indicates a Napa wine.

used the occasion of America's bicentennial to advertise his business by staging a blind tasting between California and French wines of the same type or variety. Spurrier had heard that California wines were improving in quality, and he procured six California Chardonnays and six California Cabernet Sauvignons, putting them up against France's best wines and using respected French judges. To the chagrin of the French, the California wines came out on top. To the joy of Napa producers, the top wines were both from Napa: a 1973 Chateau Montelena Chardonnay, which was just the fourth vintage from that winery, and a 1973 Stag's Leap Wine Cellars Cabernet, from a winery that had opened its doors only a year before. The results, based on Spurrier's rankings (which Ashenfelter and Quandt, n.d., suggest are broadly sound statistically), are listed in Table 7.1, with Napa wines marked by an asterisk. It is worth noting that of the six California Chardonnays, four were from the Napa Valley, as were five of the six California Cabernets. Clearly, even in the mid-1970s, Napa was perceived as the quality leader in California.

Spurred by the "Judgment of Paris" and increasing consumer interest in wine, the California wine boom continued. By 1980, California totaled 508 wineries, ninety-five of which were in Napa County. The decade of the 1980s saw accelerating growth, with the state's total growing to 807 wineries and Napa's to 176 by 1990 (*Wines and Vines*, 1980 and 1990). Thus, in a twenty-year period from 1970 to 1990, the number of wineries in Napa increased fivefold. This expansion created a need both for trained enologists and viticulturists to operate the new facilities and for continuing education for owners and would-be winemakers, who needed to gain an understanding of the winemaking process and business.

Dan Duckhorn, who had come to the Napa Valley in 1968 with an MBA from UC Berkeley, worked for various wine companies for several years, and then started Duckhorn in 1976, commented that when he moved to the Napa Valley there were only "two sources of information: UC Davis and Gallo" (Duckhorn, 2012). Of the two, UC Davis was by far the most approachable, and winery owners traveled both to Davis in search of talent and information and to the Oakville Station or the Farm Advisor office in Napa for more local advice.

The first choice for an investor without technical knowledge who wished to start a winery and vineyard was to hire an experienced winemaker or viticulturist—but in the early days of California's wine boom, such individuals were rare. The second choice was to hire a recent graduate from UC Davis, and Davis graduated twenty to forty students each year, fewer in the early years. Some, like Craig Williams (BS, UCD 1976), who became the winemaker at Joseph Phelps in 1983, were undergraduates who had decided on fermentation science as a major. Others, such as Cathy Corison (MS, UCD 1975), discovered wine after graduation. Armed with a BS in biology from Pomona College, Corison came to Davis to pursue an MS degree and became the winemaker for Chappellet Vineyards, where she worked for ten years before starting her own winery in 1987. Others were scions of already established wineries. Michael Martini, the third generation of winemakers in his family, graduated from Davis with a BS in fermentation science in 1977. Down the road from the Martini winery, Bruce Cakebread, whose parents Jack and Dolores Cakebread had established Cakebread Cellars in 1973, graduated from Davis with a BS in fermentation science a year after Martini in 1978.

A third group was comprised of individuals who had gravitated to wine or grape growing, showed strong promise, and were encouraged by their employers to pursue a degree at Davis while continuing to work for the firm. This was the case for Zach Berkowitz, who had graduated from UCLA with a degree in sociology and arrived in the Napa valley in 1973. He began working for Domaine Chandon in 1974 while completing an AA degree in viticulture at the Napa Valley Community College. Berkowitz became the Domaine Chandon vineyard manager in 1976, and his French employers offered to pay for him to complete a second undergraduate degree, encouraging him to go to Davis because, as Berkowitz put it, "Davis was the gold standard." Berkowitz received his BS in plant science with an emphasis in viticulture in 1980 (Berkowitz, 2012). Similarly, Bill Dyer had graduated with an undergraduate degree in philosophy from UCSC, became intrigued with wine, and had been hired by Ric Forman (MS, UCD 1967) to be cellar foreman at Sterling in 1977. Following Forman's departure to establish Newton Vineyards, Sterling encouraged and funded Dyer's master's in fermentation science at Davis. Following the completion of his degree in 1985 he became winemaker, and four years later he was named vice president for wine production (Dyer and Dyer, 2012). Although individual stories varied, a degree from UC Davis was a guarantee to a prospective employer that the individual was both well trained and capable of solving problems.

Not everyone interested in commercial winemaking and grape production had sympathetic employers or the time to commit to a formal education at UC Davis. For these individuals, UC Davis University Extension, the self-supporting continuing education arm of the Davis campus, offered short courses in wine and grape production. The Department of Viticulture and Enology had throughout the 1950s and 1960s offered occasional "short courses" in wine production and wine analysis intended as updates for industry members. Beginning in 1978, the Department of Viticulture and Enology partnered with UC Davis University Extension to offer courses aimed both for commercial producers and for individuals seeking to enter the wine industry. In the seven years between 1978 and 1985, approximately twenty to thirty courses were offered each year, totaling over 5,500 enrollments for the period (unpublished information derived from UC Davis enrollment records).

Some courses, such as Economics of Small Wineries, Fundamentals of Table Winemaking, Wine Microbiology, Wine Filtration, or Wine Grape Production, were multiday programs lasting three to five days. Others, such as Grape Disease Management, Legal Aspects of Establishing a Winery, Spectrophotometers for Wine Analysis, Introduction to Wine Chemistry, Trends in Winery Equipment, or Cooperage Care and Construction, were one-day classes. Most were repeated and updated each year. For individuals interested in investing in a winery but not necessarily in being the actual winemaker, the introductory technical courses provided an overview of winemaking processes while the Economics of Small Wineries course, which was offered four times, reviewed costs of production and sales as well as capital requirements for equipment and inventory. For winemakers and vineyard owners, courses such as Wine Filtration,

Canopy Management, or Phenolics in Wine and Grapes provided an update on most recent research coupled with application. Enrollments came from throughout California and beyond, but an analysis of enrollments shows that participation from Napa wineries and vineyards was especially high, coming to over 18 percent of all enrollments during the period, approximately equal to Napa's share of California wineries in 1980.

Napa winemakers and growers not interested in making the one-hour drive to Davis could also turn for advice closer to home by visiting their viticulture farm advisor or dropping by the Oakville Experiment Station. The University of California's Cooperative Extension service (UCCE) traces back to the federal Smith-Lever Act of 1914, which provided funding to hire university-trained individuals distributed geographically, often referred to as county farm advisors, to extend science-based information to farmers. Farm advisors were allocated based on the crops that were grown in a particular county, and in 1952 Jim Lider became Napa's first farm advisor for viticulture. Lider had grown up on a farm in Esparto, north of Davis, and graduated with a BS from Davis. He was later to complete a master's in viticulture from Davis in 1965. His brother, Lloyd Lider, received a PhD in plant sciences from Davis and became a professor of viticulture in the department in 1953, so Jim Lider was well connected to the department. As a farm advisor, Lider worked individually with Napa's vineyard owners and managers to decrease costs and to increase production through the planting of virus-free variety selections. In 1961 he advised Nathan Fay to plant Cabernet Sauvignon on Fay's property in the Stag's Leap district, which had been considered too cool for Cabernet. The advice had historic repercussions. Warren Winiarski purchased the property adjacent to the Fay Vineyard and planted Cabernet because of the quality of the Cabernet from the Fay vineyard (Napa Valley Wine Library Association, 2011a,b). Without Lider's advice, Winiarski might never have produced the Cabernet that took first place in Paris. And, in another connection to the University of California, the Cabernet budwood came from Martha's Vineyard in Oakville, which had in turn accessed budwood from the Oakville Station (Napa Valley Wine Library Association, 2008).

The Oakville Station, comprised of two twenty-acre blocks, is in the middle of the valley and was easily accessible to Napa grape growers. For many years, the station was run by Keith Bowers, who had received his BS from Davis in viticulture following WW II and who became the manager of the Oakville Station in 1949 (*St. Helena Star*, 2008). Bowers helped Tom and Martha May plant Cabernet Sauvignon in the thirty-five-acre parcel adjacent to the South Vineyard, a vineyard now known as "Martha's Vineyard" and made famous by Joe Heitz in 1966 (Napa Wine Library Association, 2008). It was the 1970 vintage from Martha's Vineyard that was tasted in the Paris judging. Bowers completed his master's in viticulture in 1965 and became the Napa County farm advisor in viticulture in 1972, when Lider retired, a position he maintained until his own retirement in 1987. As a farm advisor, Bowers's main interaction was with individuals, but in the mid-1970s he also helped create a viticultural version of the Napa Valley Technical Group. Phil Freese (PhD, UCD 1973), who was directing CalPlan, a major vineyard management firm in the Napa Valley and who in 1982 became the Robert Mondavi Winery's vice president of winegrowing, remembers a lunchtime meeting at Bowers's office in Napa with Bob Steinhauer of Beringer and Will Nord of Domaine Chandon. By the end of lunch they had made a collective decision that a once-a-month lunch meeting for vineyard managers would help disseminate UC research as well as pass on information derived from local vineyards. They decided that the meetings would last only an hour and would be intended for individuals with at least a BS in plant science or viticulture (Freese, 2012). Bowers organized the meetings, bringing researchers from UC Davis to meet with Napa Vineyard managers. Thus began the Napa Valley Vineyard Technical Group, which still meets once a month on Mondays. In 1979 the vineyard manager from Joseph Phelps, Ed Weber, joined the group, fresh from his BS from Davis. Ed would complete his MS in viticulture from Davis in 1982 and become the new Napa farm advisor in 1988, following Bowers's retirement.

During the 1980s, the vineyard technical group had a great deal to discuss. In 1980, Dr. Mark Kliewer, a professor of viticulture at Davis, had begun a major vineyard trial at the Oakville Station. The five-acre Cabernet Sauvignon trial was designed to explore the major management factors effecting canopy growth. It included two trellising systems to determine the effect of light penetration, three different row spacings to determine the effect of vine density in vineyards, and five pruning levels to determine the effect of crop load. It was a major experiment that continued until Kliewer's retirement in 1994. One of the major findings was the importance of filtered light on grape clusters. Most growers at the time were using a trellis system often referred to as "the California sprawl" that buried the grape clusters in foliage. The trial revealed that moderate light exposure improved cluster color, led to earlier ripening, lowered potassium levels in the berries (and thus in the resulting wine), lowered the grape pH, reduced vegetative aromas in Cabernet, improved the tannin levels, and largely eliminated Botrytis rot. As Kliewer put it, the trial "opened some eyes" (Kliewer, 2012). It also opened some winery checkbooks.

In 1982, shortly after joining the Robert Mondavi Winery, Freese organized the North Coast Viticultural Research Group (NCVRG), for the purpose of funding university research on the production of premium grapes for wine or, as it is now referred to, "winegrowing." The member wineries included Christian Brothers, Sterling, Beringer, Domaine Chandon, Joseph Phelps, and Robert Mondavi from Napa and Jordan and Simi from neighboring Sonoma County.[4] The wineries agreed to contribute funds each year to support university researchers, to make their vineyards available as research sites, and to produce experimental wines from the trials. The research would ultimately be published in scientific journals, but the member wineries followed the research as it was conducted and gained site-specific information about their own vineyards. The focus of the research was on how viticultural factors affected grape attributes and the resulting wine.

The NCVRG funded several Davis faculty members. Kliewer's research became focused on light penetration and canopy management. With his graduate student, Nick Dookozlian, Kliewer examined the effect of such viticultural practices as shoot thinning, pruning levels, leaf removal, and timing of hedging, all with the purpose of understanding how changes to the canopy microclimate effected the grapes and wine. Dookozlian completed his PhD in 1990 and joined the department as an extension viticulturist (Dookozlian, 2009).

The NCVRG also funded Dr. Mark Matthews's experiments on water management in vineyards, which ultimately showed that grape composition and quality were enhanced by limiting the amount of water to the vines, a practice which is now referred to as "deficit irrigation." The experiments on canopy management and irrigation helped Napa viticulturists transition from being grape growers to becoming winegrowers by showing how human decisions affected the qualities of the resulting wine. The research also resulted in practical tools such as pressure bombs that could be used in the vineyard to measure leaf water potential and point quadrants that quantified levels of light penetration into the canopy. Ultimately the research created metrics for predicting wine quality in the vineyard.

The decade of the 1980s was a period of continued growth for the Napa Valley. In January of 1981, the Napa Valley's importance as a grape growing region was recognized when it became the first California region to become an American Viticultural Area, a designation created by the federal government in response to the growing economic importance of grape location in the marketing of wine. During the decade, eighty-one new wineries were established, bringing the total to 176, which represented over 20 percent of California's 807 wineries (*Wines and Vines*, 1990). University research was unraveling the interaction between grape environment and resulting wine quality. University Extension and Cooperative Extension were disseminating the research findings and teaching how tools could be used and metrics applied in the vineyard. The enologists and viticulturists, many of whom had been educated at Davis, were taking the new ideas and tools and putting them into practice in Napa's vineyards and wineries. No one suspected that lurking in the soil was an insect that would ultimately cause the replanting of most of Napa's vineyards within a decade.

"RESET": THE AXRI CRISIS AND THE TRIUMPH OF CABERNET SAUVIGNON

In 1983, a Napa grower noticed that some of his grapevines were declining. The cause wasn't obvious. After examining the roots, university viticulturists were both surprised and dismayed to discover that phylloxera was feeding on the rootstock, a variety called "AxR1" (Phylloxera Task Force, 1988). AxR1 had been recommended by the university and had been widely planted throughout California during the vineyard boom of the 1970s. It was estimated that approximately 70 percent of Napa's vineyards were planted with AxR1. What had happened, and how had the university failed California growers?

Phylloxera is an insect native to the eastern United States, where it feeds on the roots of native grape species, which, through coevolution with phylloxera, have developed varying degrees of resistance to the insect. During the nineteenth century, amateur botanists in Europe moved exotic plant species to Europe, including American grape vines. Attached to the roots of some of the specimens was phylloxera, which promptly spread to the European wine grape, *Vitis vinifera*, in the 1860s in France. Not having any natural resistance to phylloxera, *vinifera* was killed by the insect. French scientists responded to the crisis in a variety of ways, but the solution that was finally chosen was to graft a *vinifera* scion to a resistant rootstock, thus allowing wine production to continue. Some American species of *Vitis* are more resistant than others; some don't root or graft to vinifera easily; and others, when grafted, impart varying degrees of vigor and yield in the scion. For this reason, French, and later American, scientists conducted breeding and rootstock trials to discover the best rootstocks for general use.

One way to improve a non-*vinifera* species' ability to graft with *vinifera* is to create an interspecies hybrid. In 1879, the French viticulturist, Victor Ganzin, crossed the *vinifera* variety, Aramon, with a selection of the American species, *Vitis rupesteris*. Nine seedlings were produced, numbered one through nine, and three were for a time recommended by French nurseries, although ultimately all were rejected by French viticulturists because of insufficient resistance to phylloxera. The experience in California was somewhat different. AxR1 was included in a 1904 USDA rootstock trial and again in a UC trial begun in 1911. In 1929, UC Professor Harry Jacob began a massive rootstock trial conducted in seventeen locations throughout California. In none of the trials or locations did AxR1 succumb to phylloxera. Jacob's trial was completed more than twenty years later by Professor Lloyd Lider, who published his finding in the 1958 *Hilgardia* article "Phylloxera-resistant grape rootstocks for the coastal valleys of California." Based on trunk growth and grape yield, Lider concluded that AxR1 was the best general choice for coastal vineyards. In several of the locations, phylloxera was observed on AxR1 roots, but the plant itself was fine, indicating some degree of resistance. In his article, Lider alluded to the failure of AxR1 in France and described AxR1's resistance only as "moderate." He concluded that AxR1 should be used in vineyards with deep soils and irrigation, where environmental stress was low (Wolpert et al., 1994).

In retrospect, any rootstock with *vinifera* genetics is suspect, but the fact that AxR1 was part *vinifera* made the rootstock easy to propagate and graft. It quickly became the favorite rootstock for nurseries, which were called on to produce tens of millions of grafted plants during the planting boom of the 1970s. In describing the benefits of AxR1, Freese commented that "it was hard to kill, grew well, gave good yields and made life simple. With AxR we didn't have to focus on viticulture" (Freese, 2012). Tim Mondavi reinforced the economic advantage of AxR1, succinctly stating, "The grape industry liked the yield" (T. Mondavi, 2012). But in 1983, AxR1's advantages paled against its failure to withstand phylloxera. UC Davis entomologist Jeffrey Granett examined the phylloxera discovered in Napa and by 1985 had determined that a new biotype of phylloxera, which he named "type B," had evolved to exploit the AxR1 rootstocks. It was estimated that 40,000 acres of vineyards in Napa and Sonoma were planted to AxR1 and would eventually need to be replaced (Wolpert et al., 1994). Replanting in Napa began in the late 1980s and was generally concluded by the mid-1990s.

In 1991, Mike Fisher's estimate of the cost solely for Napa's replanting put the amount at $250 million (Fisher, 1991). Over a decade later, wine writer Rod Smith said that most estimates put the total cost, including lost sales, at "around $3 billion" (Smith, 2007). More recently, in 2011 *The Economist* magazine, in an article titled "Gripe Grapes," placed the "damage" at $6 billion (*Economist*, 2011). In economic terms the "loss" associated with this event would need to assess replanting costs that occurred sooner than would have been necessary without phylloxera as well as including costs associated with lower yields during the first years of production. However, against these costs one must balance higher grape prices due to reduced output and include the value of cultural improvements that were adopted earlier than would have been the case had replanting not been necessary. A true accounting, which has not been done, would measure the grower's net returns rather than gross costs. Whatever the true cost, the replanting was expensive. Although the result of a mutation, many growers viewed the phylloxera epidemic as a human-made disaster that had been caused by the UC Davis recommendation of the rootstock.

Yet, today, most winery owners and viticulturists point to the AxR1 rootstock failure as the key event that catapulted Napa wine into the same heights as Burgundy and Bordeaux. Dan Duckhorn referred to AxR1 as "a blessing in disguise" (Duckhorn, 2012), and the French international consultant Michel Rolland stated, "If phylloxera hadn't happened, Napa Valley couldn't be where it is today" (Franson, 2008). Although an economic disaster at the time, the phylloxera epidemic forced a major replanting of the Napa Valley much sooner than would have normally occurred. Most vineyards have an economic life of thirty years, and so vineyards established in the 1970s would not normally have been replaced until the first decade of the twenty-first century. The forced replanting allowed growers and wineries to incorporate the new ideas about canopy management, vine density, and irrigation when they set out their new vineyards. New rootstocks were matched to soil types, and new clonal selections became available (Martini, 2012). Berkowitz (2012) described "the whole valley as a series of experiments" and Tim Mondavi (2012) commented that the "replanting was done with a focus on diversity and geography. It was an epidemic, and we all shared information." Phil Freese (2012) referred to the phylloxera replanting as "a reset, a synchronizing event" that forced Napa growers and wineries to reach beyond California for answers and to broaden their worldview of fine wine. Vineyards replanted to new trellis systems and densities using controlled irrigation of virus-free clonal selections resulted in wines that ripened more fully, allowing for greater fruit and wine intensity.

Replanting also allowed Napa wineries and vineyard owners to focus more on the production of red wine. The wine boom of the 1970s had been predominantly a white wine boom that had caused vineyard owners to plant in-demand white varieties in areas of the valley that were too hot for high-quality white wine production. Cathy Corison (2012), who came to the Napa Valley in 1978, recalls that growers were "trying to grow Cabernet in Carneros and Riesling in Calistoga." Andy Hoxsey (2012) "looked at the crisis as an opportunity." In the 1970s, his family's vineyards, located near Oakville in the heart of the valley, were 75 percent white varieties. Today those same vineyards are planted to Cabernet Sauvignon. (The replanting of the Napa Valley to Cabernet is graphically depicted in Figure 7.3.) Since 1990, starting from a base of just over 7,000 acres, Napa has added almost 12,000 additional acres of Cabernet. Conversely, Chardonnay, which counted almost 8,000 acres in 1990, has declined by 1,000 acres over the same time period (California Department of Food and Agriculture, *Grape Acreage Report*, 1990 and 2010).

The decision to replant to Cabernet was driven by grape prices, which were in turn driven by consumer demand. In 1990, the average prices of Napa Cabernet and Chardonnay were almost equal: Chardonnay averaged $2,267 a ton, 94 percent of the average price of Cabernet. Twenty years later, the average price per ton of Chardonnay had remained essentially static at $2,170 but was now less than 50 percent of the average price per ton of Cabernet, which had risen to $4,731. During the 1990s, America experienced a second wine boom, but this time it was focused on red wine. Between 1990 and 2000, per capita consumption of white wine remained static, but per capita consumption of red wine tripled.[5] The white wine boom of the 1970s had been made possible by winemaking technology that allowed the production of fruity and flavorful white wines. White winemaking processes such as barrel fermentation, the use of malolactic bacteria to induce a buttery flavor to the wine, and lees stirring, which added a rich mouth feel to white wine, imparted flavors separate from the fruit itself. These processes could be used on grapes from any location, thus reducing the importance of place and lowering the price premium that Napa growers normally received.

Unlike Chardonnay, which gains significant flavor from processing choices external to the grape, Cabernet derives most of its flavor from the grape variety, which in turn is influenced not simply by where the grape is grown, but by how the grape is grown. Napa is an excellent location for Cabernet production, and in the decade of the 1980s Napa growers had begun to learn how to maximize the benefits from those grape qualities. The American demand for high-quality red wine that emerged in the 1990s coincided with the need to replant Napa's vineyards. With few exceptions, the most expensive wines throughout the world are red wines. High wine prices create high grape prices, which in turn encourage growers to spend more dollars on viticultural practices to enhance quality. In the short term, phylloxera was an economic disaster for growers and wineries, but it cleared the way for a dramatic improvement in Napa red wine. As Michel Rolland put it: "It is the best sad story. Now Napa has some of the best vineyards in the world" (Franson, 2008).

From 1990 to the present, the Napa Valley has focused on red wine production, primarily Cabernet Sauvignon. In 1990, in the middle of Napa's replanting, Cabernet Sauvignon sales totaled just over $52 million, approximately 25 percent of Napa's total value of $210 million. Twenty years later, in 2010, Cabernet Sauvignon sales totaled over $243 million, representing 55 percent of the value of Napa's total grape revenue, which in turn accounted for over 98 percent of Napa's farm income (California Department of Food and Agriculture and Napa Agricultural Commissioner, various years). (See Figure 7.4.) In 2010, Napa counted 733 wineries, an increase of 400 percent in twenty years. If phylloxera was a disaster for some individual firms, Rolland was correct in describing it as "the best sad story" for the Napa Valley as a whole.

"WE ARE BOTH HOSTS": NAPA AND UC DAVIS

John Williams, a transplanted New Yorker who received his MS from Davis in 1977, founded Frog's Leap Winery in 1981. Williams is known for taking a holistic view and, when asked to characterize the relationship between UC Davis and the Napa Valley wine industry, replied: "It is a symbiotic relationship, we are both hosts" (Williams, 2012). Davis supplies ideas and well-educated graduates to the industry, and the industry

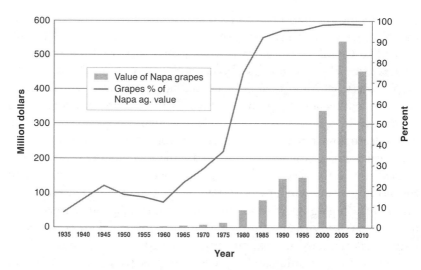

FIGURE 7.4. Value of Napa grapes and grape value as a percentage of total Napa agricultural value.

SOURCE: Napa Department of Agriculture, Weights and Measures. 1940–2010. *Agricultural Crop Report*. Napa.

raises questions and sometimes funds the research necessary to answer the questions. For Williams, grape growing and winemaking cannot be static. Rather, they incorporate constant improvements that come from critical thinking. It is the role of the university not just to train people to become competent technicians—and, after all, when stripped of its romance, wine-making is really a branch of food processing—but to be critical thinkers. As Williams (2012) asked, somewhat rhetorically, "Can you think of a great winemaking region that doesn't have a university associated with it?"

The importance of Davis to the Napa Valley is reflected in the high percentage of Davis graduates working in the Napa Valley as winemak-ers. A 2012 unpublished review of 395 Napa winery websites conducted by the authors showed 231 wineries listing their winemaker by name and education. Of the 231, 180 claimed their winemaker had attended Davis.[6] The next greatest numbers were fourteen from the University of Bordeaux and nine from CSU Fresno. Clearly, UC Davis graduates dominate wine production in the Napa Valley and have for at least a generation. As Bill Dyer put it, "Today, both the Old Guard and the Young Guard are from Davis" (Dyer and Dyer, 2012). These trained and creative graduates are one of the most important elements in the interaction between Davis and the Napa Valley. Although the number of wineries has grown dramatically in California, reaching well over 3,000 by 2010, the number of department faculty has remained static for two decades. It is impossible for faculty to visit every winery in California, and Davis research, although presented at academic meetings and industry short courses, is often disseminated through personal connections with former students and by recent graduates as they enter the wine industry.

An example of the interaction between industry, faculty, and students can be seen in the development and dissemination of an assay for tannin that is now known as the Adams-Harbertson assay, named after Dr. Doug Adams of the department and his former graduate student, and now professor, Dr. James Harbertson. In 1995 Adams, a biochemist who studies grape ripening, met with the North Coast Viticultural Research Group over lunch to discuss possible research topics. Toward the end of the meeting, one of the group commented that what viticulturists needed was an easy, quick and accurate assay for tannins. Tannins are compounds that bind with proteins, such as human saliva, thus imparting astringency to wines. They are part of a broader group of compounds, phenols, which also include anthocyanins, the pigments responsible for color in wines. Adams (2012) recalled an article that had used a ninety-six-well plate that bound tannin to the plastic, allowing rapid determination of tannin.[7] By chance, a UC Davis undergraduate with a joint major in biochemistry and art, Jim Harbertson, had recently taken VEN003, the introductory class on wine and winemaking, and was interested in working on a project on grapes. Adams had Harbertson attempt to use the procedure described in the article to measure grape tannin. It didn't work, but it was the start of an eight-year collaboration between the two that culminated in 2003 when Harbertson submitted his doctoral dissertation, "The Measurement of Tannins and Polymeric Pigments During Grape Ripening and Winemaking."

During their eight years of research together, Adams and Harbertson developed an assay that measured total phenols, anthocyanins (pigments), tannin, and polymeric pigments (anthocyanins bound to tannins). For grape growers, such measurements allow objective comparisons between vineyards and varieties. For winemakers, the assay can be used to know how much tannin and color is available for extraction into wine, as well as determining when enough has been extracted for a given wine style. Most of the graduate and undergraduate students in the department were aware of the research, if only because Adams tested commercial wine samples and then asked students to taste the samples to correlate measurements with perceived astringency. As students entered the industry, some wanted to run the assay in an industrial setting in order to make production decisions. They contacted Adams, who made the assay available on his lab website, and in the mid-2000s Adams participated in panels with commercial winemakers to discuss how the assay is run and how commercial winemakers use it to make decisions about particular lots of grapes and wines. One particular example was Theresa Heredia, a doctoral student agricultural chemistry at Davis, who was a teaching assistant with Harbertson and thus familiar with his research. When Heredia was hired as a research chemist at Joseph Phelps in 2001, she began using the Adams-Harbertson assay at Phelps. Other Napa wineries such as Rubicon and Stag's Leap were also early adopters of the assay (personal communication with James Harbertson). Dr. Steve Price, a biochemist who taught viticulture at Oregon State University and who is now a private consultant, credits the Adams-Harbertson assay for "greatly broadening the range of people using tannin as a basis for making enological decisions," although he finds the assay complex (personal communication with Steve Price).

The assay is an involved wet-chemical procedure, and operator precision is important in producing reliable results. Dr. Roger Boulton of the department has been working for a number of years to measure wine and grape phenolics through the use of a spectrophotometer to measure absorbance at visible and ultraviolet (UV) wavelengths. The advantages of such a procedure are speed and the elimination of wet chemicals. The problem is to correlate absorbance at specific frequencies with precise measurements of phenolic groups. Boulton's graduate student, Kirsten Skogerson, used the Adams-Harbertson assay to measure classes of phenolic compounds in commercial wines and correlated these with absorbance in the wines, ultimately creating a predictive model that worked well for predicting tannin, total phenols, and anthocyanin. Skogerson completed her MS in 2006 and published her findings in the *American Journal of Enology and Viticulture* in 2007. Recently, Scott McLeod (2012), the former winemaker at Rubicon, and his partner Giovanni Colantuoni have commercialized the technology with the development of their company, Wine X Ray. They create unique databases for wineries by analyzing wine and grape samples from a winery and correlating these with visible spectrum and UV readings for the same wines. This then allows wineries to take their own spectrophotometer readings, which are then sent to Wine X Ray, who compares them to past samples and generates predictive values for the wines and grape samples.

The business is in its infancy but promises to allow wineries to receive phenolic values for their wines rapidly enough to make real-time winemaking and viticultural decisions without performing their own wet chemistry and becoming expert in the assay. Ultimately this will be another tool for the winemaker to use in crafting wine.

The Adams-Harbertson assay is just one example of a measurement tool that was developed or adapted by UC faculty as a research instrument and then transitioned into the wine industry and used by grape growers and winemakers. Other examples include pressure bombs, which determine vine water status, and point quadrants, which help measure canopy density. All have allowed grape growers and winemakers to improve their wines. Dawnine Dyer (Dyer and Dyer, 2012), who for many years was the winemaker for Domaine Chandon, believes that "one of the biggest improvements" in the industry during her professional career, "is understanding grape phenolics and ripeness." That understanding has helped to improve wine quality throughout California, but it has particularly benefited Napa red wine producers, which compete at the top end of world production. For this reason, Napa wineries have been earlier adopters of analytical tools to improve grape and wine quality. Just as high grape prices allow grape growers to invest more in viticultural practices to assure high quality, so too do high wine prices allow wineries to spend money and effort in improving their wine.

Napa produces expensive wines that compete at the highest prices in the world market. To remain competitive, Napa winery owners have invested not only in land and technology but also in a creative and scientifically trained workforce. Michaela Rodeno, the founding CEO of St. Supery for almost thirty years, commented that "information has always been in short supply in this business" and that in her opinion UC Davis's most important contribution to the Napa Valley wine industry had been "educating a cadre of top flight winemakers" (Rodeno, 2012). Tim Mondavi (2012) believes that "the most important attribute that Davis brought to the California industry was instilling curiosity in its students." The faculty taught him critical thinking and a scientific way to solve enological and viticultural problems that were specific to a vineyard or winery. As T. Mondavi (2012) put it, "We did trials and we learned." For Bill Dyer (Dyer and Dyer, 2012), the education he received at Davis "provided a safety net" that allowed him to try native yeast fermentations at Sterling. He speculated that a well-educated winemaker "can take more risks because you know where the edge is." Bruce Cakebread (2012), who employs several Davis graduates at his winery, spoke of "the deep understanding of science" exhibited by UC Davis graduates and their ability to incorporate new ideas. Bob Steinhauer (2012), who has worked in the Napa Valley since 1971 and who was vice president for viticulture for Beringer for most of his time in the valley, certainly thinks that the Davis faculty research was extremely important, but ultimately concludes that "students are the biggest attribute that Davis has." John Williams (2012) concurs with his fellow winemakers, saying that Davis's major accomplishment in the Napa Valley has been that it "educated and fostered three generations of winemakers. It taught them how to communicate and advance knowledge."

Tip O'Neill is credited with the observation that "all politics is local." Perhaps the same is true for research, which ultimately must be translated into action in a given setting if it is to be of use. The Napa Valley is an excellent location to grow grapes, and wine has come to dominate the Napa economy as nowhere else in California. But wine quality is ultimately defined by the consumer, and environment alone is not sufficient to create wine that consistently sells at the highest prices. Environment is certainly one of three key factors to Napa's success, but the other factors are human. Creative, wealthy, and dedicated owners, who are willing to spend what it takes to pursue excellence and to promote the resulting wine to the world, comprise the second key factor in Napa's success. Without the financial resources and a desire and commitment to compete at the highest level on the part of its winery owners, Napa could not have succeeded as it has.

The third key factor must be the influence of UC Davis, through its research, its outreach, and its teaching. Davis research, from early clonal selections through vineyard irrigation and canopy trials to assays to assess grape attributes such as tannin and color, has provided new ways to measure, understand, and improve grape and wine quality. University outreach, through the Cooperative Extension viticultural farm advisor, the Oakville Experiment Station, and University Extension, has provided individual and group education for Napa grape growers and wineries, helping them to incorporate new ideas and to understand the need for improved quality. Education for undergraduate and graduate students has not only documented best practices but, more importantly, has supplied Napa, California, and the world with individuals capable of conducting their own investigations to advance quality wherever they are located.

In these three aspects of its mission, UC Davis and the Department of Viticulture and Enology have played a crucial role in the success of the Napa Valley and in the defining of wine quality in the United States and the world. Robert Mondavi was thus correct in his statement that "UC Davis has been a true partner in building the international reputation of the California wine industry."

NOTES

All of the individuals interviewed graciously gave of their time. They average at least thirty years of personal experience with Napa grape growing and winemaking and in total amount to over 600 years of experience. Their insights were invaluable for writing this chapter.

1. The book to which Mondavi refers was written by Professor W. V. Cruess in 1934. Later editions were titled *The Technology of Winemaking* and were coauthored by Cruess, Amerine, Berg, Kunkee, Ough, Singleton, and Webb.

2. In this chapter, "table wine" refers to wine with an alcohol concentration of under 14 percent, as opposed to "fortified" wines that have had their alcohol concentration increased by the addition of distillates. "Table wine" is not a quality assessment, as it is in Europe. "Dry" refers to the absence of sugar in the resulting wine, as all of the grape sugars are converted to alcohol by the yeast during alcoholic fermentation.

3. Over time, genes in grape varieties mutate, leading to differences such as leaf shape, berry color, disease resistance, ripening date, or cluster size and shape. Because grapes are heterozygous and do not breed true to type from seed, they are propagated by cuttings to maintain their varietal characteristics. Selections of vines of the same variety but with different characteristics are referred to as "clones."

4. All of the representatives were university trained, most with degrees from Davis. Rollin Wilkenson (Christian Brothers) had a BS from UCD in viticulture, where he had worked with Olmo. Tucker Catlin (Sterling) had a BS in plant science with an emphasis on viticulture from UCD. Bob Steinhauer (Beringer) had an MS from Fresno State University. Will Nord (Domaine Chandon) had a UCD master's in vocational agriculture with a focus on horticulture. Ed Weber (Joseph Phelps) had both a BS and an MS from Davis in viticulture. Phil Freese (Robert Mondavi) had a PhD in biochemistry from Davis. Zelma Long (Simi) had a BS from Oregon State University and studied but did not complete a masters in enology at UC Davis. Rob Davis (Jordan) had a BS in fermentation science from UCD.

5. It is beyond the scope of this chapter to address why red wine consumption tripled. Some observers have suggested that aging baby boomers began consuming red wine to lower risk of heart attacks and strokes, which had been highlighted by Morley Shafer report on "The French Paradox" on the program *60 Minutes* in 1991. The decade from 1991 to 2001 was also a period of economic prosperity.

6. We have used "attended" because it is not clear that all have matriculated.

7. A well plate is a flat plate with minidepressions, or wells, that act as miniature test tubes and allow rapid processing of multiple samples at one time.

Reference Matter

References

Abate, T. 2001. Chips off the old block: Alums of Genentech, Chiron, Cetus make Bay Area the capital of biotech industry. *San Francisco Chronicle*, April 2.

Abbate, J. 1999. *Inventing the Internet*. Cambridge, MA: MIT Press.

Abidi, A. n.d. [probably 2006]. Integrated circuits and systems: Beginnings, growth, and ascendancy. Collection of Christophe Lécuyer. Stanford, CA: Stanford University.

———. 2007. Interview conducted by Christophe Lécuyer. February 26 and 27.

Ackwood, S. 1992. Letter to Kenneth Farrell. February 27. Presidential Papers, folders on MICRO. Oakland, CA: University of California Office of the President.

Adams, D. 2012. Interview conducted by James Lapsley, March 26. Davis, CA.

Agarwal, A., and Henderson, R. 2002. Putting patents in context: Exploring knowledge transfer from MIT. *Management Science*, 48 (1), 44–60.

Ainsworth, B. 2002. Technology trailblazers: At UCSD institute, academic and business worlds converge on a new frontier of innovation. *San Diego Union-Tribune*, May 5, A-1.

Akasaki, I. 2000. Progress in crystal growth of nitride semiconductors. *Journal of Crystal Growth*, 221, 231–239.

———. 2007. Key inventions in the history of nitride-based blue LED and LD. *Journal of Crystal Growth*, 30, 2–10.

Akasaki, I., and Amano, H. 2006. Breakthroughs in improving the crystal quality of GaN and invention of the PN junction blue-light-emitting diode. *Japanese Journal of Applied Physics*, 45, 9001–9010.

Alley, L., and Golino, D. A. 2000. The origins of the grape program at Foundation Plant Materials Service, pp. 222–230 in *Proceedings of the ASEV 50th Anniversary Meeting, Seattle , Washington, June 19–23, 2000*. Davis, CA: American Society of Enology and Viticulture.

Almeida, P., and Kogut, B. 1999. Localization of knowledge and the mobility of engineers in regional networks. *Management Science*, 45, 905–917.

Amerine, M. A., and Winkler, A. J. 1944. Composition and quality of must and wines of California grapes. *Hilgardia*, 15(6), 493–673.

Anderson, N. S. 1993. *An Improbable Venture: A History of the University of California, San Diego*. La Jolla, CA: University of California San Diego Press.

Arditti, S. 1993. Letter to Jim Costa. June 22. Presidential Papers, folders on MICRO. Oakland, CA: University of California Office of the President.

Ashenfelter, O., and Quandt, R. E. n.d. Analyzing a wine tasting statistically (wherein we rigorously analyze the famous 1976 Paris tasteoff!). Downloaded March 26, 2012, from www.liquidasset.com/tasting.html.

Aspray, W. 2000. Was early entry a competitive advantage? US universities that entered computing in the 1940s. *IEEE Annals*, 22(3), 42–87.

Association of University Technology Managers (AUTM). 2010. The AUTM licensing survey, FY 2010. Norwalk, CT: AUTM.

Babcock, C. 2006. What's the Greatest Software Ever Written? Downloaded on February 24, 2012, from www.informationweek.com/news/191901844.

Bailey, D. K., Bateman, R., Berkner, L. V., Booker, H. G., Montgomery, G. F., Purcell, E. M., Salisbury, W. W., and Wiesner, J. B. 1952. A new kind of radio propagation at very high frequencies observable over long distances. *Physical Review*, 86(2) (April), 141–145.

Baker, D. 2012. Bright possibilities; LED lighting; Fremont startup firm figures the price point is right. *San Francisco Chronicle*, February 8.

Balconi, M., and Laboranti, A. 2006. University–industry interactions in applied research: the case of microelectronics. *Research Policy*, 35(10), 1616–1630.

Baldwin, C. Y., and K. B. Clark. 1995. Sun Wars: Competition within a Modular Cluster, 1985–1990. Unpublished paper. Downloaded on July 27, 2012, from www.people.hbs.edu/cbaldwin/DR2/Sun_Wars.pdf.

Bardini, T. 2000. *Bootstrapping: Douglas Engelbart, Coevolution, and the Origins of Personal Computing*. Stanford, CA: Stanford University Press.

Barrett, P. H. 1987. Departmental history. Santa Barbara, CA: UCSB physics department basement archive.

Barus, C. 1987. Military influence on the electrical engineering curriculum since World War II. *IEEE Technology and Society Magazine* (June), 3–9.

Bascomb, N. 2011. *The New Cool: A Visionary Teacher, His FIRST Robotics Team, and the Ultimate Battle of Smarts*. New York: Crown Publishers.

Bassett, R. 2002. *To the Digital Age: Research Labs, Start-Up Companies, and the Rise of MOS Technology*. Baltimore, MD: Johns Hopkins University Press.

Bechtolsheim, A. 2006. Sun Microsystems Founders Panel Video. Downloaded on April 18, 2012, from www.youtube.com/watch?v=dkmzb904tGo&feature=related.

Bekkers, R., and West, J. 2009. The limits to IPR standardization policies as evidenced by strategic patenting in UMTS. *Telecommunications Policy*, 33(1–2) (February–March), 80–97.

Belanger, D. O. 1998. *Enabling American Innovation: Engineering and the National Science Foundation*. West Lafayette, IN: Purdue University Press.

Berkowitz, Z. 2012. Interview conducted by James Lapsley, February 17. Napa, CA.

Berg, P., and Singer, M. 1995. He recombinant DNA controversy: Twenty years later. *Proceedings of the National Academy of Science*, 92, 9011–9013.

Berlin, L. 2005. *The Man Behind the Microchip: Robert Noyce and the Invention of Silicon Valley*. New York: Oxford University Press.

Berman, E. P. 2012. *Creating the Market University: How Academic Science Became an Economic Engine*. Princeton, NJ: Princeton University Press.

Bernstein, D. F. 2001. Internet Host SMTP Server Survey. Downloaded on February 25, 2012, from http://cr.yp.to/surveys/smtpsoftware6.txt.

Booker, H. G. 1954. What is wrong with engineering education? *Proceedings of the Institute of Radio Engineers*, 42, 513.

———. 1963. University education and applied science. *Science*, 141(3580) (August 9), 486–488, 575–576.

———. 1970. Cut-back in AP&IS. Dec. 12 memorandum to Herbert York and John L. Stewart, Office of the Chancellor (RSS 1), Applied Physics and Information (Box 22, Folder 5). San Diego: UCSD Special Collections.

Borrus, M. 2010. Industrial influence: Sangiovanni as entrepreneur and consigliere. *IEEE Solid State Circuits Magazine*, Summer.

Bowers, J., 2007. Interview conducted by Christophe Lécuyer. January 18.

Bowles, K., 2003. Computers: 50+ years coping with science vs. technology. *Chronicles: Newsletter of the UCSD Emeriti Association*, 3(1) (October), 4–7.

Braunerhjelm, P. 2006. Specialization of regions and universities: The new versus the old. *Industry and Innovation* 15, 253–275.

Brayton, R., 2010. Summer of '81. *IEEE Solid State Circuits Magazine*, Summer, 26–31.

Broad, W., 1985. First of the "superchips" arrive. *New York Times*, July 23.

Broadcom. 1998. SEC prospectus. Irvine, CA: Author.

———. 1999. SEC prospectus. Irvine, CA: Author.

———. 2000. SEC prospectus. Irvine, CA: Author.

Broadcom turns defense technology knowhow into communication ICs. *Electronic Business Buyer* March 1995, 57–58.

Brock, D., and Lécuyer, C. 2012. Digital foundations: The making of silicon gate manufacturing technology. *Technology and Culture* 53, 561–597.

Brown, E. 1981. Statement. January 7. Presidential Papers, folders on MICRO. Oakland, CA: University of California Office of the President.

Brown, G., and Hewlett, W. 1956. Report to Dean M. P. O'Brien. May 31. CU-149, box 40. Berkeley, CA: Bancroft Library.

Brueckner, K. A. 1994. First years at the University of California at San Diego, 1959 to 1965. UCSD Libraries. Downloaded on June 28, 2013, from http://libraries.ucsd.edu/historyofucsd/brueckterfirstyears.html.

Brueckner, L., and Borrus, M. 1984. Assessing the commercial impact of the VHSIC (Very High Speed Integrated Circuit) Program. BRIE Working Paper, December 1, Berkeley: University of California, Berkeley.

Buchin, M.1974. Report. UArch 12 Office of Public Information Subject Files, Box 56 Folder "Physics—Scientific Instrumentation 1973–1975." Santa Barbara: UCSB Library Special Collections.

Burger, R. 1998. *Cooperative research: The New Paradigm*. Durham, NC: Semiconductor Research Corporation.

Burke, J., 1997. A tale of two Henrys. *Red Herring*, July.

Bursky, D. 2000. Extra aluminum enhances power handling of AlGaN/Gan HEMTs. *Electronic Design* 10 (January). f

Bush, V. 1945. *Science: The Endless Frontier*. Washington, DC: U.S. Government Printing Office.

Cakebread, B. 2012. Interview conducted by James Lapsley, February 13. Rutherford, CA.

California Department of Food and Agriculture. (1980–2010). *Grape Crush Report*. Sacramento.

———. (1980–2010). *Grape Acreage Report*. Sacramento.

California Healthcare Institute (CHI). 2004. *California's Biomedical Industry, 2004*. La Jolla, CA: California Healthcare Institute.

Calit2. 2012. Calit2: California Institute for Telecommunications and Information Technology. Downloaded on June 28, 2013, from www.calit2.net/about/.

Cambrosio, A., and Keating, P. 1995. *Exquisite Specificity: The Monoclonal Antibody Revolution*. New York: Oxford University Press.

Campbell-Kelly, M., and Garcia-Swartz, D. D. 2008. Economic perspectives on the history of the computer time-sharing industry, 1965–1985. *IEEE Annals of the History of Computing*, 30(1), 16–36.

Carrick, R. 1980a. Letter to John Neisheim. December 8. Presidential Papers, folders on MICRO. Oakland, CA: University of California Office of the President.

———. 1908b. Letter to Thomas Skornia. December 30. Presidential Papers, folders on MICRO. Oakland, CA: University of California Office of the President.

Carter, T. 1992. Mirage relies on light to create illusion. *Lexington Herald-Leader*, November 24.

Casper, S. 2007. How do technology clusters emerge and become sustainable? Social network formation and inter-firm mobility within the San Diego biotechnology cluster. *Research Policy*, 36, 438–455.

———. 2009. The marketplace for ideas: Can Los Angeles build a successful biotechnology cluster?" Report written for the John Randolph Haynes Foundation.

———. 2013. The spill-over theory reversed: The impact of regional economies on the commercialization of university science. *Research Policy*, 42(8), 1313–1324.

Cavin, R.K., Sumney, L.W., and Burger, R.M. 1989. The Semiconductor Research Corporation: Cooperative research. *Proceedings of the IEEE*, 77(9), 1327–1344.

Chadis, E. 2004. Virgil Elings (Ph.D. '66) $3.5 million gift to name the center for theoretical physics. Downloaded on May 23, 2012, from web.mit.edu/physics/giving/profiles/elings.html.

Chang, W. 2007. Interview conducted by Christophe Lécuyer. February 6.

Choi, H. 2007. The boundaries of industrial research: Making transistors at RCA, 1948–1960. *Technology and Culture* 48, 758–782.

Clarke, P. 2011. GaN startup raises $38 million to transform power conversion. *Electronic Engineering Times*, August 1.

Codd, E. F. 1970. A relational model of data for large shared data banks. *Communications of the ACM*, 13(6), 377–387.

Cohen, W. M., Nelson, R. R., and Walsh, J. P. 2002. Links and impacts: The influence of public research on industrial R&D. *Management Science* 48, 1–23.

Coldren, Larry, 1989. Optical waveguide phase-shifters in GaAs/InP for high-speed communication. *MICRO.*

Cole, B. 1985. Letter to Peter Jegers. May 15. Presidential Papers, folders on MICRO. Oakland, CA: University of California Office of the President.

Colyvas, J., Crow, M., Gelijns, A., Mazzoleni, R., Nelson, R. R., Rosenberg, N., and Sampat, B. N. 2002. How do university inventions get into practice? *Management Science*, 61–72.

Computer History Museum. 2007a. RDBMS Workshop: IBM, moderated by Burton Grad. Mountain View, CA: Computer History Museum Reference number: X4069.2007.

———. 2007b. RDBMS Workshop: Ingres and Sybase, moderated by Doug Jerger. Mountain View, CA: Computer History Museum Reference number: X4069.2007.

———. 2007c. RDBMS Workshop: Financing, moderated by Luanne Johnson. Mountain View, CA: Computer History Museum Reference number: X4069.2007.

Corison, C. 2012. Interview conducted by James Lapsley, February 22. St. Helena, CA.

DenBaars, S. 2007. Interview conducted by Christophe Lécuyer. January 9.

Department of Economic and Business Development, State of California. 1981. MICRO. January 7. Presidential Papers, folders on MICRO. Oakland, CA: University of California Office of the President.

Digital Instruments. 1989. Exclusive license agreement for atomic force microscopes, University of California Agreement Control Number 89-04-0016, July 14, 1989, found in U.S. Patent and Trademark Office file for Patent No. 4935634.

———. 1996. DI and Sematech in join development for 2D Dopant profiling. *Nanovations*, 3 (Winter), 1.

Digital Instruments v. Topometrix, 1993. Docket No. C93-20900 RMW in U.S. District Court for Northern District of California—San Jose, filed November 24.

Dookozlian, N. 2009. Integrated canopy management: A twenty year evolution in California, pp. 43–52 in *Proceedings of Recent Advances in Grapevine Canopy Management, Davis, California, July 16, 2009*. Davis: University of California, Davis.

Duckhorn, D. 2012. Interview conducted by James Lapsley, February 13. St. Helena, CA.

Dunn, James. 2004. Interview by Joel West, January 30. San Diego: UCSD Libraries.

Dupuis, R. 2009. Harold M. Manasevit (1927–2008). *Interface* Summer, 23–24.

Dupuis, R., and Krames, M. 2008. History, development, and applications of high-brightness visible light emitting diodes. *Journal of Lightwave Technology* 26, 1154–1171.

Dyer, B., and Dyer, D. 2012. Interview conducted by James Lapsley, February 29. Calistoga, CA.

Eckdahl, D. E., Reed, I. S., and Sarkissian, H. H. 2003. West Coast contributions to the development of the general-purpose computer. *IEEE Annals of the History of Computing*, 25(1), 4–33.

Economic & Planning Systems. 2010. A study of the economic and fiscal impact of the University of California, San Francisco. Report prepared for UCSF. Downloaded from www.ucsf.edu/media/pdf/eir/ucsf_2010_economic_impact_report.pdf.

Economist, 2011. Grape gripes: How an aphid changed viticulture. *The Economist*, July 21.

Eisenberg, R. 1996. Public research and private development: Patents and technology transfer in government-sponsored research. *Virginia Law Review*, 82, 1663–1727.

Electrical Engineering and Computer Sciences, Department of (EE&CS). 2012. Industrial Liaison Program website. Downloaded on 9 July 9, 2012, from www.EE&CS.berkeley.edu/IPRO/memberships.shtml.

Elings, V. 1981. Review of *The Art of Electronics* by Horowitz and Hill. *Physics Today*, 34 (March), 68–70.

———. 1995. "Invent or die" is the key to success in science. *R&D Magazine*, March, 21.

———. 1996. The year in review. *Nanovations*, 3 (Winter), 1.

———. 2012. Interview conducted by Cyrus Mody, May 9. Santa Barbara, CA.

———. n.d. (probably mid-1970s. Advertisement for MSI program. Santa Barbara, CA: UCSB physics department basement archive.

Elings, V. B., Jahn, G. E., and Vogel, J. H. 1977. A theoretical model of regionally ischemic myocardium. *Circulation Research*, 41, 722–729.

Elings, V. B., and Landry, C. J. 1972. Optical Display Device. U.S. Pat. 3,647,284.

Elings, V., and Phillips, D. 1973. An interdisciplinary graduate curriculum in scientific instrumentation. *American Journal of Physics*, 41, 570–573.

———. 1977. Apparatus and method for measuring cardiac output. U.S. Pat. 4,015,593.

Elings Park, 2012. Elings Park: The largest privately funded public park in America. Downloaded May 23, 2012, from www.elingspark.org.

English, R. 1972. Press release. Scientific instrumentation: "Practical scientists" produced by new UCSB program, November 7. UArch 12, Public Information Office Subject Files, Box 56 Folder "Physics—Scientific Instrumentation 1973–1975." Santa Barbara: UCSB Library Special Collections.

———. 1973. Press release. It's called a Chromophone: Invention enables deaf to "see" sounds on color TV, February 12. UArch 12, Public Information Office Subject Files, Box 56 Folder "Physics—Scientific Instrumentation 1973–1975." Santa Barbara: UCSB Library Special Collections.

———. n.d. (probably mid-1970s). Fishy "swingshift" is investigated. Santa Barbara: UCSB physics department basement archive.

Estrada, A. 2000. Surfing Silicon Beach: The ever-expanding dot-com revolution catches a new wave in Santa Barbara. *Santa Barbara Magazine*, December 13.

Etzkowitz, H. 2002. *MIT and the Rise of Entrepreneurial Science*. London: Routledge.

Everhart, T. 1971. Letter from Tom Everhart, UC Berkeley, Department of EE&CS, Industrial Relations Committee to John Pierce, 4/30/71. John Pierce papers, Box 5, blue binder "Correspondence—External—August 1969–March 1971." San Marino, CA: Huntington Library.

———. 1975. Letter to Ernest Kuh, October 27. CU-39.3, box 1. Berkeley, CA: Bancroft Library.

———. 1977. Letter to Alberto Sangiovanni-Vincentelli. May 3. CU-39.3, box 1. Berkeley, CA: Bancroft Library.

Fasca, C. 1998. Veeco deals for Digital Instruments. *Electronic News*, February 16.

Fatt, I., Hahn, E. L., and Jackson, J. D. 1974. Evaluation of the graduate program of the Department of Physics, University of California, Santa Barbara, June 11. UArch 13 Academic Senate Records, Box 88, Folder 9 "Doctoral Program Evaluation Final Report, Graduate Council, August 1, 1977." Santa Barbara: UCSB Library Special Collections.

Feldman, M.P. 2000. Location and innovation: The new economic geography of innovation, spillovers and agglomeration, in G. L. Clark et al. (Eds.), *The Oxford Handbook of Economic Geography*. Oxford, UK: Oxford University Press.

Fidelman, M. 2012. Why the real wireless capital of the world is San Diego—not Silicon Valley. *Forbes*, June 27. Downloaded on June 28, 2013, from www.forbes.com/sites/markfidelman/2012/06/27/why-san-diego-beats-silicon-valley-as-the-wireless-capital-of-the-world/.

Fikes, B. 1999. Why San Diego has biotech. *San Diego Metropolitan*. Downloaded from www.sandiegometro.com/1999/apr/biotech.html.

Fisher, M. 1991. The financial impact of phylloxera—An update. *MKF Wine Industry Update*, March, 1–2.

Flamm, K. 1988. *Creating the Computer: Government, Industry, and High Technology*. Washington, DC: The Brookings Institution.

Florax, R. 1992. *The University: A Regional Booster? Economic Impacts of Academic Knowledge Infrastructure*. Aldershot, UK: Avebury.

Franson, P. 2008. A blending session with Michel Rolland. *Napa Valley Register.com*, June 28.

Freese, P. 2012. Phone interview conducted by James Lapsley, February 12.

Fried, F. 2000. Start-up Innovent targeting Bluetooth chip market. *CNET News*, June 2.

Friedbacher, G., and Fuchs, H. 1999. Classification of scanning probe microscopies. *Pure and Applied Chemistry*, 71, 1337–1357.

Funding Universe. 2012. Ligand Pharmaceuticals company history. Downloaded from www.fundinguniverse.com/company-histories/Ligand-Pharmaceuticals-Incorporated-company-History.html.

Furber, S. 2011. Interview by Jason Fitzpatrick. *Communications of the ACM*, 54(5), 34–39.

Furman, J., and MacGarvie, M. 2007. Academic science and the birth of industrial research laboratories in the U.S. pharmaceutical industry. *Journal of Economic Behavior & Organization* 63, 756–776.

Galison, P. 1997. *Image and Logic: A Material Culture of Microphysics*. Chicago: University of Chicago Press.

Gans, J., Murray, F., and Stern, S. 2008. Patents, papers, pairs & secrets: Contracting over the disclosure of scientific knowledge. Cambridge, MA: MIT Sloan Working Paper.

Garoyan, L. 1975. *California's Grape Industry: Some Economic Considerations*, Bulletin 1875. Division of Agricultural Sciences, University of California.

Geiger, R. L. 1986. *To Advance Knowledge: The Growth of American Research Universities, 1900–1940*. New York: Oxford University Press.

Gelsinger, P., Kirkpatrick, D., Kolodny, A., and Singer, G. 2011. Such a CAD! Coping with complexity of microprocessor design at Intel. *IEEE Solid State Circuits Magazine*, 32–43.

Gilead Sciences. 2006. *Annual Report, 2006*. Foster City, CA: Gilead Sciences.

Gillmor, C. S. 1986. Federal funding and knowledge growth in ionospheric physics, 1945–81. *Social Studies of Science*, 16(1), 105–133.

———. 2004. *Fred Terman at Stanford: Building a Discipline, a University, and Silicon Valley*. Stanford, CA: Stanford University Press.

Goldberger, M. L., Maher, B. A., and Flattau, P. E. 1995. *Research Doctorate Programs in the United States: Continuity and Change*. Washington, DC: National Research Council.

Gordon, W. E. 2001. Henry G. Booker. *Biographical Memoirs*, 79. Washington, DC: National Academies Press.

Gossard, G. 2007. Interview conducted by Christophe Lécuyer. March 1.

Gray, P. 1998. Oral history interview conducted by Robert Walker. August 21. Silicon genesis collection. University archives and special collections. Stanford, CA:.Stanford University.

Gray, P., McCreary, J., and Hodges, D. 1978. Weighted capacitor analog/digital converting apparatus and method. U.S. Patent No. 4,129,863. Granted December 12.

Greenstein, S., 2010. The emergence of the Internet: Collective invention and wild ducks. *Industrial and Corporate Change*, 19(5), 1521-1562.

Gubbins, E. 2006. A new life for an all-optical technology. *Telephony*, October 9.

Hall, S. 2002. *Invisible Frontiers: The Race to Synthesize a Human Gene*. New York: Oxford University Press.

Hansma, P. 2006. Interview conducted by Cyrus Mody, August 7. Santa Barbara, CA.

Harbertson, J. 2012. Personal e-mail communication from James Harbertson to James Lapsley. March 14.

Haycock, T. L. 1989. Leveraging external R&D funding: Harris Semiconductor's approach to university programs, in *Proceedings of the Eighth Biennial University/Government/Industry Microelectronics Symposium, June 12–14*, pp. 24–29.

Heeger, A. 2006. Interview conducted by Cyrus Mody, March 16. Santa Barbara, CA.

Heintz, W. F. 1990. *Wine Country: A History of the Napa Valley*. Santa Barbara: Capra Press.

Hicks, D., T. Breitzman, D. Olivastro, and Hamilton, K., 2001. The changing composition of innovation activity in the US—A portrait based on patent analysis. *Research Policy* 30, 681–703.

Higgins, M. 2005. *Career Imprints: Creating Leaders Across An Industry*. Cambridge, MA: Harvard University Press.

Hiltzik, M. A. 1999. *Dealers of Lightning: Xerox PARC and the Dawn of the Computer Age*. New York: Harper Business.

Hoagland, A. S. 1998. A Paradigm Shift: Digital Magnetic Recording. PowerPoint Presentation, 100th Anniversary Conference on Magnetic Recording and Information Storage. Santa Clara, CA: Santa Clara University. Downloaded on February, 10, 2012 from www.magneticdiskheritagecenter.org/ 100th/ Progress/Hoagland/alhoagland.htm.

———. 2010. The mechanical heart of the information storage revolution: The magnetic disk drive. Magnetic Heritage Disk Center. Downloaded on December 6, 2011, from www.magneticdiskheritagecenter.org/MDHC/Book .pdf.

Hodges, D. 1980a. Letter to David Saxon. September 12. CU-39.3, box 1. Berkeley, CA: Bancroft Library.

———. 1980b. Proposed state program to stimulate research and development. October 28. CU-39.3, box 1. Berkeley, CA: Bancroft Library.

Hodges, D. A., 1981. Letter to George Turin. April 27. CU-39.3, box 2. Berkeley, CA: Bancroft Library.

———. 1998. Unpublished table provided to authors by Hodges.

———. 2008–2010. Oral history interview conducted by Christophe Lécuyer. Berkeley, CA: Bancroft Library.

———. 2012a. E-mail communications to Christophe Lécuyer. November 16, 18, and 19, and December 22, 2012.

———. 2012b. Various e-mail communications. April 6, May 6, and July 9, 2012.

Hodges, D.A., Gray, P., and Brodersen, R. 1978. Potential of MOS technologies for analog integrated circuits. *IEEE Journal of Solid State Circuits* 13(June), 285–294.

Hodges, D.A., and Newton, A. R. 2007. Donald Oscar Pederson, pp. 89, 285–304 in National Academy of Sciences, (Ed.), *Biographical Memoirs*. Washington, DC: National Academies Press

Hoff, M. n.d. Interview. Downloaded on September 29, 2012, from http:// engineering.stanford.edu/research-profile/marcian-%E2%80%9Cted% E2%80%9D-hoff-phd-62-ee.

Hoffman, M. B. 2007. Oral History of Mark B. Hoffman, interviewed by Burton Grad. June 13, 2007. Mountain View, CA: Computer History Museum CHM Reference number: X4019.2007.

Hoh, J. 2002. Interview conducted by Cyrus Mody, June 10. Baltimore, MD.

Holbrook, D., Cohen, W., Hounshell, D., and Klepper, S. 2000. The nature, sources, and consequences of firm differences in the early history of the semi-conductor industry. *Strategic Management Journal*, 21, 1017–1041.

Hollingsworth, J. R., and Hollingsworth, E. 2012. *Fostering Scientific Excellence: Organizations, Institutions, and Major Discoveries in Biomedical Science*. New York: Cambridge University Press.

Holson, L. 2000. Networking in Southern California: "Anti-Silicon Valley" Broadcom chief rules in the wired world. *New York Times*, June 26, C1.

Hoxsey, A. 2012. Interview conducted by James Lapsley, February 17. Oakville, CA.

Hu, E. 2007a. E-mail communication to Christophe Lécuyer. February 26.

———. 2007b. Interview conducted by Christophe Lécuyer. February 27.

Hughes, S. 2011. *Genentech: The Beginnings of Biotech*. Chicago: Chicago University Press.

———. 2005. Axel Ullrich, molecular biologist at UCSF and Genentech. Oral History published by the UC Berkeley Bancroft Library. Downloaded from http://bancroft.berkeley.edu/ROHO/projects/biosci/oh_list.html.

International Solid-State Circuits Conference. Various Years. San Francisco, CA.

Iowa State University Foundation. 2006. Virgil Elings pledges $5 million for Iowa State's new Agricultural and Biosystems Engineering Facility. Downloaded on May 23, 2012, from www.foundation.iastate.edu/site/News2?page=NewsArticle&id=5857.

Jensen, R., and Thursby, M. 2001. Proofs and prototypes for sale: The licensing of university inventions. *American Economic Review*, 240–259.

Johnson, G. 1986. Hybritech shareholders OK Eli Lilly acquisition. *Los Angeles Times*, March 19.

Johnstone, B. 2007. *Brilliant! Shuji Nakamura and the Revolution of Solid State Lighting*. Amherst, MA: Prometheus Books.

Jones, M. 2005. Biotech's Perfect Climate: The Hybritech Story. Unpublished doctoral dissertation, University of California, San Diego.

Jong, S. 2006. How organizational structures in science shape spin-off firms: The biochemistry departments of Berkeley, Stanford and UCSF and the birth of the biotechnology industry. *Industrial and Corporate Change*, 15, 251–283.

Joy, W. N. 1995. Reduced instruction set computers (RISC): Academic/industrial interplay drives computer performance forward. Downloaded on April 17, 2012, from www.cs.washington.edu/homes/lazowska/cra/risc.html.

Kaiser, D. 2002. Cold War requisitions, scientific manpower, and the production of American physicists after World War II. *Historical Studies in the Physical Sciences*, 33, 131–159.

Katz, R. H. 2010. RAID: A personal recollection of how storage became a system. *IEEE Annals of the History of Computing*, 32(4), 82–87.

Kennedy, J. 1980. Memorandum. December 22. Presidential Papers, folders on MICRO. Oakland, CA: University of California Office of the President.

Kenney, M. 1986. *Biotechnology: The University Industrial Complex*. New Haven, CT: Yale University Press.

——— (ed.). 2000. *Understanding Silicon Valley: Anatomy of an Entrepreneurial Region*. Stanford, CA: Stanford University Press.

———. 2011. How venture capital became a component of the U.S. NSI. *Industrial and Corporate Change*, 20(6), 1677–1723.

Kenney, M., and Goe, W. R. 2004. The role of social embeddedness in professorial entrepreneurship: A comparison of electrical engineering and computer science at UC Berkeley and Stanford. *Research Policy* 33(5), 691–707.

Kenney, M., and Patton, D. 2005. Entrepreneurial geographies: Support networks in three high-tech industries. *Economic Geography* 81, 201–228.

———. 2009. Reconsidering the Bayh-Dole Act and the current university invention ownership model. *Research Policy* 38(9), 1407–1422.

———. 2011. Does inventor ownership encourage university research-derived entrepreneurship? A six university comparison. *Research Policy* 40(8), 1100–1112.

Khazam, J. and Mowery, D. 1994. The commercialization of RISC: Strategies for the creation of dominant designs. *Research Policy* 23, 89–102.

Kiley, T. 2006. Brook Byers: Biotech venture capitalist 1970-2006. Oral History Published by the UC Berkeley Bancroft Library. Downloaded from http://bancroft.berkeley.edu/ROHO/projects/biosci/oh_list.html.

Klass, P. 1986. Contractors use different techniques to meet VHSIC-2 objectives. *Aviation Week and Space Technology*, October 20.

Klepper, S. 2011. Nano-economics, spinoffs, and the wealth of regions. *Small Business Economics*, 37(2), 141–154.

Kliewer, M. 2012. Interview conducted by James Lapsley, March 19. Davis, CA.

Kline, R. 1988. Reflections on the influence of World War II on electrical engineering education in the United States, 1925–1955. *IEEE Antennas and Propagation Society Newsletter*, August, 12–16.

Kloppenburg, J. R. 1988. *First the Seed: The Political Economy of Plant Biotechnology*. Cambridge, UK: Cambridge University Press.

Knivett, V. 2008. Analog profile: Jim Solomon. *Electronic Engineering Times*, November d25.

Kroemer, H. 1963. A proposed class of heterojunction injection lasers. *Proceedings of the IEEE* 51, 1782–1783.

———. 1981. Heterostructures for everything: Device principle of the 1980's? *Japanese Journal of Applied Physics*, 20 Supplement 20-1, 9–13.

———. 1992. MICRO vs. UC patent policies. October 20. Presidential Papers, folders on MICRO. Oakland, CA: University of California Office of the President.

———. 2000a. Autobiography. Downloaded on November 10, 2012, from www.nobelprize.org/nobel_prizes/physics/laureates/2000/kroemer.html.

———. 2000b. Quasi-electric fields and band offsets: Teaching electrons new tricks. Nobel Prize Lecture, December 8. Downloaded on November 10, 2012, from www.nobelprize.org/nobel_prizes/physics/laureates/2000/kroemer.html.

———. 2003. Oral history interview conducted by John Vardalas, IEEE History Center. February 12, 2003. Downloaded on November 10, 2012, from www.ieeeghn.org/wiki/index.php/Oral-History:Herbert_Kroemer.

———. 2007. Interviews conducted by Christophe Lécuyer. January 4 and February 23.

Kuczynski, J., and Thomas, J. K. 1983. Surface effects in the photochemistry of colloidal cadmium sulfide. *Journal of Physical Chemistry*, 87(26), 5498–5503.

Kuehlmann, A., 2010. Thinking big. *IEEE Solid-State Circuits Magazine*, Fall, 27–31.

Kundert, K., 2011. Life after SPICE. *IEEE Solid State Circuits Magazine* Spring, 23–26.

Lam, A. 2007. Knowledge networks and careers: academic scientists in industry-university links. *Journal of Management Studies*, 44, 993–1016.

Lapsley, J. T. 1996. *Bottled Poetry: Napa Winemaking from Prohibition to the Modern Era*. Berkeley: University of California Press.

Larson, L. 2007. Interview conducted by Christophe Lécuyer. January 11.

Lebret, H. 2007. *Start-Up: What We May Still Learn from Silicon Valley*. Lausanne: Hervé Lebret.

Lécuyer, C. 2005a. *Making Silicon Valley: Innovation and the Growth of High Tech, 1930–1970*. Cambridge, MA: MIT Press.

———. 2005b. What do universities really owe industry? The case of solid state electronics at Stanford. *Minerva*, 43, 51–71.

Lécuyer, C., and Brock, D. 2010. *Makers of the Microchip: A Documentary History of Fairchild Semiconductor.* Cambridge, MA: MIT Press.

Lécuyer, C. and Choi, H. 2012. Les secrets de la Silicon Valley ou les entreprises américaines de microélectronique face à l'incertitude technique. *La Revue d'Histoire Moderne & Contemporaine*, 59, 96–117.

Lécuyer, C., and Ueyama, T. 2013. The logics of materials innovation: The case of gallium nitride and blue light emitting diodes. *Historical Studies in the Natural Sciences* 43, 243–280.

Lee, C., and Walshok, M. 2002. *Making Connections: The Evolution of Links Between UCSD Researchers and San Diego's Biotech Industry.* La Jolla, CA: UC Connect.

Leiner, B. M., Kahn, R. E., Postel, J., Cerf, V. G., Kleinrock, L., Roberts, L. G., Clark, D. D., Lynch, D. C., and Wolff, S., 2009. A brief history of the Internet. *ACM SIGCOMM Computer Communication Review*, 39(5) (October), 22–33.

Lenoir, T. 1997. *Instituting Science: The Cultural Production of Scientific Disciplines.* Stanford, CA: Stanford University Press.

Lenoir, T., and Lécuyer, C. 1995. Instrument makers and discipline builders: The case of nuclear magnetic resonance. *Perspectives on Science*, 3, 276–345.

Leslie, S. W. 1993. *The Cold War and American Science: The Military-Industrial-Academic Complex at MIT and Stanford.* New York: Columbia University Press.

———. 2010. "Time of troubles" for the special laboratories, in D. Kaiser (Ed.), *Becoming MIT: Moments of Decision.* Cambridge, MA: MIT Press.

Lindsay, S. 2003. Interview conducted by the Cyrus Mody, January 6. Tempe, AZ.

Linvill, J. 2002. Oral history interview conducted by Christophe Lécuyer. April 30 and May 20.

Livingstone, P. 2010. Taking it one particle at a time. *R&D Magazine*, 52(4), 14–17.

Lowe, R. 2002, December. The role and experience of inventors and start-ups in commercializing university research: Case studies at the University of California. Research and Occasional Paper Series. Berkeley, CA: Center for Studies in Higher Education, University of California, Berkeley.

Lowe, R., Mowery, D., and Sampat, B. n.d. What happens in university–industry technology transfer? Case studies of five inventions Downloaded on November 10, 2012, from http://iis-db.stanford.edu/evnts/4097/DMowery_University-Industry_Tech_Transfer_Case_Studies.pdf.

Lowen, R. S. 1997. *Creating the Cold War University: The Transformation of Stanford.* Berkeley: University of California Press.

Maher, R. 2012. Interview conducted by James Lapsley, February 29. St. Helena, CA.

Manalis, S. R. 1998. Optical detection for microfabricated cantilever arrays. PhD dissertation. Stanford, CA: Stanford University.

Mansfield, E. 1991. Academic research and industrial innovation. *Research Policy*, 20, 1–12.

Mansfield, E., and Lee, J. Y. 1996. The modern university: Contributor to industrial innovation and recipient of industrial R&D support. *Research Policy*, 25, 1047–1058.

Manasevit, H. 1981. Recollections and reflections of MO-CVD. *Journal of Crystal Growth*, 55, 1–9.

March, J. G. 1991. Exploration and exploitation. *Organization Science*, 21(February), 71–87.

Markoff, J. 1991. Chip technology's friendly rivals. *The New York Times*, June 4, C1, D1.

———. 2012. Engineers take aim at barrier in LED technology. *New York Times*, February 21.

Marshall, M. 2003. Silicon Valley sees rise, fall of telecommunications, networking firms. *San Jose Mercury News*, August 17.

Martini, M. 2012. Interview conducted by James Lapsley, February 29. Calistoga, CA.

Matkin, G. W. 1990. *Technology Transfer and the University*. New York: Macmillan.

McCray, P. 2007. MBE deserves a place in the history books. *Nature Nanotechnology*, 2(May), 259–261.

McCray, W. P. 2005. Will small be beautiful? Making policies for our nanotech future. *History and Technology*, 21, 177–203.

———. 2009. From lab to iPod: A story of discovery and commercialization in the post-Cold War era. *Technology and Culture*, 50, 58–81.

McGarvey, J. 2000. Clear focus in optical is on start-ups. *Inter@ctive Week*, June 26.

McJones, P. (Ed.). 1997. *The 1995 SQL Reunion: People, Projects, and Politics SRC Technical Note 1997–018*. Downloaded on June 19, 2012, from www.mcjones .org/System_R/SQL_Reunion_95/sqlr95.html.

McKelvey, M. 1996. *Evolutionary Innovations: The Business of Biotechnology*. Oxford, UK: Oxford University Press.

McKendrick, D. G., and Carroll, G. R. 2001. On the genesis of organizational forms: Evidence from the market for disk arrays. *Organization Science*, 12, 661–682.

McKendrick, D. G., Doner, R. E., and Haggard, S. 2000. *From Silicon Valley to Singapore: Location and Competitive Advantage in the Hard Disk Drive Industry*. Stanford, CA: Stanford University Press.

McKendrick, D. G., Jaffee, J., Carroll, G. R., and Khessina, O. M. 2003. In the bud? Disk array producers as a (possibly) emergent organizational form. *Administrative Science Quarterly*, 48 (1), 60–93.

McKusick, M. 1999. Twenty years of Berkeley UNIX: From AT&T-owned to freely redistributable, in: *Open Sources: Voices from the Open Source Revolution*. Sebastopol, CA: O'Reilly & Associates. Downloaded from http://oreilly.com/ catalog/opensources/book/kirkmck.html.

McLeod, J. 1989. Synopsys: The right tools at the right time. *Electronics*, November 1, 108.

McLeod, S. 2012. Interview conducted by James Lapsley, February 24. Napa, CA.

McMahon, A. M. 1984. *The Making of a Profession: A Century of Electrical Engineering in America*. New York: IEEE Press.

Meagher, P. 2007. OOL alumni: Eric Allman the man who made e-mail go. Downloaded on February 27, 2012, from http://coe.berkeley.edu/labnotes/0607/allman.html.

de Micheli, G. 2010. Chip challenge: Alberto Sangiovanni-Vincentelli and the birth of logic synthesis. *IEEE Solid State Circuits Magazine*, Fall, 22–26.

MICRO. 1985. 1983–84 Progress Report. January 21. Presidential Papers, folders on MICRO. Oakland, CA: University of California Office of the President.

——. 1986. 1984–85 Progress Report. January 1. Presidential Papers, folders on MICRO. Oakland, CA: University of California Office of the President.

——. 1989. 1987–88 Progress Report. April 1. Presidential Papers, folders on MICRO. Oakland, CA: University of California Office of the President,

Mimura, C. 2010. Nuanced management of IP Rights: Shaping industry–university relationships to promote social impact, pp. 269–295 in R. Dreyfuss, H. First, H., and D. Zimmerman (Eds.), *Working within the Boundaries of Intellectual Property*. Oxford, UK: Oxford University Press.

Mitchell, J. 1985. Integrated circuit seeds bearing high-speed fruit. *The Dallas Morning News*, July 20.

Mock, D. 2005. *The Qualcomm Equation: How a Fledgling Telecom Company Forged a New Path to Big Profits and Market Dominance*. New York: AMACOM American Management Association.

Mody, C. C. M., 2006. Corporations, universities, and instrumental communities: Commercializing probe microscopy, 1981–1996. *Technology and Culture* 47, 56–80.

——. 2011. *Instrumental Community: Probe Microscopy and the Path to Nanotechnology*. Cambridge, MA: MIT Press.

——. 2012. Conversions: Sound and sight, military and civilian, pp. 224-248 in T. Pinch and K. Bijsterveld (Eds.), *Oxford Handbook of Sound Studies*. New York: Oxford University Press.

Mody, C. C. M., and Nelson, A. J. 2013. "A towering virtue of necessity": Computer music at Vietnam-era Stanford. *Osiris*, 28(1), 254–277.

Mondavi, P. Jr. 2012. Interview conducted by James Lapsley, February 22. St. Helena, CA.

Mondavi, T. 2012. Phone interview conducted by James Lapsley, March 6.

Monroe, L. 1990. Biotech firm takes the simple road to gene therapy success. *Los Angeles Times*, March 23.

Moore, G., and Davis, K. 2004. Learning the Silicon Valley way, pp. 7–39 in T. Bresnahan and A. Gambardella (Eds.), *Building High-Tech Clusters: Silicon Valley and Beyond*. Cambridge, UK: Cambridge University Press.

[Morton 1999b]Morton, D. 1999. Oral history conducted with Irwin M. Jacobs, October 29, 1999. *IEEE History Center*. Downloaded on June 28, 2013, from www.ieeeghn.org/wiki/index.php/Oral-History:Irwin_Jacobs.

Morton, F. M. S., and Podolny, J. M. 2002. For love or money? The effects of owner motivation in the California wine industry. *The Journal of Industrial Economics*, 50(2), 431–456.

Mowery, D. C. 2009. Learning from one another? International policy "emulation" and university–industry technology transfer. *Industrial and Corporate Change*.

Mowery, D. C., Nelson, R. R., Sampat, B. N., and Ziedonis, A. A. 2004. *Ivory Tower and Industrial Innovation*. Stanford, CA: Stanford University Press.

Mowery, D., and Simcoe, T. 2002. Is the Internet a US invention? An economic and technological history of computer networking. *Research Policy*, 31(8-9), 1369–1387.

Murray, F. 2004. The role of academic inventors in entrepreneurial firms: Sharing in the laboratory life. *Research Policy*, 33(4), 643–659.

Nagel, L. 2011a. Professor, visionary, friend: Remembering Donald Pederson. *IEEE Solid State Circuits Magazine*, Spring, 22–24.

———. 2011b. What's in a name? *IEEE Solid State Circuits Magazine*, Spring, 8–12.

Napa Department of Agriculture, Weights and Measures. 1940–2010. *Agricultural Crop Report*. Napa.

Napa Valley Wine Library Association, 2008. In Memoriam: Bernard L. Rhodes. *Summer Report*. St. Helena, CA: Napa Valley Wine Library Association.

———. 2011a. Nathan Fay. *Winter Report*. St. Helena, CA: Napa Valley Wine Library Association.

———. 2011b. Warren Winiarski. *Winter Report*. St. Helena, CA: Napa Valley Wine Library Association.

Narin, F., Hamilton, K., and Olivastro, D. 1997. The increasing linkage between U.S. technology and public science. *Research Policy* 26, 317–330.

National Research Council. 1999. *Funding a Revolution: Government Support for Computing Research*. Washington, DC: National Research Council.

National Science Board. 2012. *Trends and Challenges for Public Research Universities*. , Washington, DC: National Science Board.

National Science Foundation (NSF). 1994. *National Patterns of R&D Resources: 1994*. Washington, DC: National Science Foundation.

———. 2004. *Federal Funds for Research and Development FY 2002, 2003, and 2004*. Washington, DC: National Science Foundation.

Naval Ocean Systems Center (NOSC). 1990. *Fifty Years of Research and Development on Point Loma, 1940–1990*. San Diego, CA: Naval Ocean Systems Center.

Neal, H. A., Smith, T. L., and McCormick, J. B. 2008. *Beyond Sputnik: U.S. Science Policy in the 21st Century*. Ann Arbor: University of Michigan Press.

Nee, E., 2000. Anything you can do, Nick can do better. *Business 2.0* July.

Nelson, A. 2012. Putting university research in context: Assessing alternative measures of production and diffusion at Stanford. *Research Policy* 41(4), 678–691.

Nicoli, D. F., Barrett, P. H., and Elings, V. B. 1978. Masters in instrumentation. *Physics Today*, 31 (9), 9.

Noble, D. 1977. *America by Design: Science, Technology and the Rise of Corporate Capitalism*. Oxford, UK: Oxford University Press.

Norberg, A. L. 1976. The origins of the electronics industry on the Pacific coast. *Proceedings of the IEEE*, 64(9), 1314–1322.

Nordmann, A. 2009. Invisible origins of nanotechnology: Herbert Gleiter, materials science, and questions of prestige. *Perspectives on Science*, 17(2), 123–143.

O'Brien, M. P. 1988. Morrough P. O'Brien: Dean of the College of Engineering, Pioneer in Coastal Engineering, and Consultant to General Electric: An Interview Conducted by Marilyn Ziebarth. Berkeley, CA: UC Berkeley, College of Engineering Oral History Series, Regional History Office, Bancroft Library.

Oldham, W. 1980. Letter to David Hodges and George Turin. September 30. CU-39.3, box 1. Berkeley, CA: Bancroft Library.

O'Neill, A. 2008. Asad Abidi recognized for work in RF CMOS. *Solid-State Circuits Magazine* Winter, 57–58.

O'Rourke, T. 2002. Oral history of Tom O'Rourke, interviewed by Luanne Johnson, March 13, 2002. Mountain View, CA: Computer History Museum Reference number X3778.2007.

Owen-Smith, J., and Powell, W. 2004. Knowledge networks as channels and conduits: The effects of spillovers in the Boston biotechnology community. *Organization Science*, 15, 5–21.

———. 2006. Accounting for emergence and novelty in Boston and Bay Area biotechnology, in P. Braunerhjelm and M. Feldman (Eds.), *Cluster Genesis: The Emergence of Technology Clusters and their Implication for Government Policies*. New York: Oxford University Press.

Pang, A. S. K. 1990. Edward Bowles and radio engineering at MIT, 1920–1940. *Historical Studies in the Physical and Biological Sciences*, 20(2), 313–337.

Patterson, D. A. 2007. Oral history of David Patterson, interviewed by John Mashey, September 13, 2007. Mountain View, CA: Computer History Museum CHM Reference number: X4150.2008.

Patterson, D. A., Gibson, G., and Katz, R. H. 1988. A case for redundant arrays of inexpensive disks (RAID). *International Conference on Management of Data (SIGMOD)*, (June), 109–116.

Pederson, D. 1984. A historical review of circuit simulation. *IEEE Transactions on Circuits and Systems* 31, 103–111.

Penner, S. S. 1999. Stanford S. Penner interviewed by Stanley Chodorow, May 5. San Diego: UCSD Library Oral History Archives.

Perry, T. 1998. Donald O. Pederson. *IEEE Spectrum*. June 22–27.

———. 1999. Henry Samueli. *IEEE Spectrum*, September, 70–75.

———. 2002. Not just blue sky. *IEEE Spectrum*, June.

Phylloxera Task Force. 1988. *Phylloxera and the Use of AXR#1 Rootstock in California Vineyards: A Statement of the Phylloxera Task Force, University of California, Davis*. Davis, CA.

Piercy, J. 2010. UC San Diego's Doctoral Programs Win High Marks in Prestigious NRC Study. Press release, University of California, San Diego, September 28.

Potter, M., 2001. I don't do operational stuff. *San Diego Reader*, January 25. Downloaded on June 28, 2013, from www.sandiegoreader.com/news/2001/jan/25/i-dont-do-operational-stuff/.

Powell, W. 2002. The spatial clustering of science and capital. *Regional Studies*, 36, 299–313.

Powell, W., Packalen, K., and Whittington, K. 2009. Organizational and institutional genesis: The emergence of high-tech clusters in the life sciences. Working Paper. Stanford, CA: Stanford University.

Powell, W.W., Koput, K. W., and Smith-Doerr, L. 1996. Interorganization collaboration and the locus of innovation: Networks of learning in biotechnology. *Administrative Science Quarterly*, 41, 116–145.

Prater, C. 2001. Interview conducted by Cyrus Mody, March 19. Santa Barbara, CA.

Price, S. 2012. Personal email communication from Steve Price to James Lapsley, March 10.

PricewaterhouseCoopers. 2013. *PricewaterhouseCoopers Moneytree Report*. Downloaded on June 28, 2013, from www.pwcmoneytree.com/MTPublic/ns/index.jsp.

———. Various years. PricewaterhouseCoopers MoneyTree. *MoneyTree Report*. Downloaded on December 2012 from www.pwcmoneytree.com/MTPublic/ns/index.jsp.

Rabinow, P. 1996. *Making PCR: A Story of Biotechnology*. Chicago: University of Chicago Press.

Rad, R. c. 2000. 7 visionary entrepreneurs, 5 major acquisitions. *Silicon Iran*. Downloaded on January 10, 2007, from www.siliconiran.com/magazine/leadership/issue1.shtml.

Rainbow Enterprises, 1973. Letter from Advertising Department, Re: Display advertising in *Probe the Unknown* magazine. American Religions Collection, MSS 48 Santa Barbara Parapsychology Collection, Box 1, Folder 3. Santa Barbara: UCSB Library Special Collections.

Raitt, H., and Moulton, B. 1967. *Scripps Institution of Oceanography: First Fifty Years*. Los Angeles, CA: Ward Ritchie.

Ranelletti, J. 2001. An interview with John Ranelletti by George Michael. Downloaded on July 10, 2001, from www.computer-history.info/Page1.dir/pages/Ranelletti.html.

Ranji, D. 2000a. Cree brightens prospects; Nitres may help backlog problem. *The News and Observer*, April 12.

———. 2000b. Durham, N.C., semiconductor company to buy California firm. *The News and Observer*, April 12.

———. 2001. Durham, N.C., firm develops brighter light device. *Knight Ridder Tribune Business News*, February 8.

Raymond, E. S. 2003. The art of Unix programming. Downloaded on February 10, 2012, from www.faqs.org/docs/artu/index.html.

Reese, Phyllis L. 1972 (September). Forward to annual report on activities financed from extramural funds. UArch 87 Office of Research Collection, Box 1, Folder "Annual Report on Activities Financed by Extramural Funds, Sept. 1972." Santa Barbara, CA: UCSB Library Special Collections.

Revelle, R. 1985. Untranscribed interview with Roger Revelle by Kathryn Ringrose, UCSD 25th Anniversary Oral History Project, May 15. San Diego: UCSD University Library Archives.

Riordan, M. 2007. A new blue laser. *IEEE Spectrum*, March.

Rodeno, M. 2012. Interview conducted by James Lapsley, February 17. Oakville, CA.

Rohrer, R. 2011. Growing SPICE. *IEEE Solid State Circuits Magazine*, Spring, 25–30.

Rohrer, R., Nagel, L., Meyer, R., and Weber, L. 1971. CANCER: Computer Analysis of Nonlinear Circuits Excluding Radiation. Paper Presentation, International Solid State Circuits Conference, February 18. Reprinted in 2011. *IEEE Solid State Circuits Magazine* Spring, 31–33.

Rosenberg, N. 1992. Scientific instrumentation and university research. *Research Policy* 21(4), 381–390.

Rosenberg, N., and Nelson, R. R. 1994. American universities and technical advance in industry. *Research Policy* 23(3), 323–348.

Rowe, L. A., and Stonebraker, M. 1984. The commercial INGRES epilogue, pp. 63–82 in M. Stonebraker (Ed.), *The INGRES Papers: Anatomy of a Relational Database System*. Reading, MA: Addison-Wesley Publishing Company.

Ruttan, V. W. 1982. *Agricultural Research Policy*. Minneapolis: University of Minnesota Press.

Salus, P. H. 1994. *A Quarter Century of UNIX*. Reading, MA: Addison-Wesley Publishing Company.

Samueli, H. c. 2000. Video interview. Collection of Christophe Lécuyer. Stanford, CA: Stanford University.

———. 2007. Interview conducted by Christophe Lécuyer. January 20.

SANDAG. 2012. *Info: Traded Industry Clusters in the San Diego Region*. December.

Sangiovanni-Vincentelli, A. 2010. Corsi e ricorsi: The EDA story. *IEEE Solid State Circuits Magazine*, Summer, 6-25.

Santa Barbara News-Press, 1975. Two UCSB students develop device to aid blind with sound meters. 30 March.

———. n.d. (probably mid-1970s). Oil company gives computer to UCSB. Santa Barbara: UCSB physics department basement archive.

Sapolsky, H. M. 1990. *Science and the Navy: The History of the Office of* Naval *Research*. Princeton, NJ: Princeton University Press.

Saxenian, A. 1994. *Regional Advantage: Culture and Competition in Silicon Valley and Route 128*. Cambridge, MA: Harvard University Press.

Schonfield, E. 1999. Leading the next chip revolution Broadcom's chips run high-end communications products. *Fortune Magazine*, May 10.

Shanghai Jiaotong University. 2012. Academic ranking of world universities. Downloaded from www.shanghairanking.com/ARWU2012.html.

Shimizu, H., and Kudo, S. 2011. How well does knowledge travel? The transition from energy to commercial application of laser diode fabrication technology. Paper Presentation, Business History Conference (downloaded on October 12, 2011, from www.thebhc.org/publications/BEHonline/2011/shimizuandkudo .pdf.

Shor, E. N. 1978. *Scripps Institution of Oceanography 1903–1978*. La Jolla, CA: Scripps Institution of Oceanography.

Simard, C. 2004. From weapons to cell-phones: Knowledge networks in the creation of San Diego's Wireless Valley. Unpublished PhD dissertation, Department of Communication. Stanford, CA: Stanford University

Simard, C., and West, J. 2003. The role of founder ties in the formation of San Diego's "Wireless Valley." DRUID Summer Conference on Creating, Sharing and Transferring Knowledge, June 14, 2003.

Simonyi, C. 2008. Oral history of Charles Simonyi, interviewed by Grady Booch. February 6, 2008. Mountain View, CA: Computer History Museum Reference number: X4428.2008.

Singleton, V. 2012. Interview conducted by James Lapsley, February 4. Davis, CA.

Smith, R. 2007. Post-phylloxera: A new Napa Valley. *Wine and Spirits*, Fall, 40–41.

Spinrad, P., and Meagher, P. n.d. Project Genie: Berkeley's piece of the computer revolution. Downloaded on December 6, 2011, from http://coe.berkeley.edu/news-center/publications/forefront/archive/forefront-fall-2007/ features/ berkeley 2019s-piece-of-the-computer-revolution.

Stephan, P. E., Gurmu, S., Sumell, A. J., and Black, G. 2007. Who's patenting in the university? Evidence from the Survey of Doctorate Recipients. *Economics of Innovation and New Technology*, 16, 71–99. Boston.

Steinhauer, B. 2012. Interview conducted by James Lapsley, February 13. St. Helena, CA.

Stern, S. 2004. Do scientists pay to be scientists? *Management Science*, 50(6), 835–853.

Stewart, I. 1948. *Organizing Scientific Research for War*. Boston: Little Brown and Company.

St. Helena Star. 2008. Keith Bowers. May 29.

Stonebridge Research Group. 2012. The economic impact of Napa County's wine and grapes. Private study prepared for Napa Valley Vintners. November.

Störmer, H. 1998. The fractional quantum hall effect. Nobel Lecture. December 8. Downloaded on November 10. 2012, from www.nobelprize.org/nobel_prizes/ physics/laureates/1998/stormer-lecture.html.

Strassenburg, A.A., 1973. Preparing students for physics-related jobs. *Physics Today*, 26 (October), 23–29.

Sturgeon, T. 2000. How Silicon Valley Came to Be. in M. Kenney (Ed.), *Understanding Silicon Valley*. Stanford, CA: Stanford University Press.

Sullivan, C. L. 2008. *Napa Wine: A History from Mission Days to Present*, 2nd ed. San Francisco: The Wine Appreciation Guild.

Swift, M. 2012. Google Ventures, Kleiner Perkins lead funding for energy company Transphorm. *San Jose Mercury News*, February 23.

Synopsys launches logic synthesis software. *Electronics Weekly*, July 26, 1989, 22.

Taylor, R. 1989. Robert Taylor interviewed by William Aspray, February 28, 1989. Palo Alto, CA.

Tenorio, V. 2000. Agility quickly finds $70M to finance lasers. *Daily Deal*, October 6.

Terman, F. E. 1976. A brief history of electrical engineering education. *Proceedings of the IEEE*, 64(9), 1399–1406.

Torous, J. B. 2006. Clarence Cory and a history of early electrical engineering at UC Berkeley. Unpublished paper prepared for History 199 June. Berkeley, CA: UC Berkeley, Department of History.

Trujillo, R. 2012. Manufacturers test Goleta, Calif. based company's high-tech lasers. *Santa Barbara News-Press*, November 29.

Turin, G. 1980a. Letter to F. M. Long. October 13. CU-39.3, box 1. Berkeley, CA: Bancroft Library.

——. 1980b. Letter to Lowell Paige. November 6. CU-39.3, box 1. Berkeley, CA: Bancroft Library.

——. 1981a. Letter to Karl Pister. January 20. CU-39.3, box 2. Berkeley, CA: Bancroft Library.

——. 1981b. Letter to Karl Pister. February 9. CU-39.3, box 2. Berkeley, CA: Bancroft Library.

——. 1981c. Letter to Chancellor Heyman. October 15. CU-39.3, box 2. Berkeley, CA: Bancroft Library.

——. 1981d. Letter to Steve Jobs. October 29. CU-39.3, box 2. Berkeley, CA: Bancroft Library.

——. 1981e. Letter to Karl Pister. October 30. CU-39.3, box 2. Berkeley, CA: Bancroft Library.

——. 1982a. Letter to James Dao. April 8. CU-39.3, box 2. Berkeley, CA: Bancroft Library.

——. 1982b. Memorandum. May 7. CU-39.3, box 2. Berkeley, CA: Bancroft Library.

——. 1982c. Letter to Lester Hogan. October 8. CU-39.3, box 2. Berkeley, CA: Bancroft Library.

——. 1982d. Letter to Andrew Grove. October 21. CU-39.3, box 2. Berkeley, CA: Bancroft Library.

——. 1982e. Letter to Chancellor Heyman and Vice-Chancellor Park. November 2. CU-39.3, box 2. Berkeley, CA: Bancroft Library.

——. 1982f. Letter to Karl Pister. November 29. CU-39.3, box 2. Berkeley, CA: Bancroft Library.

——. 1982g. Letter to Chancellor Heyman. December 21. CU-39.3, box 2. Berkeley, CA: Bancroft Library.

——. 1983. Letter to MICRO Policy Board. January 11. Presidential Papers, folders on MICRO. Oakland, CA: University of California Office of the President.

Tuzi, F. 2005. The scientific specialization of the Italian regions. *Scientometrics* 62, 87–111.

——. 2001b. A personal interview with the Mondavis, September 19.

U.S. General Accounting Office, 1985. GAO assessment of DoD's Very High Speed Integrated Circuits (VHSIC) Technology Program. May 8. Washington, DC: Author.

U.S. Patent and Trademark Office (USPTO). 2013. Number of patents granted as distributed by year of patent grant breakout by U.S. state and foreign country of origin. Downloaded on June 30, 2013, from www.uspto.gov/web/offices/ac/ido/oeip/taf/cst_utlh.htm.

University of California, Research Administration Office. 1985. Memo Operating Requirement No. 85-2, Subject: Microelectronics Innovation and Computer Research Opportunities (MICRO). (February 4, 1985). Downloaded on July 9, 2012, from www.ucop.edu/raohome/cgmemos/85-02.html.

UCB, 1985. Material for Chancellor's talk to the Engineering Alumni Society. CU-39.3, box 2. Berkeley, CA: Bancroft Library.

UC Davis News. 2001a. $35 million Robert and Margrit Mondavi gift to benefit Institute for Wine Food Science and Center for Performing Arts. September 19.

UCSB Office of Public Affairs, 2007. *Press Release*. Retrieved on May 22, 2009, from www.ia.ucsb.edu/pa/display.aspx?pkey=1610.

UCSB Office of Public Information. 1973. Press release. Physics student wins DuPont Fellowship, October 12, 1973. UArch 11, Public Information Office Biographical Files. Box 11, Folder "Elings, Virgil." Santa Barbara, CA: UCSB Library Special Collections.

UCSB Office of Research and Development, 1973. UArch 87 Office of Research Collection, Box 1, Folder "Organized Research Units, UCSB 1973–1974, Nov. 1973." Santa Barbara, CA: UCSB Library Special Collections.

UCSB Physics. c. 1975. Brochure. Graduate study in physics. UArch 122, UCSB Dept. of Physics Collection, Box 1, Folder "*'Graduate Study in Physics' Booklets, c. 1970s.*" Santa Barbara, CA: UCSB Library Special Collections.

———. 1976. Physics 13 Spring 1976 "Environmental Physics". UArch 122, UCSB Dept. of Physics Collection, Box 1, Folder "Course Flyers, 19761990." Santa Barbara, CA: UCSB Library Special Collections.

———. n.d. (c. late 1970s or very early 1980s). Undergraduate brochure. UArch 122, UCSB Dept. of Physics Collection, Box 1, Folder "Brochures, c. 1970s." Santa Barbara, CA: UCSB Library Special Collections.

UCSB Technology Management Program, 2008. Interview with Virgil Elings. Downloaded on July 16, 2012, from www.youtube.com/watch?v=H9aQBF7rIg8.

Veeco, 1998. SEC Filing, schedule 14A, filed May 29, 1998. Downloaded on July 16, 2012, from www.sec.gov/Archives/edgar/data/103145/0001047469-98-019196.txt.

Vettel, E. 2006. *Biotech: The Countercultural Origins of an Industry*. Philadelphia: University of Pennsylvania Press.

Veysey, L. R. 1970. *The Emergence of the American University*. Chicago: University of Chicago Press.

Viswanathan, C. 2007. Interview conducted by Christophe Lécuyer. February 5.

Walker, M. A. 2000. UC Davis' role in improving California grape planting materials, pp. 209–215 in *Proceedings of the ASEV 50th Anniversary Meeting, Seattle, Washington, June 19–23, 2000*. Davis, CA: American Society of Enology and Viticulture.

Wagner, K., 2005. The future depends on innovation: An interview with Irwin M. Jacobs. *IEEE Design & Test of Computers*, 22(3) (May–June), 268–279.

Walshok, M., Shragge, A., 2013. *San Diego's Innovation Heritage*. Stanford University Press, Stanford.

Wardani, L. 2005. Interview by Joel West, August 25. San Diego: UCSD Libraries.

Wells, J. V. 1978. The origins of the computer industry: A case study of radical technical change. PhD dissertation, Yale University, New Haven, CT.

West, J. 2008. Commercializing open science: Deep space communications as the lead market for Shannon Theory, 1960–1973. *Journal of Management Studies*, 45(8) (December), 1506–1532.

———. 2009. Before Qualcomm: Linkabit and the origins of the San Diego telecom industry. *Journal of San Diego History*, 55(1–2) (Winter/Spring), 1–20.

West, J., and Dedrick, J. 2001. Open source standardization: The rise of Linux in the network era. *Knowledge, Technology, & Policy*, 14 (2), 88–112.

Whinnery, J. 1994. Researcher and educator in electromagnetics, microwaves, and optoelectronics, 1935–1995; dean of the College of Engineering, UC Berkeley, 1950–1963. Typescript of an oral history conducted in 1994 by Ann Lage. Berkeley, CA: Regional Oral History Office, Bancroft Library, University of California, Berkeley.

———. 1996. Oral history interview conducted by Ann Lage. Berkeley, CA: Bancroft Library.

Wiener, N. 1958. *Nonlinear Problems in Random Theory*. Cambridge, MA: MIT Press.

Wildes, K. L., and Lindgren, N. A. 1985. *A Century of Electrical Engineering and Computer Science at MIT*. Cambridge, MA: MIT Press.

Williams, J. 2012. Interview conducted by James Lapsley, February 22. Rutherford, CA.

Wilson, M. 1997. *The Difference between God and Larry Ellison: God Doesn't Think He's Larry Ellison*. New York: William Morrow & Company.

Wines and Vines. 1940, 1950, 1960, 1970, 1980, 1990, 2000, 2010. *Directory and Buyers Guide*. San Rafael, CA: Wines and Vines.

Wisnioski, M., 2003. Inside "the system": Engineers, scientists, and the boundaries of social protest in the long 1960s. *History and Technology*, 19, 313–333.

———. 2005. *Engineers and intellectual crisis of technology, 1957–1973*. PhD dissertation. Princeton University.

Wolpert, J., et al. 1994. *Rootstocks and Phylloxera: A Status Report for Coastal and Northern California*. Davis, CA.

Wolpert, J. A. 2000. *Oakville Experimental Vineyard: Past, Present and Future*. Davis, CA: Department of Viticulture and Enology.

Wong, E. 1985. Letter to Karl Pister. October 18. CU-39.3, box 3. Berkeley, CA: Bancroft Library.

———. 1987a. Letter to Karl Pister. January 20. CU-39.3, box 3. Berkeley, CA: Bancroft Library.

———. 1987b. Letter to Karl Pister. March 16. CU-39.3, box 3. Berkeley, CA: Bancroft Library.

———. 1988. Letter to George Leitman. December 15. CU-39.3, box 3. Berkeley, CA: Bancroft Library.

———. 1989. Letter to Karl Pister. February 3. CU-39.3, box 4. Berkeley, CA: Bancroft Library.

Wright, B. D. 2012. Grand missions of agricultural innovation. *Research Policy* 41(10), 1716–1728.

Yablonovitch, E., 2007. Interview conducted by Christophe Lécuyer, January 19.

Zate, M., 2001. San Jose, Calif.-based Calient lands first sale of telecom switch. *Santa Barbara News-Press*, November 9.

———. 2002a. Optical networking firm picks up Agility Communications' lasers. *Santa Barbara News-Press*, 5 September 5.

———. 2002b. San Jose, Calif.-based photonic switching systems firm begins to ship product. *Santa Barbara News-Press*, February 7.

Zucker, L., Darby, M., and Armstrong, J. 2002. Commercializing knowledge: University science, knowledge capture, and firm performance in biotechnology. *Management Science*, 48, 138–153.

Index